GOD IN ALL THINGS

www.gerardwhughes.com

In the process of writing this book, a website has been set up to help make my writing more accessible and to give simple instruction on some methods of prayer to encourage visitors to find their own way of praying. It will also explore questions that arise from peoples' experience of prayer and its connection with everyday life.

The more I think about this website, the more I dream about its possibilities and hope it will move far beyond anything I have written. I would like it to become interactive, welcoming all who are looking for meaning in their lives. I hope and pray it will be a means of helping those who use it to discover for themselves the attractiveness of God.

My thanks to Chris Townsend who originally suggested the idea of a website to me and who has organised and launched this site on my behalf.

Gerard W. Hughes

GOD IN ALL THINGS

The sequel to *God of Surprises*

GERARD W. HUGHES

Hodder & Stoughton
LONDON SYDNEY AUCKLAND

Bible quotations are taken from the Jerusalem Bible, published and copyright © 1966, 1967 and 1968 by Darton, Longman and Todd Ltd.

Copyright © 2003 by Gerard W. Hughes

First published in Great Britain in 2003

The right of Gerard W. Hughes to be identified as the Author of the Work has been asserted by him in accordance with the Copyright, Designs and Patents Act 1988.

10 9 8 7 6 5 4 3 2 1

British Library Cataloguing in Publication Data
A record for this book is available from the British Library

ISBN 0 340 86135 5

Typeset in AGaramond by Avon DataSet Ltd,
Bidford-on-Avon, Warwickshire

Printed and bound in Great Britain by
Clays Ltd, St Ives plc

The paper and board used in this paperback are natural recyclable products made from wood grown in sustainable forests. The manufacturing processes conform to the environmental regulations of the country of origin.

Hodder & Stoughton
A Division of Hodder Headline Ltd
338 Euston Road
London NW1 3BH
www.madaboutbooks.com

CONTENTS

To Michael and Mary,
Maggie and James.

PREFACE

IN 1985 I WROTE *God of Surprises*, a guidebook for the inner journey in which we are all engaged, whatever our religious beliefs or lack of them. I wrote that book for bewildered, confused or disillusioned Christians, who have a love-hate relationship with the Church to which they belong, or once belonged. *God in All Things* develops and enlarges upon some of the themes of *God of Surprises*, and draws on my experience of working in the field of ecumenical spirituality in a number of countries over the past eighteen years.

During this period I have been working particularly with those who are actively engaged in the fields of justice, peace and reconciliation, and I have become increasingly convinced that Christianity today has reached the most critical moment in its history. It is more critical than the eleventh century, when Eastern and Western Christianity divided, and far more critical than the Protestant/Catholic split of the sixteenth-century Reformation. The institutions, forms and structures that served us well in earlier centuries no longer answer the needs of our day. Our nervous systems, gradually evolving through the millennia to deal with the gentle pace of natural and human development, are now subjected to abrupt and massive change. The population of the world has doubled in the last thirty years – Church and State are shaken and confused, their cohesive forces ruptured. Reactions vary: some people are crushed by all these experiences and despair; others refuse to face the fact of change and insist on carrying on as before. There are some who relish change and remain full of hope for the future. The outbreak of fundamentalism in society and in all the religions of the world is an inevitable reaction to such rapid change. Such a reaction is very understandable: fundamentalism represents a desperate attempt to find some point of anchor as our familiar securities are swept away. But the fundamentalist reaction is about as helpful as King Canute's order that the advancing tide should ebb!

Where are we to find security today? Where are we to find God? For Christians, God is always in the facts. It therefore follows that in today's confusion we are being invited to grow. We can become too attached to our securities, including our forms of religious worship; too attached to the way in which we formulate our beliefs and understand God and God's creation. Today, those securities are being shaken, not in order to destroy our faith in God, but as a means of helping us to rediscover our real security, which nothing can destroy, not even death itself. True security enables us to live at peace in insecurity, offers us certainty in uncertainty, comfort in confusion; it helps us to spot creativity in chaos, and to smile even in the tears of things.

God is very near, is at hand. 'The Word became flesh and dwelt among us.' But in spite of God's continuous efforts to make this known to us, we have nevertheless managed to make God remote, and we take remarkable care to keep God at a distance! The first three chapters of this book enlarge on the ways in which we do this. This split in our spirituality impoverishes us, preventing us from recognising God at work within us and around us. We are divided from God, from other people, and from ourselves. As a result we become frightened creatures, so intent on our own security that we try to make ourselves invulnerable both individually and collectively. We are wedded to violence, which always devours its lovers in the end; in the name of freedom, we oppress, exploit, or get rid of those who thwart us. As long as our spirituality is split in this way, we cannot know our inner wealth and ultimate identity. That ultimate identity is to 'become God'.

One of the joys of working ecumenically is the discovery that the Holy Spirit does not appear to be a respecter of Christian denominations, but seems to be happily at work across them all, and in people of differing religious faiths and of none. Chapter 4 offers some methods of prayer that have proved helpful across the cultures and across the Christian denominations, as well as to those of differing faiths and of no formal belief. The common factor within each method is that it allows our everyday experience to become the substance of our prayer.

Where do you start when working with people of differing religious traditions and those of no formal belief? Is there anything we have in common? Desire is common to all human beings. It is the source of our actions and reactions and is fundamental to all decision-making. Our desires are many and varied and most of them are mutually incompatible. They are the source of our strength and creativity, but also of our pain and destructiveness. How, then, does God's will relate to our desires?

Desire lies at the root of all feeling and emotion, and Chapter 5 explores the nature of desire. Chapter 6 develops this by showing that the search for our deepest desire enables us to distinguish the creative movements within us from the destructive ones. It also explores ways in which we can change the potentially destructive into something creative.

How do we discover the roots of peace and of violence and the relationship between inner and outer peace? And how do we find peace within our warring selves? This is our greatest challenge and a constant question among those active in the promotion of peace. It is the theme of Chapter 7.

Pilgrimage has been described as 'the poor person's substitute for mysticism', and it is far from coincidental that the practice of going on pilgrimage has become so popular in recent years. When we find ourselves confused, bewildered and directionless it can be very helpful to decide on a destination and to walk there, if at all possible. Pilgrimage is a way of externalising our inner confusion, countering that confusion by setting ourselves a destination, and then learning the lessons about life that the journey can teach us. This is the subject of Chapter 8.

The Christian Church has been described as the 'pilgrim people of God'. Chapter 9 explores the Church in light of this description: the call of the Church to unity, not only between Christians, but with all peoples in every circumstance of their lives. It is in discovering our unity with all peoples and with all creation that we can come to discover ourselves within the God of unity and compassion.

A common reason given for the abandonment of Christian belief is the impossibility of believing in a 'loving' God who allows the innocent to suffer and evil to triumph. Chapter 10 looks at pain, suffering and death in the light of a Christian belief, which can help us to appreciate and value every minute of life now, and enable us to face the future with hope.

The final chapter draws together the various themes of the book. How can we allow God to be the God of love and compassion in our own lives, in the life of the Church, and in the lives of all peoples? How can we let God out of our religious cupboards, in such a way that we can come to know the God of freedom, who loves all creation and loves each one of us in every aspect of our being.

God in All Things has been written in order to help readers to discover – or rediscover – for themselves the treasure that each one possesses. This treasure has been freely given. It is not something we create, or earn by our good behaviour: it is God's gift of Godself. Consequently, we can be confident that God is within our present crises, both the crisis of Christianity and its future, and the crisis of human survival on our planet, which is so deeply threatened by our greed, violence and timidity. We are being invited into a deeper understanding of the meaning of Christian faith, an understanding that brings heaven closer to earth and helps us to walk the earth, not 'mourning and weeping in this vale of tears', as the ancient prayer describes it, but walking with God the foolish lover who, knowing the essential goodness within us, accepts us as we are in all our stupidity, meanness, narrowness and brutality; God, the divine alchemist, who transforms base material into the very life of God.

If you find sections of this book difficult to understand, I suggest that you skip over them and come back to them later. The most valuable part of the book lies in the exercises at the end of the chapters. There is no need to try them all, but you are likely to find it helpful if you return more than once to any exercises that you have found useful. In Appendix 1 I have provided brief practical suggestions for using the book in groups.

If you enjoy this book, pray for me. If it annoys and irritates you, pray for me even more! And I shall remember you.

ACKNOWLEDGMENTS

WE CAN ONLY MEET God in and through our experience of the world, especially of its peoples, so the first people I want to thank are all those I have encountered, friends and foes, who have helped me to recognise God in the joys and in the tears of things.

I wrote many preliminary drafts of this book and Maggie McCarthy at LSU patiently edited early drafts, cutting out many pages and the occasional chapter! I also thank her for her insights, suggestions, and careful editing of later drafts.

I thank Judith Longman of Hodder & Stoughton for her encouraging response to an early and incomplete manuscript and for inviting Teresa de Bertodano to edit the completed manuscript. I thank Teresa, who had edited *God of Surprises*, for her meticulous editing and helpful suggestions. I also thank all the staff at Hodder & Stoughton who have helped in the production of this book.

I thank Fr Ralph Woodhall, S.J. for his encouraging comment on the final version. This is the first book I have written using a computer and I thank the various members of my Jesuit community, mostly Jesuit novices, who came to my rescue. I owe special thanks to Fr Alex Ochumba, a Kenyan Jesuit, for his skill and patience in working with a slow learner in computer skills.

Finally, I thank Brendan Walsh, editor of Darton, Longman and Todd, for the very helpful and encouraging comment he gave me on an early and incomplete manuscript.

Gerard Hughes
Birmingham, 2003

SPLIT SPIRITUALITY

Spirituality Popular: Churchgoing Dwindling

'SPIRITUALITY' HAS BECOME A fashionable word. Thirty years ago it was rarely used outside religious circles: today it appears frequently in the press and in novels, plays and films. We find the word in political manifestos and in the proposals of government, education authorities and the health service. 'Spirituality' has found its way into business boardrooms, and in many large bookshops there is a prominent 'spirituality' section on the ground floor. In the same shops, 'religious' books are likely to occupy a few shelves upstairs!

Today's growing interest in spirituality is accompanied by a growing disinterest in churchgoing, with the exception of those who attend some of the black-led churches. According to the survey compiled for the BBC *Soul of Britain* series, church attendance fell by over 20 per cent in the years between 1989 and 1998. According to the same survey, more than 76 per cent of the national population had undergone a spiritual or religious experience that was still affecting them. These are remarkable statistics. I do not know the average age of the congregations to whom the churches minister, but in my experience of church meetings and church services, the average age of the regular churchgoer is about fifty-five and rising annually.

1

People are looking for spiritual guidance and the majority fail to find it in the mainstream Christian churches. Today we distinguish between being 'spiritual' and being 'religious'. In this context, the word 'religious' implies membership of a particular church, regular attendance at its services, and adherence to its regulations. It is very often the most Christ-centred and committed people who are particularly critical of the Church, as they experience it. The 'Church' is accused of being hypocritical and out of touch, and more interested in self-preservation than in caring for others. The clergy are accused of being unable to listen, unable to accept criticism, and of behaving like control freaks. In such criticisms, Church/institution tends to be identified with existing clerical structures.

Pie in the Sky?

We have a very understandable movement away from 'Church' alongside a growing interest in spirituality: this is a clear indication of a spirituality that is seriously split. Spirituality without some visible form is like breath without a body. On the other hand, a visible form (Church) without spirituality is like a body without breath.

Spiritual movements have been springing up within Christianity since New Testament times, engendering great enthusiasm, attracting thousands of very committed people, and then splitting into separate factions before disappearing altogether. Christianity is, essentially, a down-to-earth religion. In the words of St Irenaeus writing in the second century, 'God became a human being, so that human beings might become God.' The word 'spirituality' refers to the presence of God, 'the Spirit' within us and among us. God is the Spirit of unity, of love and of compassion. If our life in the Spirit is genuine, it must find expression in the way we relate to one another and the way in which we organise our lives, both corporately and as individuals.

The essence of Church is the Spirit of God, and the Church is called to be the effective sign of God's presence within us and among us. I am using the word 'Church' in the sense of the visible inter-relationship that must grow and develop among those who become aware of, and respond to, the Spirit rather than referring to any particular Church. A key function of Church is to point beyond itself and to make us more perceptive and responsive to the Spirit present in all peoples and all things. All church structures need to be provisional, and all are in continuous need of reform – if we divinise particular structures we are in danger of falling into idolatry. The Spirit is found through our relationships with other human beings, and in order to enable us to relate successfully we need an organisation that is pliant and adaptable because it is open to the Spirit. Spirituality that is not embodied in some kind of organisation easily becomes 'pie in the sky', while Church without spirituality can pose a dangerous threat to human life and freedom.

Spirituality/Church?

The *Concise Oxford Dictionary* defines the word 'spiritual' as follows:

> 1 of, or concerning, the spirit as opposed to matter. 2 concerned with sacred or religious things; holy; divine; inspired. 3 (of the mind etc.) refined, sensitive; not concerned with the material. 4 (of a relationship etc.) concerned with the soul or spirit etc., not with external reality.

According to this definition, the only link between the spiritual and the material is to be found in 'sacred or religious things'. In the light of such a definition it is hardly surprising that we should have difficulty in explaining the relationship between spirituality and everyday life. Readers may well ask themselves whether, according to this definition, they rank as spiritual persons or not. How much time, attention and energy do I give to sacred things – the Church, religion, and so on – as compared with the attention I give to material things? What would be the effect upon you and your household if you became 'spiritual' according to the dictionary definition?

Such a definition reveals the enormous split in our spirituality. By 'split' I mean that God and the things of God are divided off from ordinary everyday life. God is confined to Church, religion, the sacred and the intangible. In the light of such a definition we could be forgiven for supposing that 'spiritual' persons must have minds and emotions of a highly refined and delicate quality – so refined that they are unconcerned with other human beings or with any created thing apart from those that qualify as 'sacred' or 'religious'.

Theological Language Underpins the Split

We speak of natural and supernatural, spiritual and material, eternal and temporal, sacred and secular, grace and nature. While these can be useful distinctions, they can easily be misunderstood to indicate that there are two separate layers of reality: the natural, material layer, and the supernatural, spiritual layer. The conscientious Christian is encouraged to consider the supernatural to be of greater importance than the natural, the spiritual as more important than the material. And grace is perceived as being of infinitely greater value than nature. Such misunderstanding leads us into 'doublethink'. Imagine that you are setting off on a long-distance flight and you find yourself praying for a safe journey. What kind of pilot would you like God to provide for you? A pilot who is spiritual according to the dictionary definition, a pilot whose mind is on God, the soul, the sacred, etc., and not on material and temporal things? Or would you prefer a good solid atheist whose primary interest during the flight is concentrated on the instrument panel and bringing the material plane with its material passengers safely back to their earthly destination?

Religious Instruction Confirms the Split

I was brought up as a Roman Catholic. From an early age I knew that God was all important, and for that I am grateful. God, in my childhood memory, was as homely and familiar as the rest of my family. Saying nightly prayers was as natural as kissing my parents goodnight, although the prayers took a bit longer. On reflection, my difficulties with God began when I was given religious instruction.

The spirituality presented to the Roman Catholic Church of my generation was divisive and split. It was divisive because we were taught that there was no salvation outside the Church, which was one, true, Catholic and apostolic. So the world was divided into Catholics and non-Catholics. As Catholics, we were forbidden to take part in the services and prayers of a 'false' religion, which banned us from attendance at any other Christian Church apart from the Greek and Russian Orthodox. It was divisive within our own lives, because we were taught an extremely split and dualist spirituality. The body, of which we were most immediately aware, was considered to be a threat to the spirit. One Catechism question enquired: 'Of which must you take most care, of your body or of your soul?' The answer was: 'I must take most care of my soul. The body, if not corrected by self-denial, will certainly carry us to hell'! Such a spirituality was also divisive in leading us to think of God as separate and apart from us. In the words of the Catholic Catechism of my generation, God was 'The supreme Spirit who alone exists of Himself and is infinite in all perfections'. Not the kind of God with whom one could feel at home, or want to have around on holidays. Because the spiritual was so emphasised and separated from the material, 'worldly' matters were not considered important. Worldly matters included our total emotional life. True faith did not seem to have much relationship to our experience of life on earth. Consequently, one could be a devout and committed Catholic without any awareness that political, social, economic and cultural questions were not only relevant to living faith in God, but integral to that faith. In 1891 Pope Leo XIII had published the first great social encyclical, which came to be known as 'The Worker's Charter', but its importance and implications had still to reach most of the pews fifty years later. There was, however, a great emphasis on the 'corporal works of mercy', food for the hungry, drink for the thirsty, shelter for the homeless, etc. If Catholics did not necessarily tend to think globally, they generally acted locally with great generosity.

The previous paragraph is a deliberate caricature in order to show the extent to which my early religious instruction encouraged a 'split' spirituality. Such a caricature fails to do justice to the very attractive elements I found in Roman Catholicism, and that I still find there. It is this very attractiveness that leads me to complain constantly about the split that hides the face of God. Until we acknowledge the enormity of this split in our spirituality, we shall be unable to change; church numbers will continue to dwindle, and we shall find ourselves clinging to some Christless structure.

The Split Affects All Christian Denominations

It may be objected that the spirituality that I have been describing is no longer taught within the Roman Catholic Church. Why am I harping on about past history when today's spirituality is far less dualistic and much more integrated?

The problem of split spirituality is wider and deeper than we realise. For the past forty years I have worked with Christians of many different denominations. The details of our spiritual upbringing may be different, but, in my experience, we all suffer from a split in our spirituality.

I worked at one time with a group of Christian psychotherapists, the majority of whose clients were Roman Catholic priests or members of religious congregations. On one occasion I asked the psychotherapists whether they ever asked clients about their prayer life. Their unanimous answer was 'No'. When I asked the reason, I was told that it would be 'unprofessional' to enquire about the prayer life of clients. The reason given was that if the psychotherapist focused attention on a client's prayer, the client might use prayer as a way of escaping from the psychological problems that had to be faced. If prayer is based upon a split spirituality it is undoubtedly true that it can be used as a way of escaping the problems that beset us, but this type of prayer tries to bypass the facts. And God is always in the facts. We cannot escape God's reality checks for long!

It is possible to use forms of prayer that are 'unearthed', which bear no relation to what is, in fact, going on, as a way of escaping from our responsibilities. The psychotherapists with whom I worked were aware of this problem and their reaction was understandable, but they were wrong in assuming that their clients' prayer was necessarily split.

A divided spirituality leads us to split the spiritual from the psychological, as though the two words referred to different parts of the person. This is a dangerous misunderstanding. It can, for example, lead us to think that the only people who are suitable for spirituality work are those who are 100 per cent psychologically sound. Such a principle would have excluded many of the greatest saints from spirituality work, not to mention the vast majority of the human race! There is no inner state in any human being that can be described as 'purely psychological', for God is present and at work in all our states. The distinction between psychological and spiritual does not denote two separate areas of our human psyche. It rather indicates two different ways of approaching the single psyche. As psychologists and as spiritual guides we must not create no-go areas for God – or for the psychologist. It is, however, necessary and valid to approach those areas in differing ways. It is in this context that there is a valid distinction between the spiritual and the psychological.

The Split Continues

The majority of Christians in the developed world are not opposed to a nuclear defence policy, and an even greater majority still believe in the necessity of war to preserve peace on earth. This support for nuclear defence and for war as a means of bringing peace is an indication of the divided nature of our spirituality. We all want peace, and we reckon that the possession of a nuclear arsenal, as well as conventional arms, is the best way of ensuring that peace. Most nations subscribe to the Roman aphorism 'To preserve peace, prepare for war', an aphorism that wins the support of the majority in most Western countries. Because of our split spirituality we can both pray for peace and at the same time support a policy of national defence that militates against peace. While our reason may convince us that the possession of nuclear arms is justified, ethical and sensible, we may experience acute discomfort if we allow God to enter into our prayer for peace. When Jesus appeared to his frightened disciples on Easter Sunday evening, he said 'Peace be with you' and showed them his hands and his side (John 20:20). The world's peace is achieved through trying to become invulnerable: Christ's peace comes through vulnerability. This truth brings us to the very uncomfortable heart of the matter.

We have become so used to a split spirituality that we no longer notice the split, which divides our hearts from our heads, our reason from our emotion. Consequently, we can produce well-reasoned arguments in favour of war and of the need for nuclear arms while, at the same time, praying to God earnestly and sincerely for peace. Without realising what we are doing, we take remarkable care not to let God interfere with our practical plans for peace. The point of the peace prayer is not to argue for pacifism, but simply to illustrate the truth that because of the split in our spirituality, we do not allow God to interfere in our practical plans for peace and war, or any other matter.

The following exercise is an imaginative one. You attend a church service on Peace Sunday and listen to this peace prayer. It has been composed by someone whose reason has convinced them of the legitimacy of nuclear defence and of just war as a means of bringing peace to the world. In the prayer, the composer, aware of the split in our spirituality, allows God to enter into the reasoning behind the prayer. The exercise is simply to notice what emotional effect this prayer has on you. Does it leave you strengthened, happy and hopeful in your attitudes, or unhappy, angry and confused? The prayer illustrates what happens when we allow God access to our feelings, when we allow our prayer to become 'earthed'. Here is the prayer:

> Dear Lord, inspire our scientists that they may invent yet more lethal weaponry (so that our deterrent may prove even more effective). Protect us from any unfortunate accident in its testing (lest it destroy us and our own cities rather than our enemies). Bless our economy that we may put these weapons into plentiful production (otherwise we cannot deter). Have a special care of the hungry, the homeless, the sick and the aged of our own land and of other lands until such time as our defence commitments allow us to contribute a little more to these worthy purposes. Strengthen our leaders in a strong defence policy. Drive out from our midst any who by thought, word or deed undermine our national security, and grant us the protection of nuclear weaponry now and forever. Amen.

This prayer is not offered as an argument against nuclear deterrence, but simply as an indication of the split nature of our spirituality. How did you feel as you read the prayer, and what did you do with those feelings? Some elements in the masculine culture still regard feelings and emotions as a sign of weakness rather than a source of wisdom. We have developed ways of praying that allow us to discount feelings. We may justify such an attitude to ourselves by claiming that we are trying to free ourselves from distractions (any activity involving the material physical world qualifies as a 'distraction'). Such an elevated form of prayer has the great advantage of keeping God from interfering in our plans. Could the real reason for our split spirituality be the fact that it keeps God out of the way?

Another Example Illustrating the Present Split in Our Spirituality

Each reader will have a different way of carrying out the following exercise – and if you carry it out several times you may find yourself coming up with a variety of answers. The exercise introduces us to the use of the imagination, which can open up deep wells of spirituality within.

To begin the exercise, sit down and relax. Imagine there is a ring at your front doorbell. On answering it, you meet on the doorstep the Risen Lord himself. Somehow, you know beyond any shadow of doubt that it is he. What do you do now? How do you greet him, what do you say? Presumably, you welcome him in and you invite all your friends to come and meet him. 'You'll never guess who we have staying with us this evening!' In the course of the evening, you find yourself making fatuous statements to the Lord of all creation, such as, 'Do make yourself at home'. Jesus seems very pleased with your invitation and tells you that that is why he has come.

Now take a leap of two weeks in your imagination. Jesus is still staying with you. What is it like at home now? To stimulate your imagination, you might recall some Gospel passages, sayings you wish Jesus had never uttered such as, 'Do you suppose that I am here to bring peace on earth? No, I tell you, but rather division. For from now on a household of five will be divided: three against two and two against three; the father divided against the son, son against father, mother against daughter, daughter against mother, mother-in-law against daughter-in-law, daughter-in-law against mother-in-law' (Luke 12:51–3). And the letter to the Hebrews tells us that 'Jesus Christ is the same today as he was yesterday and as he will be for ever' (Heb. 13:8), so he is obviously not going to change! How has it been at family meals during the last two weeks? What has Jesus said or done that has caused some members to leave the table in a tantrum, slamming the door behind them? In Jesus's own lifetime, as far as we can judge from the Gospels, relations with his own family were not always easy. Apart from the infancy narratives in Matthew and Luke, the only information we have about Jesus before his public life began concerns a family row, when he goes missing for three days at the age of twelve. He is eventually found by his distraught parents, sitting in the Temple in discussion with the doctors. During his public life we learn from the Gospel of Mark that the family of Jesus thought he was possessed, and his own comments on family life are not complimentary. When told that his mother and brothers are looking for him, he replies, 'Who is my mother, my brother, my sister? Whoever does the will of my Father in heaven is my brother and sister and mother' (Matt. 12:50). So life may not be too peaceful at home, after two weeks with Jesus present.

Told to make himself at home, Jesus begins to invite his friends to your house. Who were his friends in the Gospels, what kind of people were they, and what did respectable, religious people say about them? Who is coming along your road now, what is happening to the curtains in the house opposite, and what is happening to local property values? How are things in your own family and with your own circle of friends, now that Jesus's friends are also calling in?

You may then decide that it is not right to keep Jesus confined to your own house, so you arrange for him to give a little talk in your parish church. You remember the little talk he once gave to the chief priests, the scribes and the Pharisees, assuring them that the tax-gatherers and the prostitutes would enter the kingdom of God before they did. He gives substantially the same sermon to the faithful of St Jude's parish church. There is uproar, and the parish loses its principal benefactors.

You return home with Jesus, who has now become the major problem of your life. As you ponder the question, 'What am I to do with him?', you know you cannot ask him to leave, for he is the Lord of all creation, so what are you to do? Perhaps you could look around the house carefully, find a suitable cupboard, clear it out, clean it up, decorate it, sparing no expense, and have good strong locks put on the door. You then invite Jesus to step inside, turn the lock on him, put flowers and a candle in front of the cupboard door, and every time you pass, you bow deeply. You now have Jesus in your house and he does not interfere any more!

Is this an image of what we have done with God? We lock God away in the sacred, supernatural, heavenly, spiritual cupboard, where we can show great reverence, hold splendid services of worship, singing praises and thanking God for the blessings bestowed on us and the prosperity granted us. This religious behaviour keeps Jesus out of the way, so that God no longer interferes in our everyday life.

This split in our spirituality affects every aspect of our lives. It can only begin to be healed when we acknowledge it. Reluctance to acknowledge goes deep into our unconscious and can manifest itself in righteous indignation against the apparent flippancy of this imaginative exercise.

How did you feel during the exercise, and what did you do with those feelings during the exercise and afterwards? Did you perhaps feel that it was disrespectful to make fun of sacred things and 'contaminate' spirituality with worldly material comparisons? If so, could it be that your image of God and of Jesus makes it difficult for you to feel 'at home' with God?

Ineffective Spirituality

If we isolate God by keeping him out of the way of everyday life, we also isolate ourselves, pursuing an individualistic spirituality that disconnects us from 'material, temporal things'. The split in our spirituality separates us from one another and this enables us to perpetrate appalling damage in the name of religion – the history of the twentieth century provides plenty of examples. The personal damage inflicted upon ourselves may be less obvious – the following example may help to make this point clearer:

A former military chaplain was appointed to a parish in England. He came, he saw, and he had everything reorganised within a week. The parish included a very lively Third World group. They met regularly, studied, brought visiting lecturers to the parish, ran a Fair Trade stall, and every month they had a special collection for some Third World project. The new parish priest decided unilaterally that there would no longer be a monthly collection for the Third

World: in his estimation, once a year would be sufficient.

The Third World group members were furious. They met together, seethed with anger, deplored this rampant clericalism, and decided to draft a letter of complaint to the bishop. While they were still at the drafting stage, Father made a fatal mistake. There was a men's club attached to the parish. Father changed the beer in the club without consulting the beer drinkers. There was uproar. The men rose, united as never before, and confronted the new parish priest, threatening to withdraw their money and their presence from the Church unless he restored the beer. Father relented. I never heard the end of this story, but I hope the parish priest relented, and restored the monthly collection for the Third World group, who then thanked the beer group for their intervention and invited them to become members!

What is my beer factor? What is it that really moves me into action, as distinct from the things that I claim move me into action? The Third World group were very sincere and committed people, who loved God and recognised God in the poor and the hungry, but somehow these convictions did not connect with the core of their being in the immediate way that beer deprivation connected with the core of the club members' being and resulted in immediate and effective action.

Separation of Head and Heart

A divided spirituality causes a fissure between our reasoning minds and our feelings and emotions. Emotion is the driving force in our lives and a split between thought and feeling ensures that the driving force is not directed: it is like a car with a very powerful engine, but a permanently damaged clutch. We may roar and splutter with indignation on certain issues, as the Third World group roared and spluttered about the parish priest, but our split spirituality will ensure that nothing creative happens.

The search today, among churchgoers and non-churchgoers alike, is for a more holistic spirituality, more firmly connected to life experience. A striking instance of this search is to be found in the phenomenon of New Age spirituality, which appeals across generations, races, nations and classes, and does so without any apparent central organisation.

The New Age phenomenon arouses acute discomfort among many Christians, who fear the interest in witchcraft and the occult shown by some New Age devotees. In spite of some of its zanier manifestations, there are aspects of the New Age movement that are in fact extremely healthy, and in tune with Christianity to the extent that they manifest the search for a spirituality that includes not only the spirit but body, mind and all creation. Many New Age followers have a particular interest in Celtic spirituality and in the writings of Pierre Teilhard de Chardin, the French Jesuit priest and scientist, who saw the whole of creation in terms of a gradual transformation of matter into spirit. Teilhard de Chardin combined his Christian faith and his scientific knowledge in order to produce an integrated vision of the universe, which he described in one of his books as 'The Divine Milieu'. The New Age is reminding us of the same ancient truth: God is present in all things. Our Christian spirituality must therefore be holistic, including body and mind as well as spirit, because God became one of us in the person of Jesus. And in the words of St Irenaeus quoted above, God did this 'that we might become God' – an astonishing statement that can make us feel uneasy, because we are not accustomed to thinking of God, or of ourselves, in this way.

Christians are becoming increasingly aware of the need for an integrated and holistic spirituality which, like New Age approaches, includes body, mind and spirit. An illustration of this trend is to be found in *Retreats*, the ecumenical journal of the Retreat Association. This publication lists over two hundred retreat houses and centres of spirituality. The majority are in Britain, although European retreats also appear, and in most cases the programmes of the centres are included in the advertisements.

There is a bewildering variety of retreats and courses, many of them run by laity rather than priests and nuns, and almost all are open to people of all faiths or of none. The titles of the retreats reveal the growing interest in a holistic spirituality that addresses body, mind and spirit. Titles include: Dance and Movement, Circle Dancing, Clay and Painting, Icon Painting, Dreams, Calligraphy, Aromatherapy, Massage, Healing of Memories, Healing of Life's Hurts, Myers Briggs psychological personality indicator, and the Sufi Enneagram. Elsewhere I heard of a 'Swimming with Dolphins' retreat off the coast of New Mexico.

Dolphins would appear to be the best of gurus, perhaps because they are attentive and friendly, but do not talk!

Until recently, Roman Catholic retreats lasting longer than a weekend were generally reserved for clergy and nuns. During the 1970s, individually given retreats were introduced for lay men and lay women so that someone who was not a priest or nun could stay for a week or longer in a retreat house or conference centre, and spend time each day with a personal spiritual guide. Prior to that, a Roman Catholic wanting to deepen their walk with God would be encouraged to make a weekend retreat that usually consisted of three or four conferences each day, almost always given by a priest. In between conferences, the retreatants would reflect and pray over what they had heard or read in some spiritual book. They were expected to keep silence throughout the weekend.

Being Holistic is Not the Same as Being Holy

The new developments in retreat giving are excellent in that they aim to develop the whole person, recognising the sacredness of body, mind and heart, as well as the holiness of the spirit. It is good, also, that such retreats are becoming increasingly ecumenical.

We meet God when we meet one another across the divisions of our churches: we exclude God when we refuse to communicate with one another. It is also desirable that an increasing number of married and single people should be giving retreats, for the Holy Spirit is given to each individual. In spite of all these undoubted benefits, there is, however, a danger in these modern developments. It is frequently stated nowadays that holiness means wholeness, hence the emphasis on 'holistic spirituality'. While genuine holiness will always strive to be holistic, the fact of being 'holistic' does not necessarily imply holiness. We can be whole without being holy, just as we can be holy without being whole. God told Israel to 'Be holy, as I the Lord your God am holy.' God did not say, 'Be holistic, as I the Lord your God am holistic.'

As an illustration of the difference between being holy and being holistic, here are thumbnail sketches of two characters. Which of the two do you consider to be the more 'holistic'?

The first character is a middle-aged man who is gifted, intelligent, intuitive, creative, artistic and a music-lover. He is vegetarian, teetotal and a non-smoker. He is also a powerful orator and an excellent communicator. The second is also a middle-aged man who is intelligent and intuitive. But this man is of a melancholic disposition, afflicted with suicidal tendencies and bent with rheumatism. Which of the two is the more holistic? The first seems to be the obvious candidate – but this is a portrait of Adolf Hitler. The second character is Father Henri Huvelin, a famous French spiritual director who died in 1910 and was spiritual guide to the great theologian and philosopher Baron Friedrich von Hugel (1852–1925), and to the inspirational French mystic Charles de Foucauld (1858–1916). Von Hugel describes the strange sense of peace and joy that he always experienced after visiting Father Huvelin, who lived with so much mental and physical pain.

To be holy, we must strive to be holistic, but to be holistic is not the same thing as being holy. What, then, is holiness? This is the question for the following two chapters.

Exercises

These exercises may help to reveal a split in our spirituality, and a first step towards healing it:

1 Imagine Jesus visiting your house. Do not try to reason things out, but see what your imagination suggests. Have a conversation with Jesus in your heart, telling him of your hopes and fears, needs and longings.

    Having imagined the scene, try writing a description of his visit and your own reactions. The description might be intended for a friend, or for a local newspaper.
2 What was your own *felt* reaction to the peace prayer on page 8? Why do you think that you experienced this reaction? Where does this reaction come from, and how are you going to react to it now?
3 Scribble down some examples of split spirituality that you experience in yourself. Do you want to do something about this? What do you think you can do?

WHAT IS HOLINESS?

Holiness cannot be defined and can never adequately be described, because holiness means that God is present. God, the Holy One who is always greater than anything we can think or imagine, and who can never be contained within our limited human minds. In exploring the meaning of holiness, we are not only searching for God, but also for the meaning and value of our own lives. In coming to know God, we find ourselves, because it is in God that we live and move and have our being.

Try saying aloud, 'I am holy', and note your reactions. What images come to you spontaneously, and what are you feeling and thinking? This exercise can make us more aware of the split nature of our spirituality.

The *Collins Modern English Dictionary* defines the word 'holy' as follows:

1 of, or relating to, or associated with, God or a deity; sacred.
2 endowed or invested with extreme purity or sublimity.
3 devout, godly or virtuous. 4 'holier than thou', offensively sanctimonious or self-righteous.

Such definitions are unlikely to fill many of us with the desire to be holy! What is holiness in reality? And is the question of any importance? Is holiness a quality that attracts, encourages, delights and energises? Does it fill us with gratitude and overwhelm us with a sense of wonder?

Image and Identity

The Western world is much concerned with the question of image, both corporate and individual: What do we wear? How do we look? What do we eat? Do the things we say and the way we say them correspond to current standards of political correctness? Advertising is essentially an image industry. Because we confuse image with identity, we can pursue or protect images with all the intensity of our deep-rooted instinct for self-preservation. The saying 'I wouldn't be seen dead in it' is very revealing: although the phrase is a deliberate exaggeration, it touches upon the importance of image.

Confusion of Image and Identity Equals Loss of Identity

'What then will people gain if they win the whole world and ruin their lives? Or what have people to offer in exchange for their lives?' (Mark 8:37). What does it profit us if we project all the right images, are praised and promoted, decorated and elevated, and yet suffer the loss of our very selves? For all our modern sophistication, our political correctness and our claims to enlightenment, there is still much cruelty and nastiness beneath the surface. We step on one another in our efforts to project the best image while destroying our very selves in the process. Our search for identity is a healthy and necessary activity. But when that search leads us away from our true selves and into the pursuit of images, it leads us down a cul-de-sac that can end at the cliff edge.

Who Am I?

The teacher and scholar Donald Nicholl wrote a remarkable book called *Holiness* (Darton, Longman & Todd, 1981). I remember his description of a meeting he had attended: 'It was dreadful. We all had to sit in a circle and introduce ourselves. Most people introduced themselves by stating their jobs, "I'm a professor, a lecturer, an engineer, a doctor, etc." When it came to my turn, I just wanted to say, "My name is Donald. I am a unique manifestation of God" '! The authors of the New Testament and the early Christian theologians would have applauded, for Donald would have been repeating the good news that God is our ultimate identity. We have an astonishing ability to lose sight of this central truth, thus reducing Christianity to a moral code.

God is Our Ultimate Identity

St Paul addresses his first letter to the Corinthians to 'the saints at Corinth', and then reprimands some of them for their acts of incest, fornication and idolatry – not the kind of behaviour one expects of saints! In St Paul's usage of the word, 'holiness' is not something we have to create for ourselves, nor is it a reward for our virtue. Holiness is a gift, freely given, indestructible and always accessible. We can acknowledge the gift, or we may refuse to acknowledge it. What we cannot do is get rid of it, because the gift is God! 'Spirituality' is the process by which we become more aware of this gift of holiness and increasingly conformed to it. To the extent that we acknowledge the gift, our life will be transformed, as we allow God to be the God of love and compassion both to us and through us. Christians believe that this gift is given to every single human being and that it is a continuous process of giving.

We can read St Paul in such a way as to concentrate on his passages about sin while failing to notice his emphasis on our unique identity, our individual call to unity with God. We sin when we fail to allow God to be the God of love and compassion to us and through us. Our single-minded concentration on sin is, in itself, a result of our sinfulness! In his writings to the Galatians and to the Ephesians Paul reminds us of our true identity:

> I live now not with my own life but with the life of Christ who lives in me (Gal. 2:20).

> Out of his infinite glory, may he give you the power through his Spirit for your hidden self to grow strong, so that Christ may live in your hearts through faith . . . until, knowing the love of Christ, which is beyond all knowledge, you are filled with the utter fullness of God (Eph. 3:16–19).

18

That our ultimate identity is in God is beautifully illustrated in an early Christian homily by an unknown writer who imagines Jesus after his death descending into hell where he has a conversation with Adam. The conversation ends with Jesus saying to Adam, 'Arise, let us go hence; for you in me and I in you, together we are one undivided person.' What an astonishing sentence! We have lost sight of this essential truth about our ultimate identity to the extent that we can feel uncomfortable when we read it – as though we are listening to the ravings of a religious maniac.

Holiness, therefore, concerns our ultimate identity. We are not to be defined by our image, our job, our achievements, our qualities, our defects of character, nor by our ancestry, nationality, ethnic origins or religious beliefs. Our ultimate identity is in God. We can state this truth in words, but mere words cannot convey the meaning. Our Christian faith is not primarily about creeds or doctrines; it is about faith in the living God whom words cannot contain. God is to be experienced, not talked about! We need words, and we need theology, but words must be used to point us in the direction of the living God, who is always beyond words. We need words to reveal the truth, not to obscure it.

Words serve as signposts leading us into a wordless and deeper experience of God. Signposts are important because they point us in the right direction. In much of the bitter controversy that goes on among Christians about the orthodoxy or unorthodoxy of specific Christian positions, it is often the most vigorous upholders of orthodoxy who are, in fact, the most unorthodox because they can mistake the signposts for the destination itself. Vigorous assent to particular Christian propositions does not necessarily constitute an act of faith. A faith that is primarily thought of in terms of an assent to propositions can, in fact, be idolatrous, whereas true faith is an act of surrender to the living God, present in all people, in all circumstances, and in all things.

Our at-one-ness with God is not a state that we shall enjoy only after death: it is also our present state. After death, the manner of our awareness will be different, but the God we shall meet is the God who is holding us in being at this moment. The Holy One lives in us. Is there any way in which we can verify this assertion?

As God is Transcendent, There Must be Transcendence in Us Now

In the traditional teaching of every major world religion, God is transcendent, which means that God is always greater than anything we can think or imagine. For human beings, God must always be other, mysterious, elusive and unpredictable. God is always beyond our grasp:

> . . . for my thoughts are not your thoughts,
> my ways not your ways – it is Yahweh who speaks (Isa. 55:8).

God cannot be defined, privatised, domesticated or contained in any way. God will always be beyond us and ahead of us, as the pillar of cloud was always ahead of the Israelites as they wandered through the desert.

God is Also Immanent

If God is immanent, then God is present in all things, vibrant in every atom. In St Augustine's phrase, God is '*intimior intimo meo*' – 'closer to me than I am to myself'. Early Christian theologians spoke of creation itself as a sacrament, an effective sign of the presence of God.

Our divided spirituality tends to concentrate on God's transcendence to the exclusion of God's immanence – or God's immanence to the exclusion of transcendence. The difficulty lies in holding transcendence and immanence together at all times and in all circumstances. We would prefer God either to be transcendent or to be immanent. We can manage one, or the other: we find both to be unmanageable. The truth of the matter is that we are unable to 'manage' God despite our best endeavours. We have to surrender, and if we fail to do so it is not possible for God to be God to us and through us.

We shall first reflect on the signs of God's transcendence within us now. We shall look at signs of God's immanence in the following chapter.

God's Transcendence Here and Now

If we are made not only in the image of God, but in order that we may be at one with God, then there must be some signs of God's transcendence within us. If God is our ultimate identity, then there must be some signs in us now, signs that we are being called to 'Be holy, for I, Yahweh your God, am holy' (Lev. 19:2).

Writing in the thirteenth century, St Thomas pointed out that everything we can understand comes to us first through our senses. We can only come to a knowledge of God through our sense experience of God's creation. If we try to find God by ignoring our own experience, we shall construct an abstraction. And yet, with our split spirituality, this is precisely what we attempt. We are trying to find a God who is uncontaminated by anything earthly, and in this way we construct an abstract God – a form of idolatry suitable for the very refined!

About thirty years ago, when I was in conversation with Father Columba Ryan, OP, he said, 'God is like a tangent.' As a philosopher, Columba is given to profound statements that reduce the non-philosopher to silence. It was only years later that I began to appreciate his remark.

A tangent is a straight line that touches a circumference at a single point without intersecting it. Each circumference has an infinite number of points which can be touched by a tangent. The tangent differs from the circumference in that it arrives from one direction and proceeds in another. In this context, the circumference represents the limits of our human experience in which God is totally present, although we do not have the eyes to see this. God is not our human experience, but God is present in every one of our human experiences. This book explores the manner in which God is present and the way in which that presence is manifested. Let us start with some signs of God's presence in our ordinary everyday experience.

God in Our Agnosticism

The transcendent nature of God must in some way be within us if our ultimate identity is in God and we are called to be at one with God now, and not merely after our deaths. Consider this truth and then reflect on the absurdity of so much in our everyday lives. This may reduce us to a fit of the giggles. If the transcendent element exists within us, it would seem to be remarkably well disguised!

The very fact that we can find the thought of our own transcendence absurd is only possible because we have some notion of our own limitations – not just our physical limitations, but the limitations of our minds. A knowledge of our own limitations indicates that the mind contains an element that transcends itself. If this were not the case, we could not be aware of the limitations of the human mind.

Knowing the limitations of the mind must include awareness of the limitations of our knowledge of God. We can know this only because in some very imperfect way we share in the mind of God. From this it follows that an element of agnosticism or acknowledgment that the nature of God cannot be comprehended is in fact a mark of holiness. Complete religious certainty about God without any shadow of doubt is a sign of atheism. The God we *think* we know all about cannot be the true God, because God is always greater than our powers of comprehension.

Hunger for Knowledge and Truth as a Sign of Our Holiness

The search for knowledge and truth is a further mark of transcendence. 'God' has been called 'a beckoning word', constantly calling us out beyond ourselves. The beckoning of God is seen in our relentless pursuit of knowledge and truth, especially when it appears that the knowledge acquired is unlikely to be of any obvious benefit to anyone, or that the revelation of a particular truth will offend the powerful. A divine restlessness is one of the marks of holiness in an individual, or a group. The God who led Israel out of the prison of Egypt, through the wilderness and into the promised land, is the God of the now. Whatever form our bondage may take here and now, God is still leading us out of it and beckoning us on.

God's transcendence lies at the heart of all true religion. Forgetfulness of this truth can turn religion into a lethal virus in the human mind and heart, a virus that can rob us of our humanity and convince us that we possess the absolute truth, which it is our religious duty to impose upon others. True believers will always be open to views contrary to their own and will listen carefully and respectfully. They are aware of their own limitations and ignorance, and are therefore always ready to revise their opinions in light of truth communicated to them. The true believer will always be aware of non-knowing, and in that sense will possess a strong streak of agnosticism. People with a truly religious spirit are always searching and are sufficiently confident to question, because the strength of their religion lies in the living God, their rock, refuge and strength, rather than in any particular views they may hold.

As I mentioned earlier, the Church is well described as a 'pilgrim' Church, a Church in search of a way, a Church that is constantly on a road of discovery, a learning Church. If the Church is to be faithful to the transcendent God, it must never be rigidly dogmatic, resting in its own certainties and abandoning the search for truth. Openness to truth, suppleness of mind, love of learning and the confidence to question are among the marks of holiness in the Church and in its individual members.

In recent years we have experienced an outbreak of 'fundamentalism' across the world and in all religions. The word is unfortunate because religion must always contain 'fundamental', foundational beliefs. But in modern usage the word does not refer to fundamental beliefs themselves, but rather to the particular manner in which people relate to these beliefs, clinging to some particular aspect of their faith to the exclusion of any other, and clinging with a tenacity and rigidity that cannot admit any criticism or questioning. 'Heresy' was the former name for what we now describe as 'fundamentalism'. And the word 'heresy' derives from a Greek word meaning *choice*. The heretic chooses one aspect of faith to the exclusion of every other.

The Gift of Awe and Wonder is a Sign of Holiness

We discover glimpses of the transcendent in our ability to wonder, to be awe-struck, to sense the sacredness of a particular place, or glimpse the depth of mystery in another person. We sense our unity with all that we see. According to the research for the BBC *Soul of Britain* series to which I referred in Chapter 1, the majority of adults have experienced the transcendent in one or more of these ways. But because of our modern culture, most people are afraid to speak of such experiences in case they are thought to be 'odd'. What a tragic waste! These experiences of wonder are glimpses into the truth of our being, into our oneness with God, but they are also of great practical importance. Without developing the point in any detail, just reflect on the difference it would make if we really did show reverence to one another, listening carefully, treating one another respectfully, gently and with appreciation. Our violence towards one another, our tendency to regard other people as objects to be accepted or rejected, has its origin in the way we look upon ourselves. It is not narcissistic to wonder at the mystery of my own being, to accept and appreciate it, to treat it respectfully, gently and lovingly. If such a sense of wonder springs from our awareness that it is in God that we live and move and have our being, then our appreciation of ourselves will also be an appreciation of the mystery of others. Alongside such an awareness we can, at the same time, be aware of our frailty, our failures, and our proclivity to crass stupidity. We need not hide these truths from ourselves or project them on to others. We can acknowledge them, but without panicking, or indulging in self-loathing, because our security lies no longer in our own image, our own performance, our own virtue. It rests in the reality of the God in whom we live.

Laughter as a Sign of Holiness

Our ability to laugh, especially the ability to laugh at ourselves, is another sign of the transcendent within. Humour springs from our awareness of some form of incongruity in a situation, or in human or animal behaviour. It is only because we can get beyond our normal way of seeing things that we can recognise the comedy in a situation. Perhaps we shall have to wait for the moment when we meet God face to face before we can fully appreciate the humour of our present existence! An individual's sense of humour will be one of the expressions of holiness. Intense seriousness and lack of humour is a danger sign in any religiously inclined person. In the Roman Catholic Church, a spirit of joy and merriment has been one of the special marks of those who are to be declared saints.

Human Love and Human Desire as a Sign of Transcendence

The nature of human desire is another sign of the transcendent within us. We shall be considering the importance of desire in a later chapter. It is sufficient to notice here that if we ask ourselves, 'What is my deepest desire?', we find the question most difficult to answer with any precision. Looking back on his earlier life, St Augustine reflected: 'God, you have created me for yourself, and my heart is restless until it rests in You.' In asking ourselves about our deepest desire we become aware of the transcendent nature of desire within us. No person, no created thing, and no state of affairs can ever completely satisfy our inner hunger. Because of the limitations of our human nature, we have to settle for limited objectives. But if we become so satisfied with limited objectives that we cease to dream, it is a sure sign that we have died spiritually to the desire of the Holy One moving in us. In the closing words of Dante in the *Paradiso*:

> I felt my will and my desire impelled
> by the love that moves the sun and other stars (*The Paradiso*,
> Canto 33).

In all human love we can glimpse the transcendent. Love can take us out of ourselves, it can break us free from our self-imprisonment, energise us and change our perception of reality, which now seems to have acquired an inner luminosity. Our very self is changed by love, for I begin to see the beloved as me, and myself as the beloved, each giving life one to the other, but without possessiveness. St John tells us that 'God is love' and Jesus reminds us that 'Unless you lose your life, you cannot find it'. The truth of these words is confirmed by our human experience of loving another person, or of being released from our self-centredness through some project that draws us into the service of others.

Our Longing to be Free is a Mark of Holiness

The human desire for freedom is a manifestation of the transcend-ent nature of desire. Although we frequently confuse liberty with freedom, individuals and nations have been prepared to die rather than to surrender their freedom. In our better moments we prize freedom more highly than human life itself. Another person can deprive us of our liberty – totalitarian governments and groups can imprison us, try to control our thinking, bury us under bureaucracy, or threaten us with torture. Physical conditions such as earthquakes, floods, famine and ill health can restrict our liberty. But nothing can ultimately deprive us of our freedom except our own decision. If liberty is the freedom from any form of external control, then freedom is the ability to follow our deepest desires, whatever the external constraints.

One can suffer severe restrictions upon one's liberty while remaining free. This truth is strikingly affirmed in the diary of Alfred Delp, a German Jesuit priest who was imprisoned by the Nazis and eventually executed in 1945. In an entry in his diary, which he made while imprisoned, his hands bound with chains, Delp managed to write of the great inner freedom he was experiencing. Living true to his inner convictions had brought him to imprisonment, but he delighted in it. Freedom is about being true to the deepest desires within us. Such fidelity is incompatible with servitude or coercion in any form, whether enslavement to a despot, a totalitarian government, or to a religious system.

Freedom is costly and true freedom must begin from within. There is, in all of us, a strong resistance to freedom. We do not normally admit to this resistance, or even recognise it. We can cover up our resistance by giving it complimentary names, like 'faithfulness', 'loyalty', 'obedience', 'common sense', 'reason' or 'prudence'. We can succeed in our resistance to freedom, but we can never overcome the transcendent within us. In the long run, it is much more costly to resist freedom than to abandon ourselves to it. Such resistance opposes the deepest longing of our hearts – and to resist our deepest longing is to create hell for ourselves.

God alone is holy, and human beings are called 'holy' because the Holy One dwells within them. The Holy One is both transcendent and, at the same time, immanent. We have been examining some of the signs of the transcendent, the holy, within us. These include:

- Awareness of our own ignorance and of the limitations of the human mind.

- Awareness of our inability to know God adequately, while trusting God absolutely.
- Our longings and yearnings, which can never be adequately described.
- Our distress at feelings of emptiness and meaninglessness, because the transcendent within us knows that we are made for something greater.
- Our sense of awe and wonder.
- Our experience of love.
- Our longing for freedom, and our hatred of servitude in any form.

The word holiness, or transcendence, does not therefore relate to our state of virtue or of prayerfulness. The distinction we make between God's transcendence and God's immanence does not correspond to any distinction in God, in whom there is no division. The transcendent God is always the immanent God, and the immanent God is always transcendent. In this chapter we have looked specifically at the transcendent God in order to help us to discover more easily who we are and what it is that we are called to become. In the following chapter we shall look at God as immanent in all creation.

Exercises

1 Take a piece of paper and divide it into two columns. Look back to the beginning of the chapter where I suggested that you said aloud to yourself, 'I am holy'. In the first column scribble whatever occurred to you after saying to yourself, 'I am holy'. In the second column, scribble some of the characteristics that you would expect to find in a person who 'lets God be God to them and through them'.
2 Are you aware of a desire for freedom within you? Is it a desire for freedom, or a desire for liberty? That is, is it a desire to have all external restraints removed, or is it a desire to be what your deepest desire longs for?

DOWN-TO-EARTH HOLINESS

G OD IS CONTINUOUSLY PRESENT in you and in me and in all that
is. In the last chapter we looked at this truth in order to
recognise the presence of the transcendent God in us, the God
who is always calling us beyond ourselves. The transcendent,
always beyond us, is also *immanent*. 'Immanent' comes from the
Latin word *manere*, meaning to stay or to remain. Matthew's
Gospel quotes the prophet Isaiah: 'The virgin will conceive and
give birth to a son and they will call him Immanuel', a name that
means 'God-is-with-us' (Matt.1:23).

Consider again the phrase of Irenaeus, 'God became a human
being, so that human beings might become God.' What is God
like, this God we are invited to become? The Jewish writer of the
Book of Wisdom set about answering this question, and he wrote
his answers in Greek so that the Greek-speaking world could
know what the God of Israel was like:

> In your sight the whole world is like a grain of dust that tips
> the scales, like a drop of morning dew falling on the ground
> [*an image of God's transcendence*]. Yet you are merciful to all,
> because you can do all things [*the way in which the immanent
> God relates to you and to me*] and overlook men's sins so that
> they can repent.

Yes, you love all that exists, you hold nothing of what you have made in abhorrence . . . You spare all things because all things are yours, Lord, lover of life, you, whose imperishable spirit is in all (Wisd. 11:22ff).

After reading this biblical passage, take time to notice your *felt experience* while reading it. Did the passage appeal to you? Did it move you and delight you? Did it, on the other hand, annoy you, irritate you or frighten you? The God of the Bible is communicating with you now through the medium of these words. The strength of our felt reaction to a passage indicates the importance of that passage for us. In reading and pondering the words, we can begin to recognise God at work in us now. The God of Abraham, Isaac and Jacob is loving us, cherishing us and protecting us today. Use the same method of noticing and pondering your *felt experience* after reading the other Bible passages that appear later on in this chapter.

The following pages include many quotations from the Hebrew prophets. I use the word 'Hebrew' rather than 'Old Testament' because the prophetic message is not 'old' meaning 'outdated'. It is central to our faith now, and Jesus is the fulfilment of the prophets. The quotations are selected to show the meaning of holiness in God and in us; it is shown in our effective compassion for one another, whoever the other may be.

The passage from Wisdom contains a very brief summary of the teaching of the Hebrew prophets about the God of the Covenant. Some of the prophets describe this Covenant made on Mount Sinai as a 'marriage' – a marriage originally contracted with Israel, but destined to embrace all nations and the whole of creation.

'You love all that exists'. This is a key phrase, re-echoing the final words of the first chapter of Genesis: 'God saw all that he had made, and indeed it was very good'. God's relationship to creation is a relationship of love and compassion. In the Book of Amos we experience the nature of God in relation to ourselves and to the whole of creation. God is the God of love and compassion, and God is therefore the God of wrath against those who destroy God's beloved.

The understanding of God, revealed in the Book of Wisdom, draws upon the centuries-old prophetic tradition. The earliest recorded prophet is Amos, a poor shepherd living in the eighth century BC at a time when Israel was divided into a Northern kingdom and a Southern kingdom. The North was affluent and cultured, the South was poor and backward. Amos, living in the poor and backward South, was called by God to go and preach to the North. God gave Amos an abundance of zeal, but left him short on tact! In this passage, Amos is addressing the fashionable ladies of Samaria, perhaps as they were having afternoon tea in one of their summer residences:

> Listen to this word, you cows of Bashan
> living in the mountains of Samaria,
> oppressing the needy, crushing the poor,
> saying to your husbands, 'Bring us something to drink!'
> The Lord Yahweh swears this by his holiness:
> The days are coming to you now
> when you will be dragged out with hooks,
> the very last of you with prongs . . .
> It is Yahweh who speaks (Amos 4:1–3).

God is wrathful because the rich of Samaria have been 'oppressing the needy, crushing the poor'. This is a recurrent message in the Book of Amos and in the writings of all the prophets who followed him. In chapter five Amos continues in similar vein:

> Trouble for those who turn justice into wormwood,
> throwing integrity to the ground;
> who hate the man dispensing justice at the city gate
> and detest those who speak with honesty.
> Well then, since you have trampled on the poor man,
> extorting levies on his wheat—
> those houses you have built of dressed stone,
> you will never live in them . . .
> (Amos 5:7–11).

Split spirituality is nothing new. Amos and all the other prophets fulminate against Israel's solemn religious services because the devout worshippers fail to mirror the love and compassion of God in their attitudes to one another and to the stranger. Here is Amos on the subject of solemn worship:

I hate and despise your feasts,
I take no pleasure in your solemn festivals.
When you offer me holocausts,
I reject your oblations . . .
Let me have no more of the din of your chanting,
no more of your strumming on harps.
But let justice flow like water,
and integrity like an unfailing stream (Amos 5:21–4).

It is not only our prayers and solemn liturgies that God cannot endure. Fasting, lying down on sackcloth and ashes, and other external acts of penance can also be abhorrent to God, as Isaiah makes clear:

Is not this the sort of fast that pleases me
—it is the Lord Yahweh who speaks—
to break unjust fetters
and undo the thongs of the yoke,

to let the oppressed go free
and break every yoke,
to share your bread with the hungry,
and shelter the homeless poor,

to clothe the man you see to be naked
and not turn from your own kin?
Then will your light shine like the dawn
and your wound be quickly healed over (Isa. 58:5–8).

Continue to notice your *felt experience* after reading each passage.

There are three things to note in the passages from the prophets that portray God as a God of wrath and cruel vengeance.

First, there is a developing understanding of God in the Bible. The books the Bible contains were written over a period of 1,000 years. In some passages, God is presented as a very nasty character, vengeful and ruthless:

I saw the Lord standing at the side of the altar.
'Strike the capitals' he said 'and let the roof tumble down!

I mean to break their heads, every one . . .
and my eyes will be on them
for their misfortune, not their good' (Amos 9:1–4).

This God is very different from the God whom Jesus presents in
the Sermon on the Mount, a God who 'is kind to the ungrateful
and the wicked' (Luke 6:35).

Second, these threatening passages always end with the promise
of reconciliation. A few verses after the cruel threats in Amos 9,
God says, 'I mean to restore the fortunes of my people Israel'
(Amos 9:14).

In the third place, we need to notice the reason given by the
prophets for the wrath of God. God's wrath is directed against
those who are destroying the creation that Yahweh cherishes; they
oppress, exploit and destroy the poor and powerless for whom
Yahweh has a special love.

The Covenant: God's Marriage to All Creation

In the Covenant that God made with Israel, God pledges Godself
to Israel. The prophets speak of the Covenant in terms of a
marriage:

When that day comes I will make a treaty on [Israel's] behalf
    with the wild animals,
with the birds of heaven and the creeping things of the earth;
I will break bow, sword and battle in the country,
and make her sleep secure.
I will betroth you to myself for ever,
betroth you with integrity and justice,
with tenderness and love (Hos. 2:20–1).

The Covenant is made with Israel, but through Israel it is to be a
Covenant with all creation: 'with the wild animals, with the birds
of heaven and the creeping things of earth'. If Israel is to be
faithful to this Covenant, she must reflect the tenderness and
compassion of God for all creation in all her dealings; not only
her dealings with other Israelites, but in those with the stranger:
'If a stranger lives with you in your land, do not molest him. You

must count him as one of your own countrymen and love him as yourself' (Lev. 19:33–4).

The Prophetic Message Applied to the Modern World

This clear message of the prophets about the essential meaning of the Covenant has not only been quickly and effectively buried: it has also come to be considered a contamination of pure spirituality, an attempt to allow politics and social and economic reform to 'take over' from religion. What would the Hebrew prophets say if they returned to our world in which one-third of the population lives without adequate food, clothing and shelter, not because the planet cannot supply the necessary resources, but because we have devised an economy that protects and enriches the strong while impoverishing the weak and the powerless. Third World debt ensures a steady flow of goods and money from poor nations to rich ones and keeps the poorer nations securely held in the poverty trap created by the rich nations. The rich nations manufacture and arm themselves with increasingly sophisticated weapons of death, capable of destroying the main cities of any continent within minutes. They sell weapons to poor countries as well as to rich ones, thus encouraging violence between poor nations and ensuring a continuing demand for their remunerative lethal weaponry. This kind of behaviour is dressed up in the righteous language of self-defence: we are defending our freedom against wicked aggressors, rogue states and evil alliances. Our murderous policies are defended by the majority of citizens in the developed countries. We are respectable, churchgoing Christians, and too often we dismiss any questioning of our attitude upon religious grounds as 'humanist ranting'. Christians who question what we call our 'defence policy' are accused of bringing religion into politics! Our spirituality is so deeply split that we fail to perceive the illogicality of such accusations. The majority of those who object to the introduction of religion into politics are acting with sincerity, because they see religion and politics as completely separate entities. Jesus is safer in the cupboard!

In the Roman Catholic Church, candidates for sainthood are required to have performed at least one miracle after their death as a qualification for beatification, the preliminary step towards canonisation, the solemn declaration that the person is a saint. The miracle usually takes the form of some otherwise inexplicable form of healing. I wish that this criterion for canonisation could be altered in favour of concrete evidence of effective compassion practised by individuals during their lifetime. On these grounds I can think of many people who would qualify for canonisation – some of them still living. An obvious candidate would be Dorothy Day (1897–1980), the American founder of the Catholic Worker Movement which has spread from the USA to many other countries. Dorothy started centres providing food, shelter and companionship for the hungry and homeless. She edited a weekly paper on Catholic social teaching which her guests at the centres would sell. She would allow her organisation neither to receive state aid nor to be registered as a charity. Dorothy was also a pacifist. She denounced nuclear weapons, practised civil disobedience, and not infrequently came into conflict with the State and also with the Roman Catholic hierarchy. True holiness in an individual or group is always life-giving, challenging and threatening to State and religious authorities. In Jesus, his holiness led to his death.

Holiness in the Life of Jesus – His Relationship to 'Abba'

Jesus is distinguished from every other great religious leader by his relationship with God, whom he calls 'Abba', a child's name for 'father' and the equivalent of 'dad' or 'daddy'. The first recorded words of Jesus are: 'Did you not know that I must be busy with my father's affairs?' – the only quotation we have from the first thirty years of Jesus's life. He was twelve years old and had gone up to Jerusalem with his mother and father. At the end of the visit he disappeared and was found three days later by his distraught parents. Jesus had been in the Temple, listening to the doctors and asking them questions. To his mother's desperate plea, ' "My child, why have you done this to us? See how worried your father and I have been, looking for you?", he replied, "Did you not know that I must be busy with my Father's affairs?" ' (Luke 2:49).

This theme of at-one-ness with his father recurs constantly in the teaching of Jesus:

34

He who sent me is with me,
and has not left me to myself,
for I always do what pleases him (John 8:29).

If you know me, you know my Father too (John 14:7).

In the Gospel of Luke we are given the last words of Jesus before he died: 'Father, into your hands I commend my spirit' (Luke 23:46).

The Compassion of Jesus Mirrors His Relationship to 'Abba'

Because Jesus is 'the image of the unseen God', the compassion of God is his characteristic quality. The phrase 'He took pity' recurs frequently in the Gospels. The fourteenth chapter of Matthew begins with an account of the beheading of John the Baptist. When Jesus hears the news, he retires to a lonely place to grieve, and perhaps also in order to escape the attentions of Herod. The people hear that he has moved away, so they follow him. Matthew tells us that when he stepped ashore, 'He saw a large crowd; and he took pity on them and healed their sick.' As the day closes, Jesus does not dismiss the crowds as his disciples suggest. He tells the disciples to 'give them something to eat yourselves' (Matt. 14:17) and then performs the miracle of the loaves and fishes, feeding the 5,000.

The Compassion of God in the Teaching of Jesus

In the parables and in all his teaching, Jesus emphasises the compassion of God. When the Pharisees and the scribes complain that he welcomes sinners and speaks with them, Jesus offers three parables illustrating the compassion of God. The first is about the shepherd with a hundred sheep, who leaves ninety-nine of them in the wilderness while he goes off and searches for the lost one. 'And when he found it, would he not joyfully take it on his shoulders and then, when he got home, call together his friends and neighbours? "Rejoice with me," he would say "I have found my sheep that was lost." In the same way, I tell you, there will be more rejoicing in heaven over one repentant sinner than over ninety-nine virtuous men who have no need of repentance' (Luke 15:6–7).

The second parable is about the woman who loses one of her ten drachmas. She sweeps out the house and searches until she finds it. When she finds it, she calls her friends and neighbours to celebrate with her. '"Rejoice with me," she would say "I have found the drachma I lost." In the same way, I tell you, there is rejoicing among the angels of God over one repentant sinner' (Luke 15:9–10).

In the third parable God is pictured as the father of two sons, one the prodigal, the other the prig: God shows compassion to them both. God is presented as a father who spends his days waiting and watching for his prodigal son to return home, as though God had nothing better to do with his time. This point was noted by the fifteenth-century Italian mystic, St Catherine of Genoa, in terms of God's relationship to herself: 'God has nothing else to do with his time but to look after me'! The prodigal son has spent all his inheritance. He is a disgrace to the family, as the elder brother points out. But the father rushes out to meet his son, embraces him, and kisses him tenderly. When the son confesses his sins and his shame, the father appears to take no notice, but immediately tells his servants, 'Bring out the best robe and put it on him; put a ring on his finger and sandals on his feet. Bring the calf we have been fattening and kill it; we are going to have a feast, a celebration.' When the older brother complains at this indulgence, the father does not reprimand him for being unforgiving: he simply says, 'My son, you are with me always, and all I have is yours' (Luke 15:21ff).

Another striking parable illustrating the compassionate nature of God is that of Dives and Lazarus. This parable is a frightening one because Dives, the rich man who ends up in hell, is not portrayed as exploiting, oppressing or abusing the beggar: Lazarus. Dives simply does not notice Lazarus who sits at his gate, 'covered with sores . . . [and longing] to fill himself with the scraps that fell from the rich man's table' (Luke 16:20–1). Most of us know how easy it is to be so preoccupied with our immediate concerns that we fail to notice the distress of those around us. We also fail to make connections between, for example, the pictures of famine victims we see on the television and the supermarket shelves with their bewildering choice, some shelves entirely given over to varieties of pet food. It is claimed that recent famines are not the result of food shortages, but are caused by regulations covering trade and distribution that are to the advantage of richer countries. Investors are grateful for the high rate of interest earned by their shares, and can fail to make the connection between their own financial gain and the plight of starving peasants, driven off their land by multinational agricultural businesses conducted on strictly commercial principles. In the same way, we fail to connect the fate of innocent victims of landmines with the fact that Britain has exported landmines in order to boost its economy.

When Jesus told parables, revealing a God of tenderness and compassion, he infuriated the scribes and Pharisees. Such teaching undermined their authority, so they had to get rid of him. The images of God that Jesus gives us in the Gospels were to be overlaid with fearsome images of a legalistic, fearsome God who damns the majority of the human race to eternal punishment. One reason that the scribes and Pharisees receive such a bad press in the Gospels may well be that the Gospel writers saw signs of pharisaism creeping back in the early Church. Later in this book we shall be looking at our human tendency to project some of our own nastier characteristics on to God: our hatreds, our desire for revenge, and our delight in the disasters that befall our enemies. In this way we create a God of vengeance, a God whose primary interest lies in noting the sins of the people and preparing suitable punishments for them.

Our Split Spirituality Prevents God's Holiness/Compassion from Transforming Our Lives

Our split spirituality encourages us to pursue a private, individualistic spirituality. We may appear to ourselves to be models of respectability within the narrow parameters of what we consider to be our individual sphere of responsibility. For this reason, some Christians in public life can advocate inhuman policies such as capital punishment, or a market economy that ignores the plight of the powerless – compassion appears to be damaging to the national economy! There are many who are praised by their supporters for their advocacy of zero tolerance for particular criminal offences and for their support for a more punitive penal system in the interests of law and order. The crisis of our time does not lie primarily in the danger of nuclear annihilation, environmental pollution or over-population. It lies rather in our mental conditioning, our ingrained culture of violence.

It would be wonderful if we could overcome the dangers of pollution and global warming and if all nuclear weapons could be destroyed. Wonderful if every human being could have adequate food, water, shelter, education and health care and the world economy could boom. But we would not be secure until we had tackled and eradicated the roots of our own violence, hatred and aggression. Holiness is about this eradication. Holiness is like a light that uncovers our pretence and our hypocrisy; it is a fierce hurricane that sweeps away the false securities of our society, constructed so carefully in order to ensure that the rich grow richer and the poor grow poorer. In the Western world our worth is measured by our intellectual and material possessions. In this way we become a competitive society and the more competitive we become, the more losers there are bound to be. The more desperate the struggle to survive, the more violent we shall become. The greatest danger facing the human race is the world-view that sees human life in terms of a power struggle. We are convinced that in order to survive we must compete rather than co-operate. This is like a lethal virus infecting the human race. When the Church forgets the real meaning of holiness, that virus is just as likely to flourish within the Church as outside of it.

God's Compassion Embraces All Peoples, Including the Wicked

Because God, the Holy One, is a God of compassion, the kingdom of God is intended to be an inclusive kingdom, open to all. If the Church is to be an effective sign of God's presence, then the Church must also be inclusive so that every human being is welcomed, regardless of race, class, colour, belief or lack of belief. This inclusivity may occasionally be expressed in words, but our divided spirituality ensures that the universality and all-inclusiveness of the Church is seldom experienced by those who do not belong. The essential inclusivity of God's kingdom is strikingly illustrated in the parable of the wedding feast (Matt. 22:1–14).

In this parable, God is represented as a king who throws a feast for his son's wedding. Many of those who were invited do not accept the invitation. The king is not pleased at these refusals, and sends out his servants, telling them, '". . . go to the crossroads in the town and invite everyone you can find to the wedding". So these servants went out on to the roads and collected together everyone they could find, bad and good alike; and the wedding hall was filled with guests' (Matt. 22:9–10).

This parable is astonishing and scandalous when compared to the normal image of God with which most of us are familiar. God invites everyone. This must have infuriated the Pharisees and scribes, and it still infuriates those fundamentalist Christians who consider any move towards ecumenism to be the work of the devil. The scribes and Pharisees must have been still more infuriated and scandalised by Jesus presenting a God who fails to correct those servants who announce that they have invited everyone, 'good and bad alike'. One can imagine the spluttering indignation, the huffs and puffs of the outraged faithful, the pronouncements of church authorities and the leading articles in the religious press, assuring readers that anyone who speaks like this of a God who does not exclude the bad must be of the devil.

In later chapters on church unity and on the Eucharist we shall be returning to this theme of the essential inclusiveness of God's kingdom. It is sufficient to note here that inclusivity is a mark of God's kingdom, a mark of holiness in individuals and in groups.

How Do We Relate to God? Primarily by the Way We Relate to Others and to Their Needs

In Matthew 25 Jesus gives his own answer to our question 'what is holiness?' in his description of the Final Judgment. The saved will be told, 'Come, you whom my Father has blessed, take for your heritage the kingdom prepared for you since the foundation of the world. For I was hungry and you gave me food; I was thirsty and you gave me drink; I was a stranger and you made me welcome; naked and you clothed me, sick and you visited me, in prison and you came to see me.' When the saved ask God, 'When did we see you like this?' God tells them, 'In so far as you did this to one of the least . . . you did it to me.' The lost are told by God, 'I was hungry and you never gave me food; I was thirsty and you never gave me anything to drink; I was a stranger and you never made me welcome, naked and you never clothed me, sick and in prison and you never visited me.' When they ask, 'Lord, when did we ever see you like this?' they are told, 'In so far as you neglected to do this to one of the least of these, you neglected to do it to me.'

What ultimately matters before God? It is a question to linger over, and we shall be returning to it in later chapters. What matters to us now? The amount we earn? What we eat? How we are clothed? Where we live? How we look? How we are thought of by others? Our financial security? What causes us anxiety, what brings us delight? What makes for our peace, what troubles us? How far does it matter to us that we belong/do not belong to a church? How far does it matter to us that we pray regularly/never pray? What, in fact, matters most?

Familiarity can dull our sense of wonder and, as a result, those of us who are familiar with the Gospels can read Jesus's description of the Final Judgment without being much affected. For this reason we need to keep praying for enlightenment, for sensitivity, and for the ability to respond to God's word. It is, for example, astonishing that Jesus, of all people, fails to make any mention of religion, religious observance, orthodox religious belief – or any other kind of religious belief. Neither does he provide a list of moral precepts on which we shall be judged. It is not that these matters are unimportant: it is simply that they are not what matters most.

The teaching is unmistakably clear. Our relationship to God is manifested primarily in the way we relate to other human beings and their needs rather than in the frequency, fidelity or fervour with which we perform our formal religious duties. But in the lives of so many clergy their primary concern is with the upkeep and development of church plant and real estate; with points of doctrine and church order; with the form of religious worship. Clergy who preach sermons expressing concern about the social/political structures that cause hunger, homelessness and poverty are frequently denounced by those in public office for contaminating true spirituality with humanist ideas.

Jesus's Teaching on Holiness in the Sermon on the Mount

We find the clearest teaching of Jesus about the meaning of holiness in his Sermon on the Mount – the Christian manifesto. 'How happy are the poor in spirit; theirs is the kingdom of heaven' (Matt. 5:3). We shall be looking at the beatitudes in greater detail later, but in this section we focus our attention on the compassion of God that underlies the teaching of Jesus.

'Poor' and 'poverty' are ambiguous words, and the phrase 'poverty of spirit' can be ambiguous. A person who has no hope, no fight left, can be said to be suffering from 'poverty of spirit'. When Jesus says 'Blessed are the poor', he is telling us that the poor are 'blissfully happy', for that is the meaning of the Greek word *makarios*. To be *makarios* is to enjoy a state of bliss that nothing can shatter, not even death itself. The blessed have so completely surrendered themselves to God, that God has become their rock, refuge and strength. They know, deep within their spirit, that God is their ultimate security, and they know, too, that whatever their circumstances at this moment, God is with them. In the words of Julian of Norwich, 'All shall be well and all manner of things shall be well.'

The phrase 'Blessed are the poor in spirit' contains the core of the teaching of Jesus. It is an invitation to surrender our whole being to God, so that God may be the God of tenderness and compassion to us and through us. In the remainder of the Sermon on the Mount, Jesus elaborates on all that follows from this initial surrender to God: 'Love your enemies, do good to those who hate you, bless those who curse you, pray for those who treat you badly. To the man who slaps you on one cheek, present the other cheek too; to the man who takes your cloak from you, do not refuse your tunic. Give to everyone who asks you, and do not ask for your property back from the man who robs you . . . Love your enemies and do good, and lend without any hope of return' (Luke 6:27–30). Why are we to behave in a way so utterly contrary to our normal manner of life? Jesus tells us that we are called to behave like this in order to become children 'of the most High, for he himself is kind to the ungrateful and the wicked' (Luke 6:35). 'Be compassionate as your Father is compassionate' (Luke 6:36). This is what holiness is about.

The Eucharist, Manifestation of the Holiness to Which We are Called

At the Last Supper, Jesus, knowing his death was imminent, takes a piece of bread, gives thanks, blesses the bread and gives it to his friends, saying: 'This is my body which will be given for you. Do this in my memory' (Luke 22:19ff). After supper he does the same with the cup of wine, and says: 'This cup is the new covenant in my blood which will be poured out for you.' In this self-giving of himself to us, Jesus expresses the very essence of God's relationship to ourselves. God gives God's very self to us. Jesus reveals this truth in his own person. His whole life is a communication of his life to us. At the Last Supper Jesus celebrates this truth in offering himself as the bread and wine to his friends. He then tells them to 'do this in memory of me'. With our split spirituality we interpret this to mean 'Keep celebrating the Eucharist in formal worship', but it means far more than that. Jesus is saying, 'Let what I have done, in giving you myself as the bread and wine, become the pattern of your lives, too, so that my self-giving becomes your self-giving to one another, so that you live for, not against, one another.'

It is tragic that this wonderful sign of the reality of God's continuous self-giving to all peoples should have become a cause of deep and bitter division, leading sometimes to death. Present-day regulations about who may or may not receive the Eucharist are still causing deep pain, scandal and division, especially within families.

The Eucharist is a sign, one that expresses a reality. The reality it expresses is God, the ground of our being, in whom we all live, and move, and have our existence. Jesus reveals the nature of God to us when he takes the bread, breaks it, and says:

> Take this, all of you, and eat it:
> This is my body which will be given up for you.

Similarly, he takes the cup of wine and says:

> Take this, all of you, and drink from it:
> This is the cup of my blood . . .

It will be shed for you and for all,
so that sins may be forgiven.

The Eucharist is not just a commemoration of a past event: it is celebrating a present reality, just as present now as it was in that upper room 2,000 years ago. The bread and wine are signs expressing the reality of God, revealed in the person of Jesus Christ; a God who is love unconditional, a God who wants to be at one with us, a God of tenderness and of compassion. God gives God's very self to each of us, not because of our virtue, our achievements or our merits – but simply because we are. In earlier centuries we put one another to death because of the way we understood the Eucharist! Thank God we no longer do this, but we remain divided from one another in our eucharistic celebrations. When one reflects and wonders at this sign of God's love and of our human destiny, we also have to wonder and be appalled at the manner in which we have understood the Eucharist, such that God's self-giving becomes a cause of division between us.

Christian division over the Eucharist reflects the depth of the split in our spirituality. Holiness, which is the presence of the Holy One, is thought of as different from spirituality, which is about the presence of the Spirit of God. Spirituality is in vogue today, holiness is not. In many modern bookshops there is a large section devoted to spirituality, with a supermarket-like display of the bewildering variety of spiritualities on offer! In the light of the previous chapters, are there any rough guidelines that can help us in our search for a spirituality today?

The 'Fourfold Grid': Guidelines for Distinguishing True Spirituality from False

I have entitled this section the 'Fourfold Grid' because it offers four essential characteristics for any genuine Christian spirituality.

1 The intra-personal

The first section of the grid is the 'the intra-personal': the way in which we relate to our own inner selves, to our moods, feelings, emotions and mental states. There is a sense in which the intra-personal is the most important part of the grid, because the source of our behaviour lies in our thinking and our feeling. The way in which we relate to ourselves governs the way that we relate to others. To what extent does the reality we are living relate to our inner experience? Our mistakes arise from our inability to know the true harmony of things and our continual attempts to impose a false harmony. It has been said that 'Wisdom is to know the harmony of things: joy is to dance to its rhythm'. Much of our pain and sorrow comes from our inability to dance to the rhythm; instead we hurl ourselves against the restraints of reality, or we try to remove them from our path.

Inner states are very important, but they can lead us to draw the wrong conclusions about our spiritual health if we consider them in isolation from the rest of the grid. Suppose that you were to ask me how I pray and I was to tell you that 'My prayer time is the most important and precious time of my life. It fills me with peace, joy and delight. I pray frequently and never fail to be helped by it.' Taking it for granted that I am speaking the truth, would it necessarily follow that my spirituality is sound? In order to answer that question, we need to look beyond the intra-personal part of the grid and examine the second, or *inter*-personal, section. We shall return to this first or intra-personal section in a later chapter.

2 *The inter-personal*

In Christian understanding, all genuine prayer is prompted by the Spirit of God, who prays in us. Our task is not therefore to 'pray', but to remain still, relaxed and aware in order to allow God to be the God of love and compassion to us, and through us. The inter-personal aspect of our spirituality includes our relationships with our own immediate circle of family, friends, relatives and the people with whom we work. Suppose you were to enquire about my inter-personal relationships and I were to answer, 'They are an impossible bunch of people. I can't stand most of them and have not spoken to them for years.' Such an answer would lead you to the correct assumption that there was something fundamentally wrong with my spirituality. Through Jesus, God tells us to 'Love your enemies, do good to those who hate you, bless those who persecute you' (Luke 6:36). In my attitude to my own immediate circle I am not letting God be God.

It does not follow that if my spirituality is genuine, my inter-personal relationships will be excellent, enriching and life-giving. They may, in fact, be extremely painful. The important thing is the fact that I am trying to let God be the God of love and compassion to those around me, however impossible I may find them. The seventeenth-century Dutch Jesuit St John Berchmans described community life as 'my greatest mortification'! As far as we can judge from the Gospels, the relationship between Jesus and his immediate circle was not always easy. If our spirituality is genuine, in the sense that we are allowing ourselves to be moved by the Spirit of God, then we shall try to be forgiving and loving towards our immediate circle, however impossible they may be.

3 The social

If you continue to talk to me about my spiritual life I might tell you that besides the excellence of my prayer, my relationships with my own immediate circle are now also very good. 'We not only get on very well, we also work happily together in a worldwide export business which God has blessed and allowed to prosper beyond all our hopes and dreams.' Assuming that your spirituality is so advanced that you still have the patience to listen to me, you might ask, 'And what is it that you export worldwide?' If I answer, 'Personnel landmines', then I have failed in the third part of the grid, called 'the social'.

This third section of the grid helps us to look at our own attitudes, values and destructive defences. These can imprison us in our fears and prejudices, separating us from the other members of the human family who are loved by God regardless of their race, status, nationality or religion. Examples of such destructive attitudes are to be found in sexism, racism, militarism, consumer-ism and narrow nationalism in the sense of 'my country right or wrong'. We have become so accustomed to such attitudes that we no longer recognise them as Godless. We shall come back to these attitudes in a later chapter.

4 *The environmental*

The fourth part of the grid concerns our relationship to the environment. God made a Covenant not only with human beings, but with all creation. 'Yes, you [God] love all that exists, you hold nothing of what you have made in abhorrence' (Wisd. 11:24). A healthy spirituality must include an increasing awareness of our inter-relatedness with all creation, with animals, plants, forests, rivers and oceans. As human beings we do not have the right to look on the rest of creation as our personal fiefdom. In this twenty-first century we are very much more aware of the close connection between our own well-being and that of the environment. We now appreciate that our greed can literally destroy us because we have poisoned our environment and depleted the ozone layer with atmospheric pollutants. We are responsible for climactic changes that threaten the well-being of the planet and condemn millions of people to hunger, disease, misery and death. As individuals, as groups, as nations, and as Church, we need to allow God to be God to us and through us. In this way we can develop an increasing sensitivity to the environment and manifest a spirit of compassion rather than a commitment to rapacious greed.

Acknowledging Our Failures is to Begin to Change

We need to be very gentle in applying the Fourfold Grid to our own spirituality. After reading through the sections of the grid I may have concluded, mistakenly, that I am not remotely spiritual in terms of the first, or intra-personal, aspect – let alone the others! My prayer rarely feels peaceful, life-giving or strengthening – and it certainly does not feel joyful. Life in my immediate circle is impossibly difficult, and I do not generally feel well disposed to those around me. My social attitudes may be more akin to the jungle than to the Gospels, and I pay no attention to environmental issues beyond becoming irritated by the dictates of environmentalists.

In our relationship to God, it is not the excellence of our performance that matters, but our faith and our reliance on God as the source of our goodness. To be aware of my own failures and to acknowledge them is a mark of God's grace. If I can keep the focus of my attention on God, then God will increasingly become the God of compassion to me and through me. When I begin to see the reality around me in a different way, then my behaviour will begin to change.

In this chapter we have looked in greater depth at the split nature of our spirituality, and at the meaning of holiness. How can we ensure that our intra-personal life, the way we think about other people and other things, is in harmony with external reality? Are there any ways of praying that can help to heal the split in our spirituality, so that our prayer makes us more perceptive and responsive to God at work in all things? This is the subject of the next chapter.

Exercises

1 Try applying the Fourfold Grid to:
    (a) spirituality as you were taught to understand it in your youth. Which part(s) of the grid were emphasised/omitted?
    (b) spirituality as you now understand it to be. Does your present understanding omit any section of the grid? Does it emphasise any particular section?
2 Read the prophecy of Amos – either in full or as quoted in this chapter – then, if you are a churchgoer, state what changes you would suggest for your parish in the light of the Fourfold Grid.
3 Look back at the scripture readings in this chapter. Read one or more and notice again your *felt experience*.

EARTHING OUR PRAYER

> as form in sculpture is the prisoner
> of the hard rock, so in everyday life
> it is the plain facts and natural happenings
> that conceal God and reveal him to us
> little by little under the mind's tooling.
>   (from 'Emergings' by R. S. Thomas)

Michelangelo claimed that he did not create his sculptures: he 'uncovered' them, hidden in the marble. R. S. Thomas may have had Michelangelo's claim in mind when he wrote 'Emergings'. God is to be found in 'the plain facts and natural happenings' that reveal God gradually when we focus our attention on the facts. In this chapter we shall be looking at 'the mind's tooling', to quote R. S. Thomas, and considering ways of seeing and responding to the things of earth. We shall be praying out of our own experience, and in this way learning how to heal the split in our spirituality.

'Raising the mind and heart to God' is a traditional and valuable description of prayer, but it can be misleading because of the split nature of our spirituality. If we think of God as 'the Supreme Spirit', transcendent, different and distant, then any thought, memory or image that comes to mind in prayer can be considered 'a distraction' – something that draws us away from God. If we understand God in this way, it is hardly surprising that so many of us are unenthusiastic about prayer; and those of us who do try to pray and to avoid 'distractions' soon become dispirited by constant failure. This chapter provides some suggestions for prayer that are based on the truth that the transcendent God is immanent – intimately and actually present in all things and in all circumstances. If we understand prayer in this way, there is nothing that we can think about or imagine that cannot become the substance of our prayer.

Prayer in General and its Relationship to Everyday Life

We receive information at different levels of our minds. We may hear a particular word or phrase – and life is changed as a result. We may, on the other hand, be told a telephone number, register it for long enough to dial it, and then forget it. We may see a film that moves us deeply – but the feelings vanish when we step out of the cinema.

In contrast to this, we are told that 'The word of God is something alive and active: it cuts like any double-edged sword but more finely: it can slip through the place where the soul is divided from the spirit, or joints from the marrow; it can judge the secret emotions and thoughts' (Heb. 4:12). But the word of God, as every regular churchgoer knows, can often be more like a sedative than a two-edged sword. Our minds and hearts can become enclosed in the armour-plating of our own self-preoccupation, so that the word of God bounces off, like seed falling on rock, or it disappears into the vortex of our busyness.

In the Gospels Jesus gives us a parable in which he compares God's work to that of a sower. Some of the seed he sowed fell upon rocky ground, but soon withered because it had no depth of earth. More fell upon the edge of the path and was eaten up by birds, and some seed fell among thorns, but the thorns choked it, and it produced no crop. But some seed fell into rich soil, producing thirty, sixty, or even a hundredfold, crop.

In this chapter we shall be looking at ways in which we can become more perceptive and responsive to the word of God, so that 'the seed' can penetrate to the core of our being and transform us. In the words of St Paul: 'Glory be to him whose power, working

in us, can do infinitely more than we can ask or imagine'
(Eph. 3:20).

This transformation does not begin and end in us; in some way
it has an effect upon the whole of creation. God's gifts are never
given simply for the good of an individual: they are given for the
well-being of all humankind, including the good estate of our
enemies!

The Cosmic Dimension of Prayer

We are interconnected in ways that our conscious minds can
rarely grasp. A respected medical writer recently asserted that there
are six trillion chemical changes per second in the human body!
God knows how he arrived at such a figure. Perhaps he was
exaggerating wildly and the real figure is a mere one trillion – one
million times one million! How many of those changes are you
aware of in your own body at this moment? Nuclear physicists
write of the close interconnectedness of all things, telling us that
when a baby throws the rattle out of its cradle, the planets rock!
We are constantly acting upon, and being acted upon by, everything else in the universe. Even our observations can effect change.

Human observation of subatomic particles can, we are told,
change the nature of the particle! In the search for the ultimate
particles of matter, it has been claimed that there are no ultimate
particles: we are told that in every particle is every other particle!
Modern physicists are beginning to sound like mystics in some of
their utterances. In every major world religion mystics have spoken
of the interconnectedness of all people, of all things, of the ability
of prayer to transcend the barriers of space and time. Prayer can
be the most effective activity in which we can engage. It can be
especially powerful in those who are sick in mind or body, and in
those who are feeling desperate for whatever reason – perhaps
weighed down by their own guilt. Why is prayer so powerful in
such people? The reason is that in their helplessness they are more
likely to allow God to be God to them and through them. God is
the God who: 'has pulled down princes from their thrones and
exalted the lowly. The hungry he has filled with good things, the
rich sent empty away' (Luke 1:52–3). It therefore follows that
prayer is the most subversive activity in which we can engage.

If all Christian leaders were asked the question 'Do you consider prayer to be important in Christian life?', it is unlikely that any of them would answer, 'Certainly not'. But suppose that all Christians, including the leaders, were asked the question, 'Apart from being taught set prayers, have you ever had any instruction in the practice of private prayer?', I suspect that less than 5 per cent of them would answer 'Yes'. I further suspect that only 5 per cent of the leaders and those who had trained for Christian ministry would be found to have had any such training. This is another result of the split nature of our spirituality; there is a division between what we profess and what we actually do.

Some Elementary, but Frequently Forgotten, Facts About Prayer

No one is able to pray! Prayer is a surrender of our whole being to God, so that God may be the God of mercy and compassion to us and through us. Too much conscious effort can kill prayer! Prayer is about letting the Spirit of God pray in us. The Spirit who lived in Jesus, and raised him from the dead, now lives in us.

Prayer is about being still, so that we can become more perceptive and more responsive to God. In prayer, 'Heart speaks to heart'. God, who is love, speaks to us, and we speak from the heart to God. Our prayer does not have to be articulate, well phrased or eloquent, but it must be sincere, honest and without pretence. Prayer may be groans and grumbles; it may be 'ahs and ohs', or it may be wordless; but it must be 'me'. Each person is unique in the sight of God and for this reason there can be no single way of praying. The simpler our prayer, the more honest and heartfelt, the better it will be. The psalmist tells us to 'Be still, and know that I am God' (Ps. 46:10).

Why Being Still is So Important

Stillness is important in prayer so that we can become more aware and sensitive to the promptings of God within us. The English cartoonist Calum specialised in God cartoons. God was usually portrayed as a tubby figure, resting on a cloud, his head haloed, hands joined on his large tummy. He would be looking down on earth and commenting on what he saw and heard. In one cartoon God is observing choirs down below singing hymns of praise, and he remarks: 'I've had a fair amount of adulation in my day'! During church services I often imagine Calum's God addressing the congregation and saying, 'For heaven's sake, shut up and stop trying so hard; be quiet and listen for a change'!

To what kind of God do we pray? Our idea of God is derived from our life experience. For those of us who are brought up with an awareness of God, this usually means that the idea comes first from our parents, then from siblings, teachers and preachers. We tend to create a God in our own image and likeness, or in that of our Church or our nation. We can therefore have some very fearsome images of God! In this way we have managed for centuries to justify killing one another, each side in war claiming to be fighting '*Pro Deo et Patria*' – 'For God and Country'. This same habit of creating God in our own image and likeness has also enabled us to foster suspicion and hatred against people of other faiths or of none, and against Christians of different denominations. We convince ourselves that we are being loyal servants of God in attacking God's 'enemies' and suspecting the worst in them.

We need to be still in prayer, so that God can teach us who God is, as distinct from us teaching God how God ought to be! It is good to begin every prayer with, at least, a short period of stillness, even if only for a few seconds.

Some ways of being still

Prolonged physical stillness is very hard for most of us, and stillness of the mind is even more difficult. Years ago I read a book on prayer which stated that the most perfect form of prayer was the prayer of quiet, without words, thoughts or images. I decided that this was to be my form of prayer in the future. In trying to drive out all words, thoughts, memories and imaginings, I found that I had hit on the most effective method of summoning to consciousness every interesting thought, memory and imagining I had ever experienced!

The quickest and most effective way of learning how to be still is to practise stillness frequently. There are many different ways of doing this. All are based on the fact that the mind is capable of concentrating on only one thing at a time. If, for example, I concentrate my whole attention on what I am physically feeling now in my body, I cannot, at the same time, be thinking about God, or anything else. There are two stages in the process I am describing – the first is to become still, and we shall then move on to more explicit ways of praying out of the stillness.

On practising stillness – Method 1

Sit with your body thoroughly relaxed, your feet flat on the ground, your back straight, but not rigid. If you are supple enough, sit in the lotus position.

When you feel ready, concentrate all your attention on what you can physically feel in your body. You may like to start with your right foot, then move around the body. There is no need to cover the syllabus! You may prefer to spend the time in concentrating on one particular part of the body.

Attend to the feeling, but don't start thinking about what you are feeling! I may, for example, start by attending to the feeling in my right foot. I experience a light tingling sensation. I may conclude that this must indicate some circulation problem and I decide to visit the doctor. My imagination then begins to visualise an operating theatre, a deathbed, and then my funeral! As soon as you become aware that your mind is straying from the immediate physical feeling, bring it gently back to attending to the feeling itself.

If any other thoughts occur to you – for example, 'this seems a great waste of time', 'is it some Eastern thing?', 'is it safe?' – then acknowledge them as interesting thoughts that can be attended to later. Then return to the present physical feeling itself.

If you experience an itch or some other form of discomfort, acknowledge it, but, if you can, try not to move, and turn your attention back to the part of the body on which you were focusing.

Now try this stillness exercise for a few minutes. Afterwards, spend a few moments reflecting on how you found it. Was it difficult or restful? When your attention strayed, were you able to bring it back to the physical feeling? How did you feel after the exercise? Peaceful? Agitated? Rested? Tired?

This type of stillness exercise is frequently used as a means of relaxing, resting, coping with stress, or learning to control pain. If you found the exercise difficult, then congratulate yourself and do not be surprised. If your attention kept straying from *feeling* the body to *thinking* about it, or thinking about a variety of other things, it is a sign that you are becoming more aware of the difficulty of being still, and this is a sign of progress. The important thing is to keep practising one of the methods of stillness.

Other methods of practising stillness

There are many variations on this stillness exercise. You can, for example, focus your whole attention on the physical feeling of breathing in, then of breathing out. Do not deliberately attempt to alter your breathing.

Another method is to concentrate all your attention on the sounds you can hear, starting with the immediate sounds around you and then moving out to more distant ones. Do not try to identify the sounds: just listen to them.

Stillness of mind can also be attained through rhythmic movement such as slow walking. While you are walking, focus your attention on the physical feeling of walking, or on your breathing as you walk. Alternatively, you might focus on the sounds you can hear. Another way of stilling the mind while walking is just to stare at the scenery as you walk. The Scots call this 'gawking', and it can be a very stilling exercise. Experiment with these exercises to discover which suits you best.

Methods of stillness: preparation for very simple forms of prayer
Go back to the first method of stillness in which it was suggested that you sit comfortably and then focus all your attention on what you can feel in a particular part of the body. When you feel relaxed, start to reflect on the phrase that St Paul uses in addressing the people of Athens:

> [God] is not far from any of us, since it is in him that we live, and move, and exist (Acts 17:28).

Because we have become more aware of what we are physically feeling in the body, we become more open to the wonder of it, the miracle of our own bodies. How is it possible to explain the extraordinary intelligence of our body, the co-ordination and communication between the billions of cells that form our body, the intricacy and complexity of a single cell, every individual cell unique to each one of us, and each cell bearing within it the design of the whole body. Each cell knows exactly how to react to the food and drink you consume. How do the cells know what to keep and what to pass on, so that each part of the body receives the nourishment it needs? This intelligent designing and ordering of the body does not proceed from our conscious minds – if it did, our lives would be very short! Where is God in all this? God is in this process, nearer to us than we are to ourselves, ground of our being, maker and sustainer of our body. God is where we are, and the only place in which any of us can meet God is within our own experience. This is a truth that we keep trying to ignore. There are people who scorn the phrase 'finding God in our own experience', as though individual experience can only have a contaminating influence upon God. People who take this view set standards for God that the God of Abraham, Isaac, Jacob and of our Lord Jesus Christ constantly fails to attain! God can communicate with us only through our own senses and our own experience.

Pondering on the closeness of God who is present to us in our own experience, we can then speak from our own heart to the Heart of all creation. We can speak to Love itself, to a Love that cannot be lessened, even by our sinfulness. If any reader feels this remark to be heretical, try to pass it over and read instead the following words from the fourteenth-century English mystic Julian of Norwich: 'The testing experience of falling [into sin] will lead us to a deep and wonderful knowledge of the constancy of God's love, which neither can nor will be broken because of sin. To understand this is of great profit' (from *Enfolded in Love*, Daily Readings with Julian of Norwich, Darton, Longman & Todd, 1980).

Similarly, the breathing exercise suggested above can become a simple prayer of surrender to God when you have focused on the physical feeling of breathing in and breathing out, and the exercise has brought you to a degree of peace and stillness. At this point, let every in-breath become a wordless expression of all that you long for. Stay with this for as long as you can. (I do not mean that you should hold your breath for as long as you can!) Keep letting every natural in-breath express the longing of your heart. Then turn your attention to your out-breath, and let it express your total abandonment of yourself to God, along with all your anxieties, worries, responsibilities, all your sins, sinfulness and guilt. Breathe out all your inner darkness into the expanse of God's goodness. If it helps, imagine God's goodness to be a boundless ocean into which you hurl all your anxiety, negativity and sinfulness.

The listening exercise can also become a more explicit prayer. It was originally suggested in terms of listening to the sounds around us while either sitting or walking. Having listened to the sounds outside and within you, pray to reach that still point within all sound, and keep praying: 'God, out of your silence, teach me'.

Repetition of a favourite phrase can also induce inner stillness. The psalmist prays constantly: 'Show me your face'. If you find this phrase attractive, keep returning to it. When I am walking, I find it very helpful to repeat the phrase '*Qu'il est bon, qu'il est bon, qu'il est bon, le bon Dieu*' in rhythm with my step. I find that the English version is less rhythmic and sounds less natural – 'How good, how good, how good, is the good Lord'.

In general terms, any way of praying is good if it helps you to become still in mind and heart. Many people are helped by using a 'mantra' – an Eastern term that refers to any sacred word or syllable that is said or sung repeatedly as a means of inducing inner stillness. A single word or phrase from a well-known prayer, such as the 'Our Father', can be used in this way.

In Christianity, many of the prayers now used in public worship were originally the prayers that pilgrims used when walking to a sacred destination. In the Roman Catholic tradition, examples include the rosary and short repetitive prayers addressed to the saints, which we know now as litanies. Many people find this sort of prayer unhelpful when recited while sitting or kneeling, but it can be stilling if recited when walking.

We try to become still in order to become more sensitive to the reality of God who alone can teach us who God is. There are many passages in both the Old and New Testaments that remind us of this:

When the Lord has given you the bread of suffering and the
water of distress, he who is your teacher will hide no longer,
and you will see your teacher with your own eyes. Whether
you turn to right or left, your ears will hear these words
behind you, 'This is the way, follow it'. You will regard your
silvered idols and silvered images as unclean. You will throw
them away like the polluted things they are, shouting after
them, 'Good riddance!' (Isa. 30:20–2).

We shall be looking at the meaning of the 'silvered idols' in a
subsequent chapter. Here it is enough to note that the 'silvered
idols' in our own lives can induce deafness and blindness so that
we no longer recognise our teacher, nor hear what it is that we are
being taught.

Recognising God in everyday events – Part 1

In an earlier chapter, I quoted Father Columba Ryan's observation
that 'God is like a tangent'. A tangent can touch the circumference
of a circle at any one of an infinite number of points, and in the
same way we can find God present in the variety of our human
experience. How do we do this?

Towards the end of each day, many of us find ourselves reflecting
on the events of the past twenty-four hours. If we have had a
major row, we recall it, remembering what was said and with what
tone and expression. We replay the scene to our advantage, adding
in the cutting remarks with which we might have demolished our
opponent, had we been sufficiently quick-witted! This power of
recall can also be used in a very creative way in order to help us to
become more aware of the reality of God's presence in our
experiences of the day.

It is good to begin all forms of prayer with a simple request
such as: 'God, let my whole being be directed to you, so that you
may be the God of compassion and love to me and through me.'
It is possible to make this prayer, however half-asleep, inadequate
or absent from God we may feel.

Having made this request, we can then play the day back
to ourselves in any order, focusing our attention on those moments
we enjoyed, appreciated or cherished, however trivial they may

seem. Avoid any self-judgment, whether of approval or disapproval.

This is a very simple and natural exercise. After doing it for the first time, most people are surprised to discover how many things they actually enjoyed during their day. The exercise also helps us to see the day in perspective, preventing some negative incident from discolouring all other memories.

This exercise anchors our spirituality in the reality of the love of God. In recalling the moments of the day for which we are grateful, we can begin to glimpse the depth of those moments. These gifts are tokens of God's love; of God wanting to give God's very self to us. Those of us who are churchgoers are accustomed to prayers and hymns praising the goodness of God. Through this exercise we can actually experience that goodness.

Such a simple exercise at the end of each day can have a transforming effect on us. During the Roman Catholic Eucharist there is a central prayer that begins with the phrase, 'It is our duty, and it leads to our salvation that we should thank you always and everywhere . . .' This is a rather solemn way of telling us that the purpose of our lives is to thank God. We cannot thank God sincerely unless we have genuinely enjoyed and appreciated God's gifts. If it is our duty to thank God, then it must also be our duty to enjoy and delight in God's creation! It has been said that at the Final Judgment God will ask us one single question: 'Did you enjoy my creation?' If my answer is, 'Certainly not, I was far too busy searching for the transcendent God', then I am likely to be in trouble!

If we make a habit of reviewing the day in this way, we shall find that it will affect the way in which we see the world and everything and everyone in it. Life is God's gift to us. God is in the gift. Through that gift we are being called into the life of God. The transcendent is in the immanent and the immanent is in the transcendent. The extraordinary is in the ordinary, the ordinary in the extraordinary. Every bush is burning if only we have the eyes to see! If we do this exercise regularly, we shall become increasingly aware of the tragedy of the split nature of our spirituality.

Recognising God in everyday events – Part 2

Having thanked God for the moments of delight, peace, etc. during the day, it is helpful to pray for enlightenment, so that we can come to glimpse God in every other moment.

God is in everything that happens, including those moments for which we feel no gratitude: the painful, disturbing, threatening events of my life. How are we to find God in the negative experiences? How is God to be discovered in impossible people, bad health, failure and my own sinfulness?

In praying for enlightenment, remember to avoid self-judgment, either positive or negative. This is important, because our own self-examination can blind us to what is really going on. By refraining from deliberate self-judgment, we are more likely to recognise the truth about ourselves. We have an extraordinary capacity for self-deception. Those aspects of ourselves that we are not prepared to acknowledge, we project on to other people. We blame them, revile them, despise them, and feel self-righteous, unaware of the damage we are doing to ourselves as well as to those we despise. We have loaded on to others the faults we cannot bear to admit in ourselves. When we do judge ourselves, we are very selective, choosing those faults that we really consider to be negligible. We shall be looking again at this tendency to be selective, because it lies at the roots of our capacity for violence.

After praying for enlightenment, look at your moods and feelings during the day, but without moralising about them. Moods and feelings in themselves are neither right nor wrong, neither true nor false: they are simply moods and feelings – signals that let us know what is happening. We have to learn how to read these signals. Rightness or wrongness, truth or falsehood belong to our reactions to these signals; not to the signals themselves. Because we do not like to admit to negative feelings such as anger or irritability, we can disregard these signals, without realising that such behaviour can be as reckless and dangerous as ignoring traffic lights.

It is undoubtedly true that our moods and feelings are influenced by what we choose to eat and drink as well as by medication and drugs – legal and otherwise. In general, however, it is desire that influences our moods and feelings, and desire that therefore leads us to eat and drink – wisely or unwisely. When our desires are satisfied, our mood is likely to be good, and we can afford to be charming. When our desires are frustrated, our feelings complain, and we are less affable to those around us. The point of looking at our moods and feelings is to help us to discover where our desire really lies. Feelings are very revealing because they can unmask our self-deceptions.

Moods and feelings in any one day are likely to be varied and complex. In looking at them, do not attempt to cover the whole syllabus, and avoid any attempt at analysis. Simply glance at the predominant moods and feelings of the day and then ask yourself what desire underlies them. Have I failed in some project? Have I made a fool of myself and been criticised? If so, why do I feel so strongly about it? The answer lies in the strength of my underlying desire. Desire for what? Do I feel strongly because whatever went wrong during the day affects God's kingdom of love, tenderness, compassion and peace? Or do I feel strongly because it touches on my own kingdom of status, reputation, security and prestige? This question – 'for whose kingdom?' – can be devastating in revealing to us our own narrowness and meanness, our own conceit and vanity, and our childish self-centredness.

Why am I so devastated when faced with these truths? If prayer is part of my life, it is probable that I keep protesting that God is my rock, my refuge and my strength, but when my securities are actually threatened I feel devastated. If prayer is not part of my life, I can still be only too well aware that moods and feelings can signal and reveal my own lack of integrity. I may like to think of myself as compassionate, open and friendly – but if I look at the desire underlying my moods and feelings, I may find that my real desires are directed primarily to what is going to be best for me.

At the end of the review of the day the most important thing is to return to the prayer with which you started: 'God, let my whole being be directed to you so that you can be the God of compassion and love to me and through me.' No matter what has come to light in the review of the day, or how devastated we may feel at our own failures, the most important thing is to return to that first prayer, this time entrusting our whole being to the goodness and the compassion of God. We can do this in spite of all our failures and the likelihood of more failures to come, because our trust is not in our own strength, but in the power of God at work within us. There is a prayer of Julian of Norwich that can encourage us: 'Our soul rests in God, its true peace; our soul stands in God, its true strength, and is deep rooted in God for endless love.'

Both the stillness exercise and the review of the day are very 'earthed' forms of prayer. But the processes of entering into stillness and reviewing the immediate past need not be restricted to times of prayer, for these are useful tools that can be helpful in all spheres of human activity. This is a manner of 'being in the world', a way that brings peace, not agitation; awareness in place of blundering insensitivity.

In these methods of prayer, the attitude needs to be one of alert passivity rather than activity. We are allowing reality to impinge on us rather than trying to impose ourselves, or our views, upon reality. Our attitude needs to be contemplative rather than analytic, intuitive rather than cerebral. In every aspect of our lives, a contemplative attitude is key to our happiness, peace and well-being. I referred earlier to the words, 'Wisdom is to understand the nature of things, and joy is to dance to its rhythm'. As we saw in a previous chapter, the emphasis in our culture is not so much on learning the harmony of things, as in trying to impose our idea of harmony upon reality. Listen, for example, to politicians and their interviewers addressing any topic on radio or television. It is rare for either interviewer or interviewee to show any sign of a contemplative attitude. Such encounters are, instead, combative, confrontational and defensive. Neither side learns from the other, but together they succeed in strengthening their individual defences against change. I mention politicians, but we are all afflicted with similar defences against change. This attitude enters into our prayer as we hurl our petitions at God, as though God were deaf, and our attention is less on God and more on our own prayerful performance! We can be so set in our own ways and so full of our own opinions that we cannot hear the still small voice of God, let alone the quite loud voices of our unfortunate neighbours.

Some ways of praying from Scripture – Part 1

Because our spirituality is so badly split, many people feel they must pray only from formally approved religious books, preferably the Bible. The Bible obviously plays an important part in Christian life, but it is also full of encouragement to use whatever we see and experience around us as aids to prayer. We find this especially in the psalms and in the parables of Jesus:

> I look up at your heavens, made by your fingers,
> at the moon and stars you set in place—
> ah, what is man that you should spare a thought for him,
> the son of man that you should care for him? (Ps. 8:3–4).

> Think of the ravens. They do not sow or reap; they have no storehouses and no barns; yet God feeds them. And how much more are you worth than the birds! (Luke 12:24).

We read the Bible not primarily to inform ourselves about the past, but to learn how we are to find God in the present. We read about the God of Abraham, Isaac and Jacob, and of the God of our Lord Jesus Christ, in order to become more aware of that same God at work in our lives here and now. We are sometimes given the impression that God shut up shop when the last of the apostles died, or the last full stop was put in the final book of the New Testament. But God is continuously communicating with us in our hearts.

Centuries before the invention of printing, monks and nuns were praying the Bible in monasteries. Bibles were handwritten, so they were in short supply and most of the monks could not read anyway. A literate monk with a scroll would address the gathered community, repeating over and again a particular short Bible passage. As he read, the monks, one by one, would return to their cells, not because they were tired of the reading, but because they had heard a word or phrase that appealed to them. They wanted to go off to ponder and pray over the phrase that had attracted or disturbed them.

In praying the Bible today, we need to choose a passage that appeals to us in some way, preferably a short passage. A list of possible texts is included both in the Appendix, and at the end of

this chapter. Many people find this text from Isaiah helpful –
words spoken to Israel when they were in captivity, without hope
of release:

> For Zion was saying, 'Yahweh has abandoned me,
> the Lord has forgotten me'.
> Does a woman forget her baby at the breast,
> or fail to cherish the child of her womb?
> Yet even if these forget,
> I will never forget you.
> See, I have branded you on the palms of my hands
> (Isa. 49:14–16).

As in all private prayer, begin with, 'God, let my whole being be
directed to you so that you can be the God of compassion and
love to me and through me'. Then be still, even if only for a few
seconds, in order to remind ourselves what we are about. The
emphasis on stillness may seem trivial, but it can be of enormous
importance. We may be aware that the span of our attention is
only milliseconds and that our consciousness is like an airport
during rush hour: thoughts, memories, imaginings, hopes and
worries arriving, departing and queuing for attention. But in
prayer we move into the core of ourselves, into the control room,
where we pray from the deepest part of our being, like the psalmist:
'Bless Yahweh, my soul, bless his holy name, all that is in me!'
(Ps. 103:1–2).

Now return to the Bible text from which you have chosen
to pray. Read it over several times. It can help to do this
aloud. Do not attempt to analyse the text or to think about it or
read a commentary – that can be done later. Read the text slowly
several times. After a few readings, notice whether any word,
phrase or image appeals to you. Let us suppose the phrase is, 'I
will never forget you'. Focus your attention on this. Hear the
phrase spoken to you now by God, the words coming to you
from the core of your being. What response do you want to
make? Just be yourself and be spontaneous in your response.
Your reply may be silence or incredulity. Perhaps it is anger,
because your personal experience is of having been forgotten
rather than remembered.

If a particular word or phrase engages your attention and you begin to have a conversation with God, you will nevertheless find that sooner or later 'distractions' are likely to occur. Distractions turn our attention from prayer to more mundane matters: 'How am I to pay next month's bills?' or 'What if my medical test results show there is something seriously wrong?' Acknowledge these 'distractions' and bring them into the prayer, if you can; share the distractions with God so that they become the substance of your prayer. If this seems an odd thing to do, we need to ask ourselves why we consider it odd. Should God not be bothered with such questions? Is God above trivia, including questions about my bodily health? It can be over-whelming to discover in my heart that God really is interested in the tiniest details of my health and well-being: that God cares about every hair on my head – or lack of it! Do we really believe in a God who can be as homely as this?

There are, however, some 'distractions' that really do turn the focus of our attention away from God. The 'distraction' may be very 'religious': something said from the pulpit, or mentioned in the religious press, which has left me hopping mad. I know that if I pursue this particular distraction, irritation and anger will prevent me from continuing in prayer. I therefore acknowledge the distraction, but let it go for the time being. This is difficult, and at times it seems impossible. But practice can enable us deliberately to focus our attention upon one thing and away from another, instead of being distracted by every new arrival and departure. When matters that arise in prayer draw us into a swirl of powerful emotions, it is important to recognise the strength of the emotions and to acknowledge the thoughts, especially the negative ones. Then hand them over to God. We are not denying the feelings and thoughts, however painful, however negative they may be. Instead we are choosing to hand them over to God rather than plunging into them. Later, when the storm has abated, we can look at them again.

Why is it helpful to read particular Bible verses repeatedly as part of our prayer and to notice any word or phrase to which we feel drawn? Our feelings are, in many ways, far more intelligent and perceptive than our conscious minds in terms of knowing and meeting our needs. Feelings, too, seem to be less bound by time and space than the logical mind. Feelings discern what is needful and register its importance by their intensity. We must of course bring our minds to bear on what we have felt and try to trace the root of the desire that has given rise to the feelings. It is as though feelings are indicating a seam of precious metal. We may spend weeks, months, years – or a lifetime – in following up that seam, which can lead us deeper into the wonder and mystery of our being.

This method of praying the Bible allows God's word to impinge upon our everyday experience. We are no longer trying to keep 'God' and 'everyday experience' strictly apart. The process of constantly allowing thoughts and feelings about everyday things to become part of our prayer is rather like the process of bread-making, which Jesus describes in the Gospel of Matthew. He tells us that, 'The kingdom of heaven is like the yeast a woman took and mixed in with three measures of flour till it was leavened all through' (Matt. 13:33). If we pray the Bible in this way, our whole being is leavened 'all through' by the word of God, not just the 'spiritual' part!

In Chapter 6 we will look at this way of praying in terms of discerning the difference between the things that are drawing us to God and those that turn us away from God.

Some ways of praying from Scripture – Part 2

Another way of praying from Scripture is through the use of the imagination. Christians are accustomed to studying the Bible and there are innumerable books and courses to help us to do this. Bible study is one thing: praying the Bible is quite another. One can qualify for a doctorate in biblical studies while remaining an atheist. The practice of praying Scripture imaginatively may prove to be the most valuable experience of our existence – and it can turn our lives upside down. Imagination is a wonderful and much neglected faculty. Our culture tends to recognise as valuable only those things that can be measured. Imagination can, however, intuit the truth of things that are often inaccessible to the logical reasoning mind. Biblical teaching is full of imagination, and the parables of Jesus are all exercises in imagination.

People often give two reasons for their reluctance to attempt to use their imagination in prayer. The first is that they claim not to have any imagination – meaning that they do not possess much visual imagination. But we can 'imagine' with all our senses, not just with sight. We can produce stories, creative ideas and theories in imagination without necessarily visualising them. Visual imagination is linked to memory; without it you could not find your way from wherever you are reading this book to your next port of call!

The second reason for our reluctance to use imagination in prayer is that we are afraid, although usually unconscious of the fear. Use of the imagination can bring us into closer touch with the reality of things, so that we become more able to recognise not only our own illusions and self-deceptions, but also our own gifts and strengths. But it is frequently more comfortable to remain out of touch with all this so that we use the word 'imagination' to imply the reverse of reality – as in such phrases as 'The pain is all in his imagination', meaning that there is nothing really wrong with him.

Christians profess that Jesus is the Lord of all things and that God dwells within us. But when we feel overcome by our own sense of insecurity and our own inferiority, we are unable to recognise the inconsistency between the truth we profess to believe and the way in which we behave when that truth is put to the test.

Imagination can be used in praying any Bible passage, but it is especially suited to Gospel scenes. As with any other method of prayer, begin with the words 'God, let my whole being be directed to you so that you can be the God of compassion and love to me and through me'. Then still yourself, taking as long as you may need. A former Archbishop of Canterbury was asked in a radio interview about the amount of time he gave to private prayer each day. His answer was, 'About five minutes, but it takes me about forty minutes before I am ready for the five!'

Once you are still, read again the passage on which you are going to pray until you are thoroughly familiar with it. Suppose, for example, you have chosen the short passage from John 20:19–21, which describes Jesus's appearance to the disciples on Easter Sunday evening:

> In the evening of that same day, the first day of the week, the doors were closed in the room where the disciples were, for fear of the Jews. Jesus came and stood among them. He said

to them, 'Peace be with you', and showed them his hands
and his side.

The disciples were filled with joy when they saw the Lord,
and he said to them again, 'Peace be with you. As the Father
sent me, so am I sending you.'

Pray for what it is that you desire in this time of prayer – for
example, 'God, let me and all peoples know your peace'.

Imagine that the scene is taking place now, and you are in it.
You don't have to imagine yourself as a Galilean of 2,000 years
ago. Just be yourself, but a participant and not a spectator. Do not
force anything. The ideal is to let imagination lead you, rather
than trying to control it. Imagination works in different ways for
different people, and it can act in very varied ways on the same
person at different times. Starting imaginative prayer can be like
switching on a defective television set: the screen may remain
blank, or indistinct. Be patient. In order to get into the scene, it
can sometimes help to imagine that we have to describe it, as
vividly as possible, to a child. The success of our prayer is not to
be measured by the vividness of our imagination, or the intensity
of our feelings. We may not be able to get 'into' the scene and
remain dry and distracted. But the important thing is to pray for
whatever it is that we have decided to pray for during this time of
prayer, however blank our imagination may remain.

In order to keep our attention on the scene, it is useful to ask
questions, such as, 'What kind of room are we gathered in? Is it
large, or small, circular or rectangular, is it light or dark? Who
are the other people in the room? What are they doing? What, if
anything, are they talking about?' Without forcing anything, see
if you can talk/interact with any of the characters. The Gospel
passage tells of the fear of the disciples. Listen to their conversation. You may like to talk with them about your own fears.
The disciples had closed the door for fear of the Jews. Are you
aware of having 'closed a door' for fear of a particular event or
person?

When Jesus appears, see the effect he has on the frightened
disciples: 'The disciples were filled with joy when they saw the
Lord.' Then see him turn to you, call you by your name, and say,
'Peace be with you', showing you his wounded hands and side.

What response do you want to make? Let your heart respond as spontaneously and honestly as you can. Talk with the Risen Lord as you would talk to a friend in whom you have absolute trust. Grumble and complain, if that is how you feel, trusting that God is big enough to take your tantrums. There is no set way of praying imaginatively, just as there is no set way of having a conversation that goes deeper than the weather.

Before beginning to pray imaginatively, or in any other way, it is good to decide beforehand how long you are going to give to prayer and to stick to that amount of time, especially if the prayer does not appear to be getting you anywhere. It can, in fact, be good to prolong the time of prayer when it is dry, difficult and apparently pointless. This is not an exercise in masochism. Our consciousness is multi-layered and transformation takes place at the deeper layers. The superficial layers of consciousness are usually the noisiest and most demanding, and the conscious mind is often unaware of any deeper levels until some crisis looms. In prayer, we journey through layers of consciousness. A period of blankness in which nothing seems to be happening is usually the forerunner of progress to a deeper layer of consciousness. If we abandon prayer whenever we experience boredom, aridity and negativity, we are unlikely to reach those layers of consciousness where transformation is likely to occur. The volume of noise and information and the rapidity of change all pound upon a nervous system that has evolved gradually over hundreds of thousands of years in order to cope with the stresses of a nomadic way of life which then became pastoral. Evolution of a new human nervous system takes millennia: the microchip culture produces instant change. In order to survive the massive surface assault upon our psyche, we need to learn how to live in the deeper and more protected regions of that psyche, where we can choose how to live and act rather than merely responding as pawns in the power struggles of the few. One way of exercising this sort of choice is to remain with our prayer when it is boring and does not seem to be getting us anywhere. It is good to end with some closing prayer such as the 'Our Father'.

On reflection after prayer

After praying, it is important to spend a few minutes looking back on the period of prayer in a relaxed way while having a cup of tea, or going for a walk. At this point, we are looking primarily at our *felt experience* during the prayer. We have already seen that our feelings are often more intelligent than our conscious minds. Feelings are a great source of wisdom, if we can learn to read them.

This period of reflection is not an analysis of the prayer. It is rather a form of contemplation, a kind of 'gawking' at our prayer experience. Was the prayer time peaceful, strengthening and joyful, or was it sad, agitated and anxious? Do not judge these feelings, just note them. As we have already seen, feelings in themselves are neither right nor wrong, true nor false: they are simply 'feelings'. The categories of rightness or wrongness, truth or falsehood can only be applied to the way in which we react to our feelings, not to the feelings themselves. It is as though the feelings are saying to us, 'What gave rise to these feelings is very important for you. You have a lot more to learn from us!' Next time you pray, come back to the phrases/words/images that gave rise to these particular feelings.

Note, too, any persistent distractions during the prayer. By distraction I mean any event, thought, memory or imagining that persisted in forcing its way into your consciousness, diverting your attention from God and turning it on to yourself.

The point of looking at persistent 'distractions' is that the things we term 'distractions' can sometimes be a nudge from God. Our first reaction to a 'distraction' should be to present it to God in prayer. The distraction may be a row we are having with someone, a difficult relationship, or some disappointment. If we bring the distraction to God during prayer and examine it in the subsequent time of reflection, we may begin to see that there is a conflict between the desire for God that I am professing in my prayer, and a particular attitude in myself to which the 'distraction' is calling my attention.

During imaginative prayer, the imagination may present us with something that seems bizarre. If so, do not dismiss the unwelcome visitor, but try to bring it into prayer, as with any other apparent distraction. One particular priest had just such an experience when praying John 1:35–9:

On the following day as John stood there again with two of his disciples, Jesus passed, and John stared hard at him and said, 'Look, there is the lamb of God'. Hearing this, the two disciples followed Jesus. Jesus turned round, saw them following and said, 'What do you want?' They answered, 'Rabbi,' – which means Teacher – 'where do you live?' 'Come and see' he replied; so they went and saw where he lived, and stayed with him the rest of that day.

The priest found himself standing beside John the Baptist. He and John had both turned into mechanical toys; each one holding up an arm, pointing first at the crowd in front of them, then at the figure of Jesus passing by, and saying together in the same dull voice, 'Behold the Lamb of God'. The gestures and the words continued relentlessly. The priest felt miserable throughout what he considered a useless prayer time.

During his prayer he had been feeling particularly wretched and sad. When he reflected afterwards on the source of these feelings, he recognised that they lay in his own sadness at his 'automaton' state. When he further reflected on the desire underlying the pain, he recognised that he wanted his whole life to be Christ-centred, but weariness was frustrating that deepest longing. Although this reflection was painful for him, it proved to be very fruitful. Instead of concluding that he was no good at praying with the imagination, the priest began to see its value. He found that he was able to pray to God in his exhaustion and he was surprised at the strength of his own longing to be Christ-centred. He became aware that his most urgent need was for a long rest in order to recover his strength.

Prayer can never fail! Whatever happens in prayer mirrors, in some way, the reality of ordinary life. The precise way in which prayer does this is known only to the individual. This overworked parish priest had been close to burnout and the mechanical figure, pointing to the crowd, then to Jesus, and saying in a dull voice 'Behold the Lamb of God', was an accurate reflection of his inner state.

We cannot learn how to pray simply by reading books on the subject or attending lectures. Prayer can only be learned by praying, because God alone can teach us how to pray. Any of the methods of prayer suggested in this chapter can help us to heal the split in our spirituality. In the following chapter we shall be looking more closely at the nature of desire – the 'control room' of our lives both in prayer and out of it.

Exercises

(There are many exercises suggested here. Take your time with them and never rush them.)

1 Practise some of the ways of being still. Do not force anything. Start by doing one of the stillness exercises on pages 53–7, and be content, *at first*, with a few minutes only.
2 Try practising, every day, the 'review of the day' on pages 57–8, but start with Part 1 only, recalling those events of the past day for which you are grateful. Relish them in memory and thank God for them.
3 Once you are familiar with Part 1, you can then add Part 2 of the 'review of the day' (pages 59–61).
4 Sometime, when you have time, practise Part 1 of the praying from Scripture exercise on pages 62–5. Use the text from Isaiah on page 63. Reflect on the prayer afterwards, as suggested on pages 69–71. In subsequent times of prayer, return to any word or phrase in the passage that moved you, whether positively or negatively. This process is called 'repetition': it allows the word of God to penetrate more deeply into our layers of consciousness in order to bring about transformation. 'Repetitions' can be the most valuable part of our prayer.
5 Practise imaginative prayer using John 20:19–21 on pages 66–7, and in future prayer periods keep returning to those images, words and phrases that affected your feelings. Always make sure you have had a conversation with God, or with Jesus, during the course of your prayer. This conversation can be spread throughout your prayer: it does not have to be left till the end.
6 Other Scripture passages for prayer can be found in Appendix 2.

ON DESIRE

A SCHOOLGIRL ONCE ASKED her teacher, a nun, why it was that St John, in his Gospel, kept repeating the same phrases. The nun explained, 'You must remember, my dear, that St John was a very old man when he wrote the Gospel, and old men tend to repeat themselves'! Some phrases can bear endless repetition: it is not so much that they convey information, but they open a door, leading us into a new and exciting world. One such phrase is that of St Augustine: 'Lord, you have created me for yourself, and my heart is restless until it rests in you.'

In Chapter 2 we looked at features of our human experience that indicate the transcendent God dwelling within us and around us. One of those features is the nature of human desire. No person, no thing, no state of affairs, can ever completely satisfy our deepest desire. In this chapter we shall further explore the nature of desire and its relevance to every other aspect of our lives as individuals, as Church and as nation.

Progress in the spiritual life has often been compared to mountaineering, as if when we come closer to God we approach the summit. How are we to climb the mountain of God? We are unable to do so, but God can get us up the mountain. In religious language, we express this reality in such phrases as, 'Without God we can do nothing', 'God is my rock, my refuge and my strength'.

Pursuing the image of the mountain climb, it is as though we are 'roped' to God, our lead climber. What corresponds to the rope in human experience? Human desire is the 'rope' attaching us to the God in whom we have every particle of our being.

I have never met anyone who could remember being taught the importance of desire. On the contrary, desire has usually been presented as a dangerous tendency; something to be curbed and brought into submission to 'the will of God', which is the only 'legitimate desire' for a conscientious Christian. As a result, the more scrupulous can find their lives blighted. When they are happy, delighted, enthusiastic and generally enjoying life, they feel that there must be something wrong. They feel bad about feeling good! This is bringing us to the heart of the split in our spirituality: on one side of the split are the longings of our heart, the core of our being; on the other side is God. I do not know whether Satan ever seeks advice. If I were Satan's adviser on the most effective method of destroying Christianity, I would advise against any persecution or even hint of opposition: instead, I would suggest that Satan ensures that Christian leaders emphasise the danger of human desire, and the need to subject it totally to the will of God, constantly warning their flock that anything they desire must be rooted in their own selfishness, which they must constantly oppose. This will ensure that they always feel bad about feeling good and will soon ensure the destruction of Christianity, because it cuts the very lifeline between human beings and God, destroying the very core of our being and leaving us without hope or enthusiasm, incapable of love or responsibility, perfect citizens of hell.

The Relationship Between Our Desiring and the Will of God

Jesus taught us to pray to God, 'Thy will be done on earth as it is in heaven'. His life was summed up in his desperate cry during his agony in the garden: 'Let your will be done, not mine' (Luke 22:42). We must do God's will and not our own. I believe that this truth lies at the heart of our faith. But what does it mean, and what is the relationship between God's will and my own will? Is it simply a question of submitting our will to the will of God? If your answer is 'Yes', then consider the following scenario.

Imagine a couple getting married. They have been encouraged by the presiding minister to use their own formulation of the marriage vows, so the groom declares 'You are my heart's delight and I love you, my dear, with all my being. However, you must understand that from this moment on, you must not expect me to have the slightest interest in your wants and desires. Henceforth, till death do us part, your whole good and your happiness consist in your doing my will with total dedication, resisting and overcoming your own.' Having solemnly declared his love so movingly, the groom awaits the bride's answer! This is the image of God that can lurk in the Christian subconscious. With such an image of God, it is not surprising that we sometimes appear to be less than enthusiastic for the things of God, and we can begin to understand the advantages of a split spirituality. If we allowed this monstrous God into every moment of our lives, life would be unendurable!

It is extraordinary how readily this phrase, 'the will of God', can trip off the tongue. It is even more extraordinary how often the will of God seems to coincide precisely with the personal preferences of those who use the phrase! God has long been recognised by tyrants as a most powerful and useful ally. To keep their subjects under control, the Roman emperors declared themselves to be divine. Thus disobedience to the civil authority was also an offence against God, whose punishments for disobedience were inescapable, pursuing the perpetrators beyond death and lasting for eternity. In Christian Europe, kings did not claim to be divine, but they claimed instead to rule 'by divine right'. In this way their orders became God's orders.

'The will of God' is a phrase with which we can control, oppress, exclude, bully, beat, enslave and even murder: it is the reason why religion can be such a danger in human life, why so many of the wars and bloody conflicts for centuries past and up to the present day have a religious element in them.

How are we to understand the relationship between God's will and my will? This question is linked to another equally fundamental question: How are we to understand the meaning of 'self'? If we describe someone as selfish, it is not a compliment, but a condemnation. In Christianity we speak in favour of self-sacrifice and of self-denial. And we emphasise the value of mortification, a word of Latin origin: it means putting to death our desires and inclinations. What is this 'self'? And what are these desires and inclinations we are to overcome, deny, get rid of?

Is it possible that God could will our happiness, our delight, our joy? If we are able to discover what it is that we really desire with the whole of our being, could we, in fact, have discovered God's will? Could it be that I have a true self, which I must never deny, but always nurture? A self that I must never try to overcome, but that I must allow to overcome me, a self that I must never try to get rid of, but with which I must always identify in everything I think and say and do?

If we could discover what we really desire, we should have found God's will: if we could really find our true self, we should have found God. St Augustine summed it all up in his words, 'Lord, you have created me for yourself, and my heart is restless until it rests in you', and in his prayer, 'Lord, that I may know you, that I may know myself'.

Without desire we quickly perish. It is sometimes said of a dying person, 'She (or he) has lost the will to live'. Desiring is as necessary to us as breathing, and our breathing expresses our longing for life. It is desire that determines the way in which we live. Desire decides our decisions, actions and reactions. No matter what we may profess, the reality of the matter is that we all do what we want – we do our own will. Those of us who claim to desire only the will of God would not be able to make this claim and carry out the perceived will of God unless we wanted to do so. Mother Teresa of Calcutta, when asked why she spent her life looking after the dying, is reported to have answered, 'Because I like doing my own thing.' Mother Teresa had discovered the deep place in herself in which her only desire was to be at one with those who were suffering. Her desire was at one with the compassionate heart of God. This was her 'thing' from which nothing could divert her.

The Fundamental Importance and Power of Human Desire

One of the most powerful descriptions of human desire appears in the autobiography of the English philosopher Bertrand Russell (1872–1970):

The centre of me is always and eternally a terrible pain – a curious wild pain – a searching for something beyond what the world contains, something transfigured and infinite – the beatific vision – God – I do not find it, I do not think it is to be found – but the love of it is my life – it's like the passionate love for a ghost. At times it fills me with rage, at times with wild despair, it is the source of gentleness and cruelty and work, it fills every passion that I have – it is the actual spring of life within me (Bertrand Russell, *Autobiography*, George Allen & Unwin, 1967).

In Christian understanding, desire is the prompting of God to draw us beyond ourselves. The ultimate object of our desire is to be at one with God, who is love, and at one with all creation. That is the literal meaning of the word 'atonement' – at-one-ment – which is used to describe the reconciliation between God and humankind.

Desire is a spring of life, but it can also be a searing pain, a destructive power that can tear us apart and cause havoc to those around us. In the Gospel of Mark the man possessed by an evil spirit is a tormented creature who 'lived in the tombs and no one could secure him any more, even with a chain; because he had often been secured with fetters and chains but had snapped the chains and broken the fetters, and no one had the strength to control him. All night and all day, among the tombs and in the mountains, he would howl and gash himself with stones' (Mark 5:3–5). When Jesus asks him his name, the possessed man, the demoniac, shows great insight, for he answers, 'My name is legion . . . for there are many of us' (Mark 5:10).

In an extreme form, the demoniac exemplifies the state of every human being. We desire happiness and peace, but our efforts to attain our own happiness can destroy peace, and our attempts at peacemaking can cause us great unhappiness. In the words of the American writer Henry Thoreau (1817–62), 'Most men live lives of quiet desperation.' How are we to live happily and at peace with this tormenting fire within that we call desire? The Stoic answer to the problem was to try to live without desire. On this ideal Jonathan Swift commented, 'The Stoical scheme of supplying our wants by lopping off our desires, is like cutting off our feet when we want shoes'!

The explosive power of human desire is like the atom. Harnessed, it can become an almost limitless source of energy:

released and uncontrolled, it can destroy all life on earth. We do not create desire, but we discover it within ourselves where it can lift us from lethargy, energise us, and draw us beyond. Desire is a yearning to be related to something or someone outside ourselves.

In Plato's dialogue *The Symposium* the setting is a party at which the guests are discussing the nature of love. Among the guests is the comedy playwright Aristophanes, who argues that human beings were originally perfect and therefore circular, because the circle was the symbol of perfection. Early in human development these perfect circles were cut in half. Since then we have been wandering the earth trying to find our other half! In all human love there is a desire for oneness, for completeness. For this reason, loneliness is deeply painful, with its sense of separation and exclusion from everything for which we long. We can only discover who we are through our relatedness. In Christian understanding, we are created in the image of God, and God is a trinity of persons, Father, Son and Holy Spirit, whose being is in their relatedness!

The desires that draw us are multiple and conflicting. If we satisfy one desire we frustrate another. At this moment I am writing. I want to write this book, but I also want not to be writing, because I hate the inner conflict that writing can bring. I feel the urge to write, but once I begin, all ideas seem to drain away and I am left facing an empty page. If I force myself to write, I fill the page with platitudes. At other times, ideas jostle with one another in my head, and what I write is incoherent. Then come the doubts as to whether I should be trying to write at all, especially about spirituality! There are lots of other things I would like to be doing: visiting friends, going for a walk, reading a novel. The conflict is not between my will and God's will: it is a conflict between one desire and another. I shall not persevere with writing unless my desire to write is stronger than my fear of inner conflict, or my desire to engage in some alternative occupation. I do not create the desire to write: the desire draws me to write.

You can explore this conflict in your own experience. Here are a few examples: We want to be truthful and transparently honest – but we also want to be popular and have lots of friends. These two good desires are rarely compatible. We may want to be slim, healthy and fit – but we may also hate taking exercise and would welcome death by chocolate. We would love to be open and welcoming to all those we encounter – but we can't stand people who bore us. Whether we believe in God or not, the conflict is rooted in the nature of desire. It is not God who makes life difficult for us!

This Conflict of Desire

We all claim to desire peace, including the arms' manufacturers. I mentioned earlier the Roman aphorism 'To preserve peace, prepare for war' – advice that has been faithfully followed to this day. How can we long unanimously for peace and yet perpetrate the acts of war that have produced a greater number of innocent victims during the twentieth century than throughout the previous millennia? As we have already seen in Chapter 1, the reason lies in our specific interpretation of 'peace', which we understand as a process of making ourselves invulnerable. Christ's peace comes through vulnerability, and our conflicting attitudes to peace and war indicate the high cost of our conflicting desires.

How do we discover our basic desire? Daydreams can be very important and there is a striking example in the life of Inigo of Loyola (1491–1556), the Basque nobleman who founded the Society of Jesus – generally known as 'the Jesuits'. As a youth, Inigo had been brought up in the Spanish court, from whence he emerged in his early twenties. At this stage of his life, Inigo describes himself as 'a man given over to the vanities of the world'. He tells us that he took special delight in the exercise of arms 'with a great and vain desire of winning glory'. He had more than a touch of Don Quixote in him.

In his late twenties Inigo was defending the Northern Spanish fortress of Pamplona against vastly superior French troops. The governor of the fortress advised surrender, but Inigo insisted in fighting on, until a cannonball broke one of his legs and severely damaged the other. The fortress surrendered and Inigo returned on a stretcher to the Castle of Loyola, where he lay for about eight months, waiting for his legs to heal.

Inigo had a great gift for daydreaming, which could absorb him for hours at a time. At first, he dreamed of the great deeds he would perform once his legs were healed, and of the great lady whose love he would win. These early daydreams were pleasant at the time, but

Inigo found that they left him bored, empty and sad, so he asked for novels. But novels were in short supply during the sixteenth century and there were none in the Castle of Loyola. The only books available were a life of Christ, and a book of saints' lives. In his boredom Inigo began reading them, and then found himself launched on a new set of daydreams. Until relatively recently, the biographies of saints gave the impression that holiness was in direct proportion to physical toughness. It could be measured by the hours the saints spent in daily prayer, the discomforts they tolerated, and the additional penances they imposed upon themselves. Saints were apparently given to fasting, whipping themselves, and standing in cold lakes reciting their prayers! In reading about these people, Inigo reflected that he was as tough as any saint! If Dominic, Francis and the rest could achieve sanctity, so could Inigo of Loyola. He now began daydreaming about 'St Inigo' and the marvellous things he would achieve!

For many weeks Inigo alternated between the two sets of daydreams: the first set about great deeds and the great lady, and the second set in which he was outdoing the saints. Eventually he noticed something that was to change his life and millions of other lives. It is the reason you are now reading this book! Inigo perceived that although both sets of daydreams were pleasant at the time, the first set left him bored, empty and sad, but the second set of daydreams, about outdoing the saints, left him hopeful, happy and strengthened. Inigo subsequently described this experience as his first lesson in 'discerning the spirits'. We might describe it as 'reading our moods'. In religious language, both these expressions come under the heading of 'discovering the will of God'. There was nothing wrong with Inigo's daydreams about the magnificent deeds he would carry out and the great lady he would win, but in reading and 'daydreaming' about the lives of the saints, a deeper layer of his desiring was revealed. In the next chapter we shall be looking at this process in much greater detail.

There are many points to notice in the story of Inigo's daydreams. Our deepest desire is not something that we create: it is something we discover. In this sense our daydreams resemble the claim of Michelangelo about his sculptures. He did not 'create' them. Instead he revealed the sculpture that was already hidden in the marble. As an artist, it was his task to uncover the hidden form. Inigo's daydreams revealed to him and to us that God is not apart from us. God is most intimately within; the very source of our being. No one has put it better than the French poet and politician, Charles Péguy (1873–1914):

> I myself will dream a dream within you
> Good dreams come from me, you know
> My dreams seem impossible,
> not too practical.
> not for the cautious man or woman
> a little risky sometimes,
> a trifle brash perhaps
> Some of my friends prefer
> to rest more comfortably,
> in sounder sleep,
> with visionless eyes
> But, from those who share my dreams
> I ask a little patience, a little humour;
> some small courage,
> and a listening heart –
> I will do the rest
>
> Then they will risk
> and wonder at their daring.
> Run, and marvel at their speed,
> Build, and stand in awe at the beauty of their building.
>
> You will meet me often as you work,
> in your companions who share the risk,
> in your friends who believe in you enough
> to lend their own hands,
> their own hearts
> to your building
> In the people who will stand in your doorway.
> stay awhile,
> and walk away knowing they, too, can find a dream.
> There will be sunfilled days,
> and sometimes it will rain,

a little variety,
both come from me.
So, come now, be content.
It is my dream you dream,
my house you build,
my caring you witness,
my love you share,
and this is the heart of the matter.

Péguy underlines the teaching of Inigo. Péguy's poem and Inigo's experience are excellent examples of the earthed nature of spirituality. Both start with dreams, but God's dreams are very earthed: they are 'the heart of the matter', and constantly transforming matter.

Inigo's dreams of carrying out magnificent deeds and winning the love of a great lady leave him bored, empty and sad. His dreams of outdoing the saints leave him hopeful, happy and contented. In the same way, the dreaming of God within us bears the mark of its own authenticity through the moods and feelings to which God's dream gives rise in us.

In both sets of daydreams, Inigo was full of conceit, ambition, and self-importance. In the case of the dreams about 'St Inigo', was it personal holiness that attracted him, or the thought that he could outdo the other saints? I love this element in the story because of the insight it gives into the nature of God. God took Ignatius as he was: conceited, vain and ambitious. And God worked on him through his weaknesses. It is so important to notice this, because much of our religious teaching and training can give the impression that we have to rid ourselves of all weakness and sin before we can make any progress whatever towards God and the things of the spirit. And as this is an endless task, most of us prefer to postpone it until the afterlife! In Péguy's poem, God does not demand that we first put our own house in order; he asks, instead, that we learn to listen and to take risks. What a refreshingly different approach from most religious teaching!

I have referred to the following exercise in previous books, and it can be extremely helpful in putting us on the track of our own basic desire. If you are familiar with the exercise, it may bear repetition.

Imagine that you have died and someone writes your obituary. The exercise is to write your own obituary notice, not the one you are afraid you are likely to receive, but the one that you long for in your wildest dreams. Do not allow reality to limit you in any way. Let your imagination run free. You do not have to show the 'obituary' to anyone, and, if you wish, it can be torn up as soon as you have completed it. If you attempt this exercise several times you may find that you produce a different obituary on each occasion.

Would it satisfy your deepest desire if it was stated in your obituary that you always looked smart, well dressed and had a steady, respectable job? Would you like your grieving family and friends to be reminded that you possessed a desirable residence, and were a model of respectability to all who knew you, including the bank manager? In day-to-day existence, these relatively superficial things can so engage and occupy our attention that we fail to notice much deeper longings. It seems a general principle that the more superficial a desire, the more demanding, noisy and disruptive it is likely to be. Just as our human consciousness is multi-layered, so too is our desiring. Relatively superficial desires and matters can occupy our attention to the extent that we are unconscious of anything deeper. Sometimes our entire attention is claimed by the way we dress, how we look: our status, possessions and reputation. But these are not our ultimate concerns, neither do they touch upon our deepest desires. Football hooliganism is one example of the overriding power of a superficial concern. Attention and desire can be so focused on a win by the supporter's team, that the sight and sound of rival supporters becomes unbearable. They must be physically silenced. Interviewed later by police, the violent attackers may say, 'I don't know what came over me. I just experienced a blinding rage.' I would doubt if even the most ardent football fan would like the epitaph engraved upon his tombstone to read 'He never failed to do physical harm to rival supporters'.

The practice of writing a personal obituary is one way of getting into touch with one's own basic desire. There are many other ways, including the regular practice of the 'review of the day' described in an earlier chapter. The daily review enables us to look at the moods and feelings of the day in order to discover the underlying desire. Another clue to our basic desire lies in the characters of the people we admire or envy – whether real people, fictional characters, or figments of our own imagination. Some of these people are sources of envy because they have possessions or qualities of character that we lack, and we are frustrated by that lack. The envy we feel may indicate frustrated superficial desires, but it may also indicate very deeply buried desires that we have neglected. The frustration can be very painful and may lead us into hatred – as we read in the Book of Wisdom:

> Let us lie in wait for the virtuous man, since he annoys us
> and opposes our way of life . . .
> Let us test him with cruelty and with torture,
> and thus explore this gentleness of his
> and put his endurance to the proof (Wisd. 2:12, 19).

Envy may start to open us to new and deeper levels of desire, as is apparent in this reading from Wisdom. But 'the virtuous man' can also provoke profound admiration. Hero/heroine worship can be a most valuable affliction, which can affect our whole future. The life of Inigo of Loyola was radically altered by his hero worship of the saints and their exploits.

Superficial desires can lead us into attitudes and actions that are destructive of other people and of ourselves. This is true of individuals: it is also true of groups, of nations, and of religious bodies. Some years ago a most unseemly row broke out in Jerusalem on Good Friday at the beginning of the Calvary procession along the route that Jesus is understood to have walked on his way to crucifixion. The disputants were Christian leaders of different denominations and they were fighting over which of them was to carry the cross!

During elections, political parties of the Western world always promise that if they are elected the voters will have more money to spend. This is not an appeal to the deepest desires of a nation, but it is an appeal that can silence deeper, stronger and more beneficial desires. Would it really satisfy the deepest longings of a nation to know that their era went down in history as the time when the average citizen of an advanced industrial nation spent and consumed conspicuously more than the average citizen of any other country in the world? Yet it is such promises of prosperity for the majority that win elections. We are told that two-thirds of the people of Britain are financially better off and that per capita consumption is higher than ever before. A recent poll indicates that the British people are less happy than at any earlier period. Is this because deep down desires are being ignored or repressed? History reminds us that when such deep desires are repressed in favour of more superficial desires, the result can be disastrous.

Resentment and anti-Semitism were not the deepest desires of the German people during the years following their defeat in the 1914–18 war. There was nevertheless a very strong sense of resentment in the country because of the terms of peace inflicted upon Germany by the Treaty of Versailles in 1919. When Hitler rose to power in 1933, this was coupled with an ancient and shameful anti-Semitism in which the German people were by no means alone in Europe. Adolf Hitler was able to tap into these resentments and the anti-Semitism. Once the mind and heart of a nation is united in desire for revenge, a terrifying, blinding and destructive force can be unleashed. But the desire of the nation at a particular moment does not necessarily represent the deepest yearning of the human spirit.

How Can We Control Our Desires So That They are Life-Giving to Ourselves and Others?

Desire can only be controlled by a stronger desire. It cannot be controlled by some extraneous force – whether we call that force 'will power' or 'the will of God'. Although God is not desire, God is *in* desire – the God who is constantly drawing all people and all things to an at-one-ness through the power of love: 'the love that moves the sun and the other stars' (Dante, *Paradiso*, xxxiii).

As we begin to focus on God, and on Jesus who is the image of the unseen God, we gradually become aware of a new and deeper stratum of desire in us. God is the source of all truth: the source of beauty and of goodness; a God of tenderness and compassion, a God who is so deeply in love with all creation that God becomes one of us in the person of Jesus. God is the joy of our desiring and is constantly drawing us onwards, in spite of our sins and sinfulness. It may take us a lifetime to discover our deepest desire. That deepest desire is not necessarily something that we feel with intensity and recognise clearly and immediately. It may be only after a long period of disappointment and suffering that we discover where it lies.

The experience of Inigo of Loyola with the two forms of

daydream eventually led him to compile a remarkable series of guided meditations that have transformed the lives of millions of people across the world, and have come to be known as the 'Spiritual Exercises'. At the start of each meditation he encourages us to, 'Ask God our Lord for the grace that all my intentions, actions and operations may be ordered purely to the service and praise of the Divine Majesty.'

In this way we are asking God to make every part of our being God-directed. We can make the request with complete sincerity, even though we know that our attention is likely to be scattered in many directions during the time of prayer. This is a point of fundamental importance, with implications for every aspect of our relationship with God and with other people. We do not have to rid ourselves of all our weaknesses and sins before we can enter into relationship with God any more than we have to become perfect before we enter into a relationship with another human being.

In Christian teaching, we are accustomed to exhortations to overcome our own desires, introduce more discipline and self-control into our lives, deny ourselves, take up our cross, and thus find God. Yet the psalmist, like the author of the Canticle of Canticles, is full of desiring. The most important thing is the direction of our desire:

God, you are my God, I am seeking you,
my soul is thirsting for you,
my flesh is longing for you,
a land parched, weary and waterless (Ps. 63:1).

Love draws us out of ourselves towards the beloved. Self-control, self-discipline, self-denial and mortification can draw us into such intense self-preoccupation that we have no energy left to love anyone or anything else. If we exercise self-control, self-discipline and self-denial without love, we can be led into profound selfishness, self-righteousness and inhumanity. Jesus was brought to his death through love of us: not through love of self-denial.

If, at this point, you are wondering whether you have any basic desire at all, never mind a basic desire for God, then the following questions about your own desires may be helpful. For the moment, leave aside entirely any consideration of your actual performance:

- Ideally, would you like to be remembered as a generous person who was open and friendly to any human being whom you encountered, regardless of ethnic origin, religious belief, political leanings or social class?
- Would you like to be remembered as always having been an effectively compassionate person?
- Would you like to be remembered as a person who was always transparently honest and whose words and actions were always in harmony?
- Would you like to be remembered as someone who always gave encouragement, hope and life, wherever you happened to be?
- Would you like to be remembered as a person who never bore grudges and was always ready to forgive: someone who was entirely free from any hint of self-importance?
- Would you like to be remembered as a person who always delighted in sharing whatever you had and was never condescending?
- Would you like to be remembered as someone who knew what it was to hunger and thirst after justice, a person who always worked on behalf of the oppressed and the marginalised?
- Would you like it to be said of you that 'love possessed, inspired, and permeated every thought and every action'?

Remember that these questions are not about your own performance, but about your desires. Do not be put off by the inner voice saying, 'But I am light years away from being anything like that and I always shall be.' This voice is totally self-centred and is speaking out of your atheist self. With God, all things are possible.

If your answer is 'yes' to all of these questions – or even to most of them – then your basic desires are in harmony with the will of God. Whenever you act in accordance with these basic desires you will experience a resonance within your psyche, which means that you will feel some measure of peace, tranquillity and strength. Our desires are like human beings – they come to life when some attention is paid to them. For this reason, daily prayer is very important because it focuses attention on our deepest desires.

Here are some further questions that can help us to find God within our own desires:

1 Would you be happy and at peace if you were given an absolute assurance that you, and you alone, would be 'saved'? That you are to be safe in this life and for ever after, while the rest of the human race perishes?
2 Would you be happy and at peace with the assurance that you, and all the friends and relatives you choose to include, can be saved – but the rest of the human race will perish?
3 Would you be happy and at peace if you knew that the vast majority of humankind would be saved, but some would be permanently excluded from achieving happiness?
4 Would you be completely happy and at peace if you knew that in some way every single human being would ultimately be saved?

If your answer to questions 1–3 is 'No', and your answer to question 4 is 'Yes', then your desire and God's will must be in harmony, for God wills the salvation of all people.

If any or all of your answers to questions 1–3 were 'Yes', and to question 4 'No', stay with those answers, bring them into prayer, and talk with God about them. Then notice, over a period, your felt reactions. Do your answers bring you peace, delight and joy, or do they bring sadness, agitation and confusion?

To sum up this chapter:

- The split in our spirituality separates God's desire from our desire, God's will from our will, so that the two seem to be in opposition. This split alienates us from ourselves, from other people, and from God.
- If we could discover the deepest longing of our heart, we should find that our longing is at one with the will of God. It is God's will that we should find the answer to the longings of our hearts. They are God's gift to us.
- Desire is like nuclear power. It is a concentrated energy that can be extremely creative or deeply destructive. How can we harness this energy?
- The answer lies in the nature of desire itself. Desire is controlled by desire, and love is controlled by love. We saw examples of this in the life of Inigo of Loyola and in the poem by Charles

Péguy. We experimented with questions and answers in order to elicit our own deepest desires.

- The more attention we can give to our basic desire, the stronger it will become. It is through the strength of our basic desire that we can learn to distinguish the creative from the destructive, both within us and outside ourselves. If we act in accordance with our basic desire, we shall respond very positively to things that feed that desire, and negatively to anything that is working against it. The stronger our basic desire, the more intense our reaction to whatever is answering that desire or opposing it.
- Are there any guidelines that can help us to recognise and distinguish creative and destructive forces in our lives? Is it possible to transform a potentially destructive force into something creative? We shall consider these questions in Chapter 6.

Exercises

1 Write your own obituary notice! (See pages 81–2).
2 The 'Two Columns' exercise:
    Take a blank piece of paper and divide it into two columns. Give one column the heading 'Things that enliven me', and the other the heading 'Things that deaden me'. 'Things' can be anything – weather, places, people, jobs, activities, books, religious services, duties, etc. Do not analyse or censor what you write, just scribble down anything that comes to mind. This exercise can be repeated throughout a person's lifetime. As you do it, the point of the exercise is likely to become clear. This exercise is a preliminary step in discernment and an introduction to Chapter 6.
3 Write down the reasons you admire or envy particular men and women – whether real people, living or dead, or fictional characters. This exercise can help us to discover the unanswered longings of our own hearts.
4 In your own life, have you noticed ways in which desire can control desire, and love can control love?

WHICH PATH TO FOLLOW?

When the Lord has given you the bread of suffering and the
water of distress, he who is your teacher will hide no longer,
and you will see your teacher with your own eyes. Whether
you turn to right or to left, your ears will hear these words
behind you, 'This is the way, follow it' (Isa. 30:20–1).

What Does 'Discernment' Mean?

How are we to distinguish the creative from the destructive in our
lives? When we have made this discovery, how can we react to
creative and destructive elements in such a way that the destructive
becomes creative and the creative remains life-giving for ourselves
and for others? The process can be summed up in the word
'discernment'. How are we to learn discernment? How can we learn
to live in such a way that our choices and decisions enrich and bring
life to ourselves and to others? Translated into religious language,
the question becomes, 'How are we to know God's will?' and 'How
are we to know whether it is, in fact, God's will that we are doing?'
How do we know that we are not simply doing our own will and
justifying our actions by describing them as 'the will of God'?

I have written about this on previous occasions and readers
have implied that I needed to explain myself more clearly. In this

chapter I shall be trying to 'unpack' and develop earlier material in the context of the guidelines for distinguishing true spirituality from false, which we examined in Chapter 3, and I shall be using some visual aids.

Discernment is an issue for every human being, regardless of whether or not we admit to any religious belief. It is obvious that government ministers and those responsible for large organisations carry heavy responsibilities, and that their decisions can enrich or impoverish the lives of millions. But my own decisions will also affect the lives of others, whether or not I am aware of this. No one can make a wholly private decision: we are interrelated beings whose every decision affects other people.

'Discernment' comes from two Latin words, *dis* = apart, and *cernere* = to separate. Donald Nicholl told me that the words 'shit' and 'discernment' have the same root – the word 'shit' being related to the Old English *sceadan*, meaning 'to separate out'! The billions of cells in our body are continuously practising 'discernment' on the food and drink we consume and on the air we breathe. Each cell accepts what it needs for the good of the whole body and rejects or passes on the remainder. Cancer could be described as a failure of discernment on the part of individual cells. They 'forget' the good of the whole body and concentrate only on their own individual good. As a result, the whole body suffers, and in many cases it dies. In human society, individuals, groups, nations and religious bodies are all liable to act within the narrow parameters of their own immediate interests. Such behaviour brings oppression, misery, starvation and death to other human beings, and in many cases to the total global environment. Discernment is as necessary for survival as air, food and water.

Creative and Destructive Forces Within

We do not require any great religious insight in order to be aware of the destructive forces that surround us. Millions of people are doomed to lives of dire poverty and starvation, not because there is insufficient food, but because the stronger and wealthier nations have exploited world resources to their own advantage, so that the poorest people are left without food or the means of obtaining it. We can see the cruel and savage destructiveness of war, fuelled by an arms trade that encourages rich and poor nations to pour their wealth into weapons of destruction. It is much more difficult to recognise that these forces of destruction are also rooted in our own minds and hearts, where they can generate forces that reverberate throughout creation. We feel helpless in the face of the violence of our society and the plight of millions because we are unable to recognise the roots of violence within our own minds. Money alone cannot free people from poverty, and superior weaponry can never bring peace because the roots of destruction are buried in our minds and hearts. They will flourish in our hearts until we recognise the damage they are doing. How can we distinguish the creative from the destructive, and how are we to react to each?

Discernment is an art to be learnt through exploration, and there is no end to the exploration. Wise discernment does not assume that all things and all events can be clearly labelled as bad/good. In the words of the prophet Jeremiah:

The heart is more devious than any other thing,
perverse too: who can pierce its secrets (Jer. 17:9).

How Do We Distinguish the Creative from the Destructive? How Should We React?

The first step in discernment is to become aware of our moods and feelings and to acknowledge them. Moods and feelings are neither right nor wrong, true nor false; but they are indicators that we ignore at our peril. In Britain, there is a tradition of facing adversity with a stiff upper lip, of learning to 'bash on' regardless of one's own feelings, or those of anyone else! Such a climate makes it difficult to acknowledge feelings! It is not easy, for men especially, to acknowledge emotions. A retired British naval officer once told me that in the Royal Navy ratings were allowed to have feelings and emotions, but not officers!

The fact of becoming aware of our feelings does not imply that we should necessarily act upon them. An awareness of feelings can, in fact, protect us from impulsive reactions. But our minds can be so conditioned by upbringing and by our own choices that we fail to notice negative and destructive feelings. Racism, sexism, militarism, religious bigotry and intolerance can be so deeply ingrained that we bristle with indignation if anyone suggests that we may have even a trace of such a defect.

Feelings are very wise and they are far more perceptive than the reasoning mind. It is for this reason that we neglect them at our peril. To acknowledge and take note of feelings is the beginning of wisdom. If you find it difficult to get in touch with feelings, the following questions may be helpful:

- Have you ever felt any of the following: afraid, agitated, aimless, angry, bewildered, bitter, bored, confused, depressed, disillusioned, envious, frustrated, guilty, helpless, inadequate, lonely, panicky? If your answer is 'Yes', then welcome to the human race; if your answer is 'No', there is no need to worry: just be patient, and at least some of these feelings will arrive in God's good time!
- Have you ever experienced any of the following, even if only very fleetingly: delight and gratitude at being alive; a sense of peace, joy, happiness and hope; a sense of unity within yourself and with everyone and everything around you; a sense of wonder at the beauty and mystery of life; a sense of liberation from yourself through the love of another person?

Such states are random examples of moods and feelings. Some are painful; some pleasant. None are right or wrong, true or false in themselves. They are signs that we have to learn to interpret, nudgings from God that we can learn to read and to follow. It is not pleasant to feel sad, but if I look at the reason for my sadness, I may find that it springs from the fact that I have neglected a friend in need. The sadness is nudging me away from self-preoccupation towards greater generosity and a freedom from self-absorption. Feeling happy is pleasant, but if I look at the reason for my happiness, I may discover that it springs from a delight in the humiliation suffered by my favourite enemy; a delight that indicates an attitude I dislike and start to resist.

The first step in discernment is the acknowledgment of our moods and feelings; the second step is to ask ourselves about the source of the moods and feelings. The third step is to notice where they are leading.

Visual Aids

The diagrams on the following pages can be helpful in understanding discernment. In reading the following descriptions,
notice if anything corresponds to your own experience. If a
particular description fails to correspond to your own experience,
ignore it and move on for the time being. It is important to start
with something that anchors you within your own experience.

Figure 1

Figure 1 is based on a reflection that came to me when I had
been watching the television programme *One Man and his Dog*
for the first time. For the benefit of those who haven't seen it, the
programme is a competition for shepherds and their sheepdogs.
Each shepherd is given a small flock of sheep to guide through
fields with the help of the dog, and the object of the exercise is to
pen the sheep in an enclosure. The shepherd and dog that perform
most effectively and quickly are the winners, and the entire
operation depends upon the relationship between shepherd and
dog. The shepherd may be a fine upstanding person and the dog
may be a champion, but if the two fail to relate well, the operation
will fail.

This television programme reflects aspects of the inner life of each human being. As in so many biblical passages, the shepherd symbolises God. The sheepdog represents our deepest desire. The classical writers describe this as 'the fine point of the soul'. The sheep represent the many desires within us that are not our deepest desire – those aspects of ourselves that reveal themselves when more superficial desires take us over: greed, ambition and vanity; the desire to be accepted and promoted; the desire to control, possess and dominate; the desire to save one's skin at all costs! The superficial desires are usually the loudest and most insistent within our consciousness. Our deepest desire seems to lie dormant much of the time, and only breaks through into our consciousness when more superficial desires have taken control and led us into actions that oppose our deepest desire. You may wish to create your own diagram, enlarging and colouring the sheep, giving them names that correspond to your inner flock of superficial desires!

In Chapter 5 we looked at the account of the healing of the man who had been possessed by an evil spirit. The 'sheepdog' part of the demoniac brings him running to Jesus, but his sub-personalities so rage within him that 'he would howl and gash himself with stones'. When Jesus asks his name, the man answers with great insight: 'My name is legion, for there are many of us.'

Pray, and Act Out of the 'Sheepdog' Part of Yourself

The 'shepherd/sheepdog' diagram underlines a most important and fundamental guideline for the spiritual journey, which is that we should always pray out of the 'sheepdog' part of ourselves – out of our deepest longing. This principle applies not only to prayer, but to every human decision. Our decisions should flow from the place of our deepest longing and not from the superficial parts of our being.

In the parable of the Pharisee and the tax-collector who both go up to the Temple to pray, the Pharisee addresses God: '"I thank you, God, that I am not grasping, unjust, adulterous like the rest of humankind, and particularly that I am not like this tax collector here. I fast twice a week; I pay tithes on all I get." The tax collector stood some distance away, not daring even to raise his eyes to heaven; but he beat his breast and said, "God, be merciful to me, a sinner". This man, I tell you, went home again at rights with God; the other did not' (Luke 18:11–13).

This is a fascinating and revolutionary parable. The Pharisee is doing all the right things. He has worthwhile virtues: he prays, he fasts, and he pays his temple tax. The tax-collector appears to be a religious and moral failure. He does nothing right – and yet Jesus tells us that it is the tax-collector who goes home at rights with God. The 'sheepdog' part of the tax-gatherer is focused on the shepherd, on God; the 'sheepdog' part of the Pharisee is focused, not on God, but on his well-behaved sheep!

To God, it is the direction of the heart that matters. It does not, however, follow from this that as long as the heart is directed aright our actions do not matter. If the heart is really directed towards God, the appropriate actions will follow. Jesus reminds us to 'set your hearts on his kingdom, and these other things will be given you as well' (Luke 12:31).

It also follows from the parable of the Pharisee and the tax-collector that appropriate actions and correct opinions are not of fundamental importance in the eyes of God. This is certainly revolutionary! How would 'good' church people receive Jesus if he was to reappear today and declare that, 'My interest is not primarily in your verbal orthodoxy, in your religious observances, your ritual fidelity, church dues, or political correctness. What matters is the disposition of your heart, your focus on God, so that you allow God to be the God of love and compassion to you and through you in all that you do.'

Christians are not only divided into separate denominations; they are frequently and more bitterly divided within the same denomination. When reading controversial Christian writings, it is often helpful to give greater attention to the tone of the writing than to the content. Books that are presented as 'orthodox' may be written with venom. Statements that are considered to be unorthodox may, nevertheless, be delivered with compassion. Our adherence to orthodoxy and our fidelity to religious ritual can flow from the 'sheepdog' part of ourselves. Such responses may indeed be focused on God, but they may also flow from the fact that I myself have chosen to follow particular observances and to adhere to specific statements of orthodoxy. My ego can become the determinant of my values, decisions and actions rather than the intrinsic value of specific observances, or the objective truth of particular statements. In the context of Christian discernment, the tone of a statement is every bit as important as the meaning of the statement. God is not an orthodox proposition!

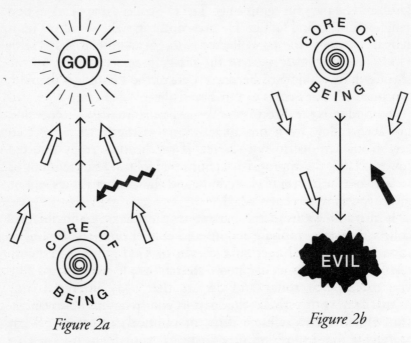

Figure 2a

Figure 2b

Figures 2a and 2b above are illustrations of the relationship we experience or 'feel' between the focus of our hearts and our minds on the one hand and, on the other hand, our decisions, actions and reactions. I have captioned the 'twirl' in the illustration 'core of being', and this corresponds to the 'sheepdog' part of ourselves. In Figure 2a, the 'core of being' is directed towards God. What does this actually mean? St Augustine provided us with one answer in his words, 'You have created me for yourself, and my heart is restless until it rests in Thee.' But in order to be directed towards God we have to discover God, and in order to discover God we need to consult our own experience. It is obviously possible to read about God in books of theology, but the living, loving God is to be found in living, loving hearts and not in books. Theology books can be valuable in helping us to become more aware of the reality of God within us and among us, but our experience of the living God can only come to us through our own minds and hearts.

Moods and Feelings Indicate the Fundamental Direction of Our Lives

In the previous chapter we looked at the nature of desire and began to track our own deepest desire. We recognised that God is to be found in love, compassion, mercy, peace, justice and truth. When the core of our being is directed towards God, and everything that God means, we shall find that our values, actions and decisions are in accordance with the God-directed core of our being. The consonance between our values and actions and our God-directed core will bring us a measure of peace, strength and tranquillity. This movement is represented by the white arrows in Figure 2a.

However, we live in a world of creative and destructive forces. If we make decisions that are consonant with our basic and God-centred desire, we shall find that sooner or later the destructive forces, represented by the black arrow, will start to oppose our decisions, causing us agitation, sadness and inner turmoil. This movement is represented by the black arrow in Figure 2a. Try to recall a specific decision that brought you some measure of peace, joy, gladness and freedom once it had been taken. Can you also recall an occasion when you were assailed by doubts, sadness and agitation after making a specific decision?

Figure 2b represents the core of our being totally turned away from God. I do not think that such a state is, in fact, possible for any human being, because there will always be some residual longing for the God in whom we live and move and have our being, no matter how wicked we may become. It is, however, possible for us to become so self-preoccupied that there is no room for God in our consciousness. The white arrows in Figure 2b represent my own decisions, actions and reactions in pursuit of personal self-aggrandisement. Such decisions, actions and reactions will bring me pleasure, delight and assurance, because they resonate with the desire for self-aggrandisement which I have chosen as my 'core' desire. Intent on my own interests, to the exclusion of those of anyone else, I may, in fact, be full of self-congratulation at having succeeded in robbing a bank of a vast amount of money. In going to sleep that evening, I am suddenly reminded of my pious old grandmother, and for a moment I feel a sharp pang of conscience. We can never escape the goodness of God, no matter how wicked we have become. Sooner or later any self-congratulation, sense of delight and satisfaction in my evil doing will be 'disturbed'. This movement is represented by the black arrow in the diagram.

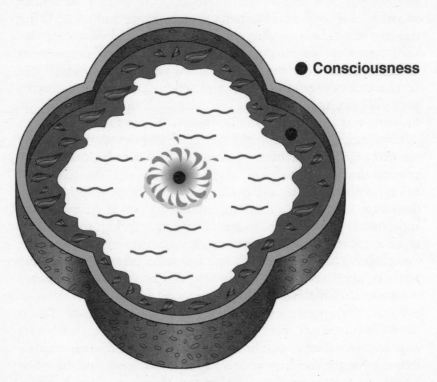

● **Consciousness**

Figure 3

Figure 3 above represents my own memory of a well that was surrounded by carved stonework. I saw it one bright autumn day close to the wall of a ruined chapel. The water at the edge of the well was covered in dead leaves and sludge. But the water at the centre was welling up with such force that it broke the surface. The sun was so bright that I could see little grains of sand dancing in the water, welling up at the centre. When I remembered this scene afterwards, I saw it as an illustration of our human consciousness. The well represents a human life. In the diagram there is a little black dot at the centre of the well that represents one of the grains of sand I saw dancing in the water. The black dot near the rim of the well represents the same grain of sand, which has now been caught in the dead leaves and sludge at the rim.

I imagined the little grain of sand, dancing in the sunlight in the middle of the well, saying to itself, 'I am feeling full of life, full of peace and joy.' The little grain generalises about its present feelings, saying, 'Isn't life wonderful? Praise the Lord, alleluia! Why can't everyone see how good life is?' Through the movement of the water the grain of sand is then moved to the rim of the well and lodges among the dead leaves and sludge. I imagined it saying to itself, 'I am trapped. I am in darkness. I feel utterly miserable . . . the situation is hopeless. There is no way out. Everything else I have experienced has been an illusion.' We all have a tendency to react like the little grain of sand when destructive forces begin to oppose our decisions.

The destructive forces may seem to be very powerful, but we need to remain aware that human consciousness is very restricted and that our knowledge is limited. It is easy to conclude that negative experiences reflect the totality of my existence – past, present and future. From such a perspective we can make false judgments and act upon them. Such judgments can be self-destructive and they can cause damage to others. Returning to the shepherd and sheepdog diagram on page 93, the sheepdog must fix its attention on the shepherd and act on the commands of the shepherd. If the dog allows its concentration to move away from the shepherd, it may start pursuing individual sheep and forget the rest of the flock. As Christians, we can become so preoccupied with the 'sheep', in the form of our own particular defects, that we turn our attention away from the love and goodness of God, the 'shepherd', and become totally absorbed in ourselves. If we do this we may end up plunged into the depths of despair at our lamentable failure to live up to our Christian ideals. We may alternatively find ourselves preoccupied with different 'sheep' in the form of our own good qualities – in which case we may find ourselves glowing with our own self-righteousness, like the Pharisee.

My Ultimate Identity Lies in God and Not in My 'False' Self

In Figure 3, the black dot at the rim of the well represents a human being caught in some kind of difficulty. Our human tendency is to jump from knowledge of our subjective state to an objective statement. Subjectively we perceive that 'I am in difficulties and cannot, at the moment, see any solution.' We therefore decide 'objectively' that 'It is hopeless. I am trapped. There is no escape.' If we feel personally responsible for the difficulty in which we find ourselves, we can further damage ourselves by our objective decision that 'It is hopeless . . . there is no escape.' We can plunge ourselves into the depths of despair. If, however, we believe that responsibility for the situation rests with another individual, or with a particular group, we can rapidly demonise them. We consider them beyond hope and relegate them to outer darkness!

For the Christian, it is a form of atheism to generalise from a subjective state to an objective assertion. Such generalisations implicitly assume that what I fail to see cannot be there, as though my limited, subjective impressions are both omniscient and infallible, rendering God unnecessary. As we have seen in earlier chapters, my ultimate identity lies in God: not in my own subjective opinion about my present identity. The sheepdog image in Figure 1 reminds me of the importance of keeping my attention fixed on the love and goodness of God rather than upon my own merits, achievements, sins and failures. Perhaps I have failed badly in something and the sense of failure so pervades my consciousness that there is little room for anything else. I assert that 'I am a failure'. If this declaration sinks into my consciousness, it can do far greater damage than the original failure that prompted the statement. Such a declaration robs me of self-confidence and thus damages the core of my being. If I say instead, 'That event, for which I was responsible, was a failure', I am, instead, making an honest acknowledgment of specific failure. The event was a failure. I am responsible. If, however, I assert that I myself am the failure, I am declaring the uselessness and hopelessness of the very source from which improvement can come. In some forms of aversion therapy the client is encouraged to discontinue particular activities by declaring, 'I am an alcoholic', 'I am a drug addict', 'I am a paedophile', etc. I believe that such declarations can undermine the very core of one's being and are likely to prove destructive in the long term.

The Importance of 'Ecstasy'!

The stillness exercises described on pages 53–7 can be very useful in terms of enabling us to 'stand aside' and to view ourselves from an exterior perspective. If we learn to do this, we are less likely to be overwhelmed by adversity, whether self-inflicted, or visited upon us by an exterior source. In order to learn contemplation, we need to practise the art of looking in at ourselves from outside ourselves. The Greeks had a word for the process: they called it *ekstasis*, ecstasy, which means literally 'to stand outside of'! Imagine yourself standing on a bridge staring at the many barges passing by in both directions. Keep staring at the barges, but do not jump into them if they look attractive, or refuse to look at them because they frighten or repel you in some way. The barges correspond to the thoughts and feelings running through your consciousness.

True Progress Lies in the Expansion of Our Consciousness

The well image in Figure 3 can provide many useful reflections. The well fills with water from a number of hidden streams flowing down the hill. Each stream is 'fed' by rain, which falls from the clouds, and the clouds originally drew up the water from the ocean. The well eventually receives and retains this life-giving water and dispenses it to give growth, cleanse, heal and refresh. The well is an illustration of the meaning of our lives.

We are told that the 'flow' of human life began with the 'Big Bang' – that explosion of dense matter that expanded and cooled into subatomic particles and eventually resulted in the formation of stars and galaxies, and then the earliest beginnings of life as we know it. These are our origins. Each one of us is a 'child of the stars'. To revert to the image of the well, each one of us is a 'stream' feeding into the well that is a source of cleansing, healing and refreshment. Our life is something given. We are receivers and transmitters of life, called to delight and to share, and thus to become one with all creation. In light of this image so much of our behaviour begins to look pretentious, absurd and laughable. Unfortunately, it is also tragic. The absurdity and the tragedy arise from our failure to recognise our own limitations and from the assumption that our narrow and individual perspective encompasses the totality of existence. If the human race is to progress in the future, our perspective must broaden immensely.

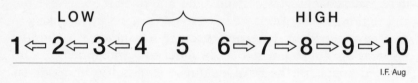

Figure 4

For my fourth diagram, Figure 4, I am indebted to my fellow Jesuit, Gerald O'Mahoney, who uses it in his book *At the Still Point – Making Use of Our Moods* (Eagle Books, Guildford, 1993). The diagram represents two ways in which we can lose touch with the 'core' of our being. Later we shall look at two countering methods for regaining contact.

We are aware of the possibility of being 'out of touch' with ourselves and we express the experience in such phrases as 'I am feeling out of sorts', 'I am not in good form', 'I don't know what came over me when I said/did X or Y'. We describe others as 'not themselves at present', but God is always God's loving self, even when we know that we are hating ourselves and/or others.

In Figure 4, number five on the grid represents the state of our inner life when we are completely 'at one' with ourselves. Numbers one and ten represent states of extreme 'out-of-touchness'. The left-hand side of the grid indicates degrees of passivity, lethargy, low spirits and the disinclination to bestir oneself. The right-hand side of the grid indicates activity, starting with 'normal' and moving to 'manic' at number ten. At the extremes of passivity on the left side, and of hyperactivity on the right, we are out of touch with ourselves, with others and with God. As we move towards the centre, we are returning to normality.

We are very complex creatures. Everything that has ever happened to us registers, in some way, in our nervous system and affects the way in which we perceive reality; the way that we act and react. On any given day, our moods and feelings are many and varied. Figure 4 is a useful preparation for the guidelines that follow. In reflecting upon them, be sure to attend only to your predominant moods and feelings.

Guidelines for Distinguishing the Creative from the Destructive

We can only learn discernment through our attempts to discern. The following guidelines are an abridged version of those given by Inigo of Loyola for the 'Discernment of Spirits' in his Spiritual Exercises. The guidelines are general, and Inigo tells us that they can help in the practice of discernment 'at least to some extent'.

1 *If the core of our being is directed to God, then the decisions we make in harmony with that fundamental desire will resonate in our moods and feelings, bringing some measure of peace, strength and tranquillity. The destructive forces, outside and within us, will oppose this decision that brought us peace, causing agitation, sadness and inner turmoil.*

'*If the core of our being is directed to God . . .*' I once attended a three-day meeting between Roman Catholics and Communists. Although we had come together to consider our respective attitudes to politics, we spent most of our time in a discussion about God. One of the Communists had a rigid notion of God – an inflexible, authoritarian, controlling God. He was a man of integrity and compassion and he was surprised to discover that the Roman Catholics present also rejected such a God. In Roman Catholic understanding, the core of a person's being may be directed towards God, even if the individual denies belief in God, either through ignorance, or because they are rejecting the notion of God that has been presented to them. People who declare themselves to be agnostic, atheist or irreligious can therefore find these guidelines very helpful. The Spirit of God is at work in every human being, irrespective of their beliefs or lack of them.

Notice Inigo's reference to '*moods and feelings, bringing some measure of peace, strength and tranquillity*'. Our nearness to God, or our distance from God, is never to be measured simply by the intensity of our feelings. We may have chosen a particular course of action or way of life, and we are convinced that our decision is in harmony with our basic desire to allow God to be the God of love and compassion to us and through us. Initially we may experience joy, strength and peace with this decision. But in life there is no guarantee that such a state of affairs will continue! We may subsequently wish that we had never decided on a particular course of action or way of life. We begin to doubt that it is the will of God; we may even doubt whether there is a God who wills anything at all. What, then, are we to do if we find ourselves in this state?

The above guideline is helpful in forewarning us that destructive forces outside and within are likely to oppose decisions that are in harmony with our basic desire for God. When we experience such doubts, we must not simply refuse to look at them. We should instead acknowledge the doubts and bring them into prayer before God. God is always gentle, always attractive. If the doubts are of God, then we shall be able to look at them without fear, and without disturbing our basic peace: if they are not of God, we shall experience some measure of agitation, darkness and inner turmoil. If we reflect on these inner reactions, we are now more likely to see the reason for the turmoil within.

Let us suppose that we have committed ourselves to a way of life or course of action and we are convinced that the decision is in harmony with the core of our being. If we are later assailed by doubts, there is a simple test in the form of the following question: 'If you could wave a magic wand, where else would you prefer to be?' While caught in the turmoil of a particular situation, the answer may be 'anywhere, except where I am at the moment', but when the turmoil has died down, the answer very often is 'despite the difficulties, this is where I want to be'. I have frequently asked this question of people who are suffering from frayed nerves and exhaustion as a result of their active engagement in work for peace and justice. Almost always they have answered, 'It is here that I want to be. If I were to withdraw, I could not live at peace with myself.' This is an echo of the complaint of Jeremiah:

The word of Yahweh has meant for me
insult, derision, all day long.
I used to say, 'I will not think about him,
I will not speak in his name any more'.
Then there seemed to be a fire burning in my heart,
imprisoned in my bones.
The effort to restrain it wearied me,
I could not bear it (Jer. 20:8–9).

2 *If the core of our being is turned away from God, any decisions we make, which are in harmony with that fundamental aversion, will comfort and console us, while the creative forces, outside and within us, will trouble us with stings of conscience.*

If the core of our being is God-centred, then decisions that are in harmony with our God-centredness will bring peace. In the same way, if our heart is turned away from God, then decisions consistent with that aversion will please us. Some Christians, on reading this guideline, can become anxious and wonder whether the core of their being really is turned towards God. Our worries can be very instructive. Out of this worry, we can learn one very important principle and some useful lessons for our spiritual journey. The principle is this: always give yourself the benefit of the doubt! If we fail to do this, we can become so accustomed to deferring to those in authority in Church or State, or to current opinion, that we cease to take charge of our own lives. As I write, a most dangerous and tragic example of this irresponsibility was the initial support given to President Bush for his 'War on Terrorism' policy, which threatens war against Iraq – if necessary without the sanction of the United Nations Security Council. The United Kingdom stands 'shoulder to shoulder' with this policy. In the words of Tacitus nearly two thousand years ago on the subject of the Roman Empire: 'They create a wilderness: they call it peace' (*Agricola* 30). The devastation of bombing can never bring true peace. Our ultimate security lies in God. It is faith that saves us, not our weapons of death and the certainty of our own righteousness.

If we find ourselves worrying about whether or not the core of our being is turned to God, we need to remember the value of returning frequently to our basic desire. The obituary exercise in Chapter 5 can be helpful here. We looked at the qualities for which we would like to be remembered: compassion, honesty, justice, etc. In the depths of my being, would I like to live *without* love, *without* compassion, truth, justice, etc? If the answer is 'No', then the core of my being cannot be turned away from God.

There is another lesson to be learned from the worry about whether or not the core of my being is God-centred. Let us suppose that I have, in fact, taken a particular decision in the belief that it is creative, when it is in fact destructive. If this is the case, then God will eventually make this clear to me, provided I continue to turn my mind and heart Godwards. It is in the light of God that we see light.

Although this guideline may seem rather threatening, it is, upon reflection, very encouraging. God is in all things. No matter how evil a person may become, he or she cannot escape the goodness of God. No person and no state of affairs can ever be hopeless. God's love for all creation is unconditional. We can certainly make things very difficult for ourselves by refusing to look beyond the narrow parameters of our own self-aggrandisement. But if we can once manage to look beyond our own prison cell and get in touch with our transcendent self, we can begin to see light in the darkness.

3 *Creative moods and feelings are to be distinguished from destructive ones, not by their pleasantness or painfulness, but by their effect. If going with the mood or feeling leads to an increase of faith, hope and love, then it is creative; if it leads to a decrease of faith, hope and love, then it is destructive.*

'Ignore your feelings' was the advice frequently inflicted on children by parents, on pupils by their teachers, and on congregations by their preachers. We have, however, seen that acknowledgment of our feelings is an essential part of any process of discernment. As I mentioned earlier, to advise someone to 'ignore your feelings' is as crassly stupid as advising motorists to ignore the traffic lights. Feelings are indicators, and they can also move us towards, or away from, a particular course of action. I can feel attracted by the sight of a large cream cake. The feeling is moving me to take it and eat it, but the doctor has told me that my cholesterol level is perilously high, so I withdraw my outstretched hand. Feelings tend to move us towards action and reaction: they draw us towards what is pleasant and repel us from what is painful. But feelings and emotions need to be discerned: where do they come from, and where are they leading? This guideline is a warning against simplistic judgments that declare whatever pleases us to be good, and whatever displeases us to be bad.

'*If going with the mood or feeling leads to an increase of faith . . .*' Faith is primarily an attitude of trust in the God in whom 'we live and move and have our being'. This must include trust in the circumstances in which I find myself, however repellent they may be. Faith is only secondarily a belief in statements about God, in formal creeds. The gift of faith can be described as the gift of recognising the sacramentality of all creation, which means seeing that all creation is an effective sign of the presence of God. Faith is the gift of being 'at home', wherever I may find myself, for God is in all things and all things are in God.

Test this guideline against your own experience. Here are two examples. The first shows how a very painful event can lead to an increase of faith, hope and love; the second shows how a pleasant experience can lead to a decrease of faith, hope and love.

In the first example we have lost someone very close to us and the experience is very painful. The pain can either push us towards despair, or it can force us to ask, 'Where is my ultimate security?' The former tendency is destructive; the latter is creative and can lead to an increase of faith, hope and love.

In the second example, we are on bad terms with someone who then fails in a particular venture. We can experience a pleasure that confirms our ill feeling. The pleasant feeling bears a hate virus within it, leading to a decrease of faith, hope and love.

4 *Moods and inner feelings, whether pleasant or unpleasant, that are drawing us towards God are called 'consolation'. Painful moods and inner feelings that are drawing us away from God are called 'desolation'.*

'Consolation' and 'desolation' are shorthand terms for all the thoughts, feelings, emotions, actions, reactions and decisions that lead either to an increase or a decrease in faith, hope and love. The

English word 'consolation' describes a warm, comforting, soothing feeling, and desolation describes gloom, sadness and low spirits. This can lead to confusion within the context of these guidelines for the discernment of spirits. This particular guideline reminds us that consolation, in the sense of an increase in faith, hope and love, can feel either pleasant or unpleasant. Desolation in the sense of a decrease in faith, hope and love always feels painful. This may seem rather gloomy. It is in fact most reassuring.

The pain we feel in desolation is a sign of spiritual health! It is important to realise this, otherwise we can misinterpret the pain we experience during desolation and tumble further into despair. We experience pain when we feel a decrease of faith, hope and love because the core of our being longs to trust, to love and to hope. If someone were to turn away from God in the core of their being, any decrease in faith, hope and love would fail to trouble them – apart from the occasional pang!

Guidelines for a Creative Reaction to What is Destructive

5 *In desolation, we should never go back on a decision made in time of consolation, because the thoughts and judgments springing from desolation are the opposite of those coming from consolation. It is, however, useful to act against the desolation. We should also examine the cause of our desolation.*

This guideline does not tell us that we should never make any decision in a time of desolation. The ban is only upon reversing a decision that has already been made in a time of consolation. The reason for the ban is that our judgment can go awry in a time of desolation. I may, for example, have decided to join some voluntary organisation. After a few months the work has lost its novelty. My prayer had originally led me to volunteer, but prayer has now become very dry and I am beginning to doubt whether my voluntary job is of any value. The guideline advises against resigning from the organisation while in a state of desolation. Once the desolation has passed, I may then consider resigning.

The guideline also advises us to act against the desolation. In this way, we can turn a destructive tendency into a creative one.

In order to understand this, we need to return to Figure 4. If the desolation is pushing us towards lethargy, inactivity and gloom, then we need to move gently in the other direction, becoming a little more active and outgoing. If the desolation takes the form of hyperactivity and obsessive behaviour, we need to counter this by slowing down, and acting against the obsession, however important we may consider it to be. Whichever form of desolation afflicts us, we must always act gently and kindly with ourselves.

The final sentence of the guideline is very wise: '*We should also examine the cause of our desolation*'. This can save us endless trouble and spiritual melodrama! When afflicted with desolation, we can tend to jump to wrong and very painful conclusions: God must have rejected us – We have no capacity for prayer – We are permanently and incurably flawed – All our previous experiences of the presence of God must have been an illusion, and we really have no faith! In terms of the image of the 'well', the grain of sand is now lodged in the dead leaves and sludge by the rim, and is indulging in oracular utterances! When afflicted with desolation, we should start by asking some very simple and practical questions about our general well-being: How am I sleeping? Am I eating properly? Am I taking the right amount of exercise – too much or too little? Am I working too hard, or am I not working hard enough?

In my experience of individual retreat-giving and spiritual direction, two of the most common causes of desolation are lingering guilt and the refusal to forgive ourselves, as well as those who have offended us.

It is healthy to experience guilt after we have done wrong. If we never experience guilt after doing wrong, this is symptomatic of psychopathic tendencies! But the life of a religious believer should not include the lingering guilt that persists long after the specific wrong has been committed and repented. Neither should it include the guilt that hovers over everything and seems to permeate our being, but is not connected to any particular wrongdoing. One remedy for lingering guilt is to imagine Jesus dying on the cross. Speak with him and tell him, 'Lord, I believe you are giving your life for the sins of the world, but you must realise, dear Lord, that you have met your match in me! You certainly won't be able to atone for *my* sins!' See how long you can keep the prayer going! If lingering guilt, or any other experience of desolation, is presented to God in prayer, it can become a means of enlightenment.

A second cause of desolation is the refusal to forgive others, or to forgive ourselves. Forgiveness is difficult: it can feel impossibly difficult. In prayer before God it is always safe to be completely honest. We can present our hurt to God and express the anger we feel about the wrong that has been done to us. One method of praying about our inability to forgive is to imagine that we are in the presence of the individual or group responsible for the offence. Jesus is also present. We express our hurt and anger to the offending party and then pause to give them the opportunity to answer. Then turn to Jesus and hear what he has to say to you and to the other party. I do not suggest this as a simple solution to any and every difficulty with forgiveness, but it is a good start to present our hurt to God in prayer.

6. *In desolation, remember two things:*
  (*a*) *Know that the desolation will pass.*
  (*b*) *If we can keep the focus of our attention on God, even if we have no felt experience of God's presence, God will teach us through the desolation. It is as though in desolation God gouges out our false securities, revealing God's self to our inner emptiness so that God may fill and possess it.*

Desolation afflicts us all and it always has the appearance of permanence. To pursue the image of the well, the grain of sand caught in the dead leaves and sludge at the rim considers its state to be permanent. It is good to remind ourselves of past occasions when the desolation did pass away. Later, we were able to see that our judgment had become extremely cloudy when we were in the desolate state.

It is difficult to keep the focus of our attention on God when we have no felt experience of God's presence, but it is possible. One method is to say the words, 'There is in me a feeling of God's absence and atheistic thoughts are in my mind.' The fact that I can say these words is an indication that the transcendent One is present within me, a presence that transcends the present awareness of my conscious mind and my range of feelings. The fact that

I am not experiencing God need not lead me to the conclusion that God does not exist.

This guideline can take us to the heart of the Christian faith – to the knowledge that God really is our rock, our refuge and our strength. God is our ultimate security, our ultimate reference point whenever we say the word 'I'! To return to the words of Irenaeus: 'God became a human being, so that human beings might become God.' Human beings need all kinds of securities in order to grow, for we are essentially inter-related. If we are to be truly free, we must not allow our *ultimate* security to rest in any person, group or created thing. The road to freedom can be very painful, because we are on a journey that strips us of our perceived securities. If we choose to remain in our perceived securities rather than take the road to freedom, we are making a deadly choice, because our ultimate freedom cannot rest in anyone or anything, but only in God.

Guideline for Getting the Maximum Benefit from 'Felt' Consolation

7 *In consolation, make the most of it! Acknowledge it as a gift, freely given, to reveal a deeper truth of our existence, namely, that we live always enfolded within the goodness and faithfulness of God. In consolation we have had a felt experience of this truth. Let this truth become the anchor of our hope in a time of desolation.*

The first six guidelines concern desolation, and the fact that we have only this one guideline on the subject of consolation can give the impression that desolation is the normal state for a Christian! In fact, the normal state of the Christian should be one of peace, trust, love and hope. But peace, trust, love and hope are not necessarily accompanied by intensely positive feelings. When we do experience strong feelings of consolation, the value of the experience does not lie in the intensity of the feeling itself, but in the fact that the feeling is reminding us of the reality of the continuous presence of God within us and among us. If we reflect in this way upon 'felt' consolation, we can come closer to the transcendent within us. In this way we can begin to 'know' God's presence at a level that is deeper than sensibility. In terms of the image of the 'well', the grain of sand can now remain at peace, even when lodged in the sludge at the rim.

Guideline on Befriending Our Fears

8 *We must face the fears that haunt us.*

Fear is a very necessary emotion: without it our lives would be short! But fear is also the most potentially destructive emotion. It can lead us to respond with mindless violence or paralytic inactivity. In the Bible, God frequently utters the words 'Do not be afraid'. As with every form of desolation, we need to acknowledge our fears and present them to God in prayer. Every fear we experience can become an opportunity for us to acquire a knowledge of the presence of God at a deeper level of our being.

When fear is acknowledged, expressed and presented to God in prayer, the fear can no longer possess us and thus rob us of our freedom. Acknowledged fear can instead become our teacher, revealing the assumptions that are hidden in our fears. If we can only acknowledge our greatest fear, it may in fact turn out to be a friend rather than an enemy. The most striking and common example is the fear of death. I experienced this powerfully when a close friend was told that she was terminally ill and that death was imminent. She had suffered trauma in her life, but she had learned to befriend death. She remained at peace with the prospect of death, and meanwhile took an even greater delight in everything and everyone around her.

'Hardening of the Oughteries': Disease or Blessing?

There is a practical and useful rule of thumb for discernment in decision-making: *God draws: the destructive spirit drives*. In his book *Clinical Theology* the priest and psychiatrist Frank Lake describes a particular spiritual disease as 'Hardening of the Oughteries'. This is a common ailment among conscientious religious people whose lives are dominated by a sense of duty. Sufferers of 'Hardening of the Oughteries' experience 'God's will' as a categorical imperative imposed from without and leaving them no choice. The condition is totally independent of any desire of their own, no matter how deeply rooted.

The guideline on befriending our fears encourages us to 'face the fears that haunt us'. In this context, the word 'fear' embraces everything that affects us deeply and arouses our fury, indignation and outrage. We need to befriend not only our fears, but also our 'hates', and everything that repels us. By 'befriend' I mean that we need to acknowledge our fears and hates and try to understand them. I do not mean that it is necessary to 'force yourself to like X or Y'. That would be the imposition of an 'oughtery'. But if we can attempt to acknowledge our own hates and aversions and try to face into them, they will be less likely to damage the core of our being.

'Hardening of the Oughteries' – For Some a Disease: for Others the Essence of Orthodoxy

God is a God of love. If God's love for us bears no relationship to our own deepest longings and desires, then God cannot be a God of love, but a God of commands. If God's will for you and for me did not bear any relationship to our own deepest longings and desires, we should be obliged to ignore the longings of our hearts and to put our trust in some authority external to ourselves. Religion would indeed become 'the opium of the people', in the words of Karl Marx (1818–83). And it is just such an attitude towards religious authority that the Jewish theologian and philosopher Martin Buber (1878–1965) had in mind when he wrote that 'nothing so masks the face of God as religion'. If it is really of the essence of religion that we ignore our own deepest inner promptings in order to surrender to an external authority, then we would be right to refuse such a surrender and to renounce religion – even at the cost of our own lives. To surrender ourselves totally to any created thing is to worship an idol. Death is preferable to the 'idol worship' of an external authority, no matter how threatening, or pious, its utterances. The alternative to death would be a life lived in denial of the God of all our desiring: a denial of the God who is closer to us than we are to ourselves. If we were ever to allow ourselves to be totally ruled by any such authority, it would be a sign of that deadly disease 'Hardening of the Oughteries' which masquerades as orthodoxy: an infection that kills the love of God and blocks communication with God in the depth of the soul. It is the disease that Jesus exposed and denounced in the Pharisees of his day, who felt that it was their religious duty to have him put to death (cf. Matt. 23).

Jesus tells us that, 'Yes, my yoke is easy and my burden light' (Matt. 11:30). Because God is the God of love, God always draws us and never drives us. God is always attractive, and if an inner prompting is of God, there will always be an element of attractiveness, no matter how demanding and painful the task in question.

We are called to 'Let God be God' at all times and in all circumstances, to let God be the God of love and compassion for all peoples rather than a God who is confined to 'the spiritual', having nothing much to do with material creation. In this chapter we have reflected on the presence of God who is active in our desiring, and active in the moods and feelings accompanying our desires: the God who is drawing us to the creative and rescuing us from the destructive. In the following chapter we shall further explore the 'earthiness' of the transcendent God.

Exercises

1 Go through the guidelines given in this chapter and note down anything in your own experience that corresponds to them.
2 Make a brief note of anything in the guidelines that you find to be unclear.
3 Try writing your own guidelines, based on your own experience.
4 Try drawing your own inner self in terms of the sheep and the sheepdog in Figure 1, naming the 'sheep' – that is, your own tendencies and sub-personalities.

THE PATH TO FREEDOM

I F WE ARE TO live in truth and integrity, if we are to discover the answer to our inner longings and so find true freedom, what kind of attitude of mind and heart does this demand? The ancient Romans had a word for it: they called it *humilitas*, a word derived from *humus*, meaning earth; therefore *humilitas* can be translated *earthiness*. We translate it as *humility*, attaching to the word meanings that have little or nothing to do with being free or living with delight in truth and integrity.

Is Humility Your Favourite Virtue?

The fate of the word 'humility' is a further instance of the split nature of our spirituality. As Christians, speaking in religious mode, we can discourse eloquently on the subject and of the wonderful humility that Jesus showed in washing the feet of his disciples on the night before his death. In some Christian traditions we pray to be 'meek and humble of heart'. But if we search our hearts and ask, 'Do I honestly want to be humble?' or 'Would humility come in the top ten of my favourite virtues?', most of us would answer 'No'. In writing your own obituary, as suggested in Chapter 5, would you delight in being described, after your death, as 'outstandingly humble', with the rest of the obituary making it clear that you had every reason for being so because there was, apparently, nothing else to commend you? Humility seems to be a quality that could be attractive only to the masochist. Why is the phrase 'false humility' so common? We seldom hear of 'false generosity', 'false courage' or 'false compassion'. In his letter to the Philippians, St Paul writes: 'There must be no competition among you, no conceit; but everybody is to be self-effacing' (Phil. 2:3). If we try to obey Paul's words to the Philippians, it somehow becomes overwhelmingly tempting to make it clear to others that we are being admirably self-effacing!

A few years ago I was invited to preach at the Church of St Mary the Virgin, in Oxford, on 'The Grace of Humility'. This sermon has been an annual event since 1684, when the Vicar of Preston, William Masters, made a bequest to the university. A condition of the bequest was an annual sermon on 'The Grace of Humility'. A further condition of the bequest was a second annual sermon on 'The Sin of Pride'. For each sermon the stipend is £5 – that sum to be equally divided between the preacher and the university! As I struggled to prepare the sermon I came to appreciate the wisdom of the Reverend William Masters in describing his chosen subject as 'The Grace of Humility' rather than 'The Virtue of Humility', because the more we practise humility and think we are succeeding, the less humble we are likely to become. Humility must be a grace, a free gift: we can no more achieve it for ourselves than we can achieve holiness.

Humility – The Foundational Attitude for Freedom in All Decision-Making

The *Collins English Dictionary* describes 'humility' as: 'the state or quality of being humble'. If we then turn to the definition of 'humble', we discover the following: 'as adjective: 1 conscious of one's failings. 2 unpretentious, lowly: *a humble cottage*. 3 deferential or servile. As a verb: 4 to cause to become humble, humiliate. 5 to lower in status'.

The dictionary definition does nothing for humility. It gives no indication that humility is the foundational attitude if we are to be free in all our decision-making, the basic attitude for all undiluted joy in our lives, enabling us to appreciate every moment of life, helping us to recognise the truth of things and to discover the extraordinariness of the ordinary, for God is in all things. Humility is the most attractive of virtues, but because it has had such a bad press, it is a virtue shunned by most of us most of the time. How has this come about?

In Appendix 3 there is a brief description of Inigo of Loyola, the Basque nobleman who became the founder of the Jesuits in the sixteenth century and wrote a book called *The Spiritual Exercises*, which is enjoying worldwide attention today in many Christian denominations, and among people of other faiths and of no faith. I mention Inigo here because his treatment of humility demonstrates its fundamental importance: and he shows us why humility has acquired such a bad name!

In his Spiritual Exercises, Ignatius has a meditation that he calls 'The Two Standards', and which precedes all the meditations on Jesus's public life and his passion, death and resurrection. The Spiritual Exercises are designed to enable a person either to make an important decision in freedom and, therefore, in accordance with the will of God, or to confirm such a decision that has already been made.

In the Two Standards meditation, Inigo presents the problem of good and evil: a theme that has engaged the human mind since the dawn of recorded time, a question that confronts every thinking human being regardless of religious belief, or the lack of it. The manner in which Inigo presents the problem is typical of himself and of his time, but the truths he is considering transcend all times and all cultures.

Since 11 September 2001, we have been very much aware of the destructive threat posed by al Qaeda. In the United States and Britain the thinking has been that the threat of terrorism can only be counteracted by the imposition of greater terror on the perceived perpetrators – as though bombs can solve the problem of evil. Inigo's Gospel-based teaching is simpler and more pro-found – and it is deeply uncomfortable. The roots of human creativity and destructiveness lie, in fact, in the human heart. The roots are normally hidden from us: destructive forces can attack good, conscientious and committed people in subtle and plausible ways that can appear very acceptable, respectable and rewarding. How are we to unmask such forces at work in our minds and hearts, how are we to react to them, and how are we to become more discerning? Humility is not the prerogative of those who have nothing else to commend them: it is the virtue on which our future as a human race depends.

The Nazi Experience – A Lesson for All Peoples

During the 1950s I studied theology for three years at the Jesuit college of Sankt Georgen, in Frankfurt. When I arrived, my mind was well stocked with uncomplimentary stereotypes about Germany and the Germans. Although I soon became aware of my own prejudices, the following question arose, and has remained with me. How could such a talented, intelligent, efficient, religious and cultured nation fall for Nazism? A number of Christians saw what was happening – Dietrich Bonhoeffer (d.1945), Paul Schneider (d.1939) and Alfred Delp (d.1945), to name but a few. They protested publicly and were imprisoned or executed. But why did the majority of Christians and Christian leaders fail to act? On asking themselves this question, the German answer very frequently was 'We lacked discernment'.

Nazism promised much, and in less than two years it had changed an impoverished and demoralised nation with over five million unemployed into a nation of full employment, economically healthy; it was proud of its identity and had great hopes for the future. There was a hunger-relief programme that included a weekly fast day when people were encouraged to limit themselves to a 'one pot' meal; the money saved to go to the hungry. Every village with a population of more than five hundred had to have a public library. There was a great emphasis on sport and body building, especially among the young, whose energies and aspirations were focused on national resurgence under their glorious leader.

Hitler won the support of rich and poor in a predominantly Christian country. The president of the German Catholic Bishops' Conference was an elderly man, who had been alive when the Catholic Church lost over 2,000 parishes in the time of the 'Iron Chancellor', Otto von Bismarck (1815–98). The Archbishop did not want to risk another such loss and used to send the Führer birthday greetings, a gesture that infuriated some of his fellow bishops.

As we saw in a previous chapter, Hitler was able to tap into German resentment resulting from the Treaty of Versailles in 1919, which had left the nation impoverished and demoralised after their defeat at the end of the 1914–18 war. He also encouraged anti-Semitism by making a scapegoat of the Jewish people, presenting them as the root cause of Germany's economic plight and of her humiliation as a nation. Resentment can produce floods of destructive energy, which sweeps away humanity and compassion; reason becomes the slave of the irrational and proposes arguments justifying savagery.

The rise of Nazism is one example of an evil into which every nation, every religion, group and every individual, is liable to fall: an evil that presents itself as attractive, respectable and desirable in order to ensnare and destroy.

Imagination Can Reveal the Reality of Christ and the Subtlety of Evil

Inigo always encourages the use of imagination. In the Spiritual Exercises he presents the problem of evil in an imaginative way. He names the devil 'Lucifer', which literally means 'the light bearer', because under the appearance of good, Lucifer brings destruction. Inigo imagines Lucifer 'in the great plain of Babylon, seated on a throne of fire and smoke, in aspect horrible and terrifying'. Lucifer summons innumerable devils and disperses them, some to one city, some to another, throughout the whole world, omitting 'no province, place, state, or individual person'. The imagery is dated and we may prefer to find our own, but before dismissing it, it is useful to notice the truths that lie behind Inigo's imagery:

From Lucifer's throne comes fire and smoke, fire that devours and smoke that blinds. His empire is worldwide and there is no corner of the world that Lucifer neglects: no Church, no State, no place is exempted. When seen in 'close-up', Lucifer is horrible and terrifying. Followers of *Lord of the Rings* will recognise the power of the imagery.

Lucifer is subtle, cunning and seductive. Ignatius imagines Lucifer giving the devils what appears at first sight to be clear, simple and relatively harmless instructions. They are to encourage people to covet riches. The next step is to encourage them to love honours. These two steps will bring people to the third step, contemptuous pride, a state in which the only passion in their lives is self-aggrandisement; leading them to treat everyone and everything else as a means of increasing their own sense of self-importance. From these three steps, the enemy, as he calls Lucifer, leads people to all other vices.

In contrast to Lucifer, Inigo imagines Jesus in a beautiful and attractive plain near Jerusalem, where he summons lots of people and sends them out all over the world to spread his teaching 'among people of every state and condition'.

Like Lucifer, Jesus also gives clear instructions to his followers, but they are *opposing* his instructions. Jesus's followers are sent to help people everywhere in three steps. First, they are to attract people to spiritual poverty, and even to actual poverty. Second, they are to attract them to a desire for 'reproaches and contempt', since from these comes the third stage, humility, which is the source of all the other virtues. In these three stages, the battle lines between good and evil are clearly drawn: Jesus's followers are attracted by poverty in opposition to riches, are drawn to reproaches and contempt rather than to honours from the world, and they choose humility rather than pride. Such a programme helps us understand why humility is not a popular virtue; but as we look more closely, we begin to see the destructiveness of Lucifer and the attractiveness of Jesus's teaching.

Inigo suggests that we start to pray the meditation on the Two Standards, with a prayer asking for insight into the deceits of Lucifer and the grace to resist them; and for insight into the genuine life that Jesus offers and for the grace to allow his ways to become our ways. Insight means having a felt knowledge of the deceits, as distinct from a merely theoretical knowledge. A felt knowledge of the deceits will include a loathing for them: felt knowledge of the life Jesus offers will include a strong attraction and love for him and his ways.

At first sight, Lucifer's programme looks far more attractive than Christ's. Can you imagine a modern politician trying to woo the electorate with the following manifesto: 'We promise all of you poverty of spirit, and, to some, actual poverty. Moreover, we shall make every effort to persuade you to come to a love of reproaches and contempt, for this will lead you to humility, the highest of the virtues and the source of them all.' What a challenge for the spin doctors to make such a manifesto attractive to the electorate! A politician offering Lucifer's manifesto would have no need of spin doctors; the message would speak for itself: 'We promise you affluence, we promise you job security and status, leading to full blown pride in your own importance and the importance of your nation'!

Why is Lucifer's Attractive Programme So Destructive, and Christ's Unattractive Programme So Life-Giving?

Wealth, in itself, is a blessing; a form of energy that is life-giving, as every hungry person knows. It is not wealth in itself that is destructive, but the way in which we relate to wealth and the ways in which it is distributed. We can relate to wealth in such a way that the preservation and accumulation of riches becomes the dominating factor in our lives; the goal to which we direct all our energies and abilities. Every other relationship and activity becomes subservient to the creation and maintenance of wealth. When we relate to wealth in this way, we measure the value of our existence in financial terms; this can then become the commonly accepted measure of the value of a human being. Absence of wealth becomes a cause of shame and can rob people of any appreciation of their self-worth. In today's cult of celebrity, personal wealth is an essential feature. If my life is dedicated to the creation and maintenance of wealth and I measure the value of my existence in financial terms, it follows that the loss of my wealth makes my life worthless. I shall fight against any threat to my wealth with all the strength and energy of my self-preservation instinct. I shall act ruthlessly towards anyone, no matter how close, if they are likely to threaten my wealth and therefore my very existence. My wealth has become my prison. I possess, therefore I am. I do not possess, therefore I am not. I have become my possessions, paying for them with my humanity. Wealth is my idol and I worship it.

The self-imposed tyranny of wealth affects both individuals and nations: elections are won and lost upon promises of economic prosperity. The desire for economic prosperity can become like a ravening, all-consuming monster that lurks hidden under the fine words of the powerful. Decisions about the health, education and social welfare of a nation can be directed primarily not to the health of a nation, nor to education or social welfare, but to economic targets. The profit motive determines, and the account-ant is the prophet! The whole process can be exceedingly subtle: we can deceive ourselves that 'hard' decisions are taken in the interest of customers/constituents when they are, in fact, driven by the profit motive.

An example of the way in which we can deceive ourselves is to be found in the rhetoric justifying the 1991 Gulf War between Saddam Hussein's Iraq and an international coalition of forces determined to compel Iraqi withdrawal from Kuwait. We were told that the war was conducted to bring down a tyrant who harbours and assists worldwide terrorist networks; who is engaged in the manufacture of nuclear weapons, of poison gas and biological weaponry – the poison gases having already been used by Saddam against his own people, and causing thousands of defenceless casualties. Similar rhetoric was constantly heard in justification of the war in Afghanistan undertaken to root out Osama bin Laden and his al Qaeda terrorists. This is not to deny the danger of Saddam or of Osama bin Laden, nor to deny the need to resist terrorism. It is rather a matter of questioning the alleged motives for the destructive retaliatory violence unleashed on both countries. Afghanistan, one of the poorest in the world and threatened with severe famine, was pounded with 'smart weapons' that included cluster bombs which, if they do not explode on impact, can act as small landmines for years after they have been dropped. The US forces also dropped 'Daisy Cutters', huge bombs designed to terrify and kill indiscriminately. Terrorism has been answered by worse terrorism, all in the name of peace and democracy: much fire and lots of smoke, as in Inigo's imaginative picture.

Had Iraq not been the most important oil-producing country in the Middle East affecting US and British oil interests, would the campaign against terrorism have been conducted as it was? Had Afghanistan not been a country of unexploited oil and mineral wealth, through which America had been planning to build an oil pipeline from Russia to the Caspian Sea, would the campaign have been conducted in this way? Would America, with Britain in support, be threatening to invade Iraq without UN sanction if Saddam does not accept the Security Council's demands for weapons' inspection?

Financial considerations can also dominate decisions concerning the life of churches. Attachment to church property and church wealth can restrict the worldwide mission of the Church, so that it becomes primarily concerned with the maintenance of local plant. The priest or nun who belongs to a religious congregation may be as poor as a church mouse because they are living in strict personal fidelity to their vow of poverty, but these individuals may be caught up in corporate acquisitiveness.

A Church Weakened Through Wealth Can be Renewed Through Poverty

I worked at one time with a Vietnamese Jesuit, Augustin, who had left his country just before the end of the Vietnam war in 1975. I asked him about the work in which he had been engaged before leaving his country. He told me that he had been working with 'Catechumens', people who wanted to become Roman Catholics. In many places in the Western world this task would make little demand on the time of a priest. I asked Augustin how many 'Catechumens' he had to instruct. He answered, 'About three hundred', and then he explained. Before the Vietnam war, the Roman Catholic Church in South Vietnam had been very wealthy and very influential. After the close of the Second Vatican Council in 1965, the Catholic Church in South Vietnam organised many conferences and seminars aimed at educating the Catholic population in the call for renewal contained in the Council documents. 'But', said Augustin, 'no renewal happened. Then came the war. The Church lost everything. Then renewal happened.' The people who ran and attended the renewal courses that were arranged after the Vatican Council were probably very conscientious; but they were so accustomed to being a large, wealthy and influential Church that they were probably unaware of the extent to which their possessions limited their vision. When circumstances stripped them of these securities, they recovered their freedom and real renewal could begin.

When money rules in any organisation, whether secular or religious, there is no more need for discernment, for wise men and women, or for philosophers: we need only accountants! The cries of the poor of our own land and overseas must be ignored. If we listen to them, they may disrupt our economy. This is not to deny that the cost of a project is an important element in decision-making: but it is not the only consideration. If we fail to be vigilant, our attachment to our wealth can cost us our compassion and our humanity.

The Meaning of 'Honour' and its Destructive Possibilities

The second step in Lucifer's destructive strategy is to lead us from love of wealth to love of honour. In this context, honour is a generic term and stands for all that gives us a sense of personal security – relationships, status in society, reputation, occupation, qualifications, achievements, the good/bad state of our health. Honour and all that honour represents is, in fact, good in itself. It is the way in which we relate to honour that can be destructive. If I find my basic security in honour and all that honour stands for, I shall be building my house on sand. What happens when the storm comes and relationships break down? Suppose that I lose my job, my status and my reputation? At this point the shallowness of what I had considered to be my own achievements is now revealed to me and to others. My security has been taken from me, so I have no alternative but to sink into despair. This scenario plays itself out in individuals – but it also happens with nations. We go to war because the nation's 'prestige' is thought to be at risk. And in modern warfare we risk not only the lives of combatants, but the lives of a far greater number of innocent non-combatants. It is claimed that prestige is one of the reasons for Britain's possession of a nuclear deterrent. Possession of the nuclear deterrent assures the nation a voice among other nations. Across the world, intelligent and well-intentioned people can thus risk the lives of millions for the sake of prestige. Does this help us to understand why earlier generations considered the devil to be a mixture of deep cunning and crass stupidity?

The devastation and destructiveness of attachment to honour becomes even more apparent when we consider it in terms of our struggles for power and desire for control. This desire affects every individual, every human grouping from the smallest to the largest, from the weakest to the strongest, the most pious to the most profane. No individual or group is exempt from this desire, which operates irrespective of ethnic origin, religious allegiance or atheistic conviction. Organisation and control are necessary among any group of people. The destructiveness lies not in organisation and control in themselves, but in the way in which we relate to these realities. Do we organise and control for the good of those we are meant to be serving, or to build up our own sense of security, whether individual or corporate?

In Inigo's image, the devils are scattered throughout the world, no person or place being excepted. Similarly, the destructive virus of power and control is also 'scattered throughout the world'. Religious groupings are by no means exempt! A friend remarked to me, after a particularly strained meeting of a spirituality group, 'There's no clash like guru clash!' Consult your own experience. So many groups start with admirable ideals of service, and finish with their energies exhausted through committee in-fighting. The noble ideals are forgotten and the intended beneficiaries are no better off.

The desire for control and domination is the deadly virus that afflicts every human assembly – and Jesus's own disciples and friends were not exempt. James and John ask Jesus to promise them top places – in the kingdom! 'When the other ten heard this they began to feel indignant with James and John, so Jesus called them to him and said to them, "You know that among the pagans the so-called rulers lord it over them, and their great men make their authority felt. This is not to happen among you. No; anyone who wants to become great among you must be your servant, and anyone who wants to be first among you must be slave to all. For the Son of Man himself did not come to be served but to serve, and to give his life as a ransom for many"' (Mark 10:41–5). If this teaching were really to be practised in every department of every Christian Church, many of the structures would come tumbling down and there would be a wonderful resurrection and revival.

The Destructive Power of Pride

Undue attachment to wealth and honour leads to an all-consuming pride, to a state of such total self-absorption that

nothing and no one possesses any value apart from the further-
ance of my personal concerns and/or the concerns of my group,
Church or nation. We saw an example of this in 1945 when the
defeat of Germany was inevitable. Adolf Hitler still gave orders
that the fighting must continue and pulled the entire nation into
even greater destruction! Pride is the refusal to let God be God:
one of its characteristics is crass stupidity. Pride displaces God by
ignoring the demands of truth, love, compassion, justice and
loyalty in so far as they affect anyone or anything apart from
myself. Full-blown pride imprisons us within our narrow selves,
leaves us hating ourselves and others: we can create our own hell.

   We have seen the utter destructiveness lurking beneath the surface
of Lucifer's seductive programme, drawing us from love of riches to
love of honour to full-blown pride. Now we shall look at Jesus's
programme as Inigo presents it in his Two Standards meditation, a
programme which, at first sight, is most unattractive; yet it is the
way to life, to freedom, the answer to our deepest longings.

Spiritual Poverty Means Total Trust in God

In contrast to Lucifer's instructions to the devils, telling them to
draw people to love of riches, Jesus urges his followers to practise
'spiritual poverty'. This implies an attitude of total trust in God,
the attitude of the psalmist when he sings, 'You are my rock, my
fortress' (Ps. 31:3). 'Yahweh is the fortress of my life, of whom
should I be afraid?' (Ps. 27:1). I may pray such psalms with
sincerity, but after my prayer I meet someone who says something
less than complimentary and all hell breaks loose! I am now in
touch with the reality of the gulf that exists between my verbal
protestations to God and the truth that is within me. The
uncomplimentary remark threatened my real security, which does
not lie in total trust in God, but in my reputation, in my own
view of myself, which I assume to be the truth of things. If I was,
in fact, 'spiritually poor' I should be able to accept the uncomplimentary remark with equanimity, because the only opinion
that matters is the opinion of God in whom I trust.

   How would we behave if we really possessed poverty of spirit; if
we really trusted in God as our rock, our refuge and our strength?
Imagine yourself at a large public gathering that is being televised

worldwide. Someone goes to the microphone and proceeds to tear your reputation to shreds, not by telling lies about you, but by revealing the truth about all your weaknesses. How would you feel towards the speaker? How would you feel about yourself? If we really possessed poverty of spirit we should presumably listen to our critic with interest, because he or she would be speaking the truth. We could wear our best half-Zen smile, thank the critic for this contribution to truth, and feel no personal rancour whatsoever!

The real truth about me is revealed in the way in which I react to events that threaten what I, in fact, consider to be the 'core' of my being, what I perceive as my ultimate security. As we have seen, this can be my wealth, status or past achievements. I can sit in an armchair and be convinced that I am not unduly attached to my wealth and possessions. I may also think that I am not unduly absorbed in my state of health, or at the prospect of death, whenever it may come. If I am suddenly deprived of my wealth, or the doctor tells me that I am terminally ill, my reactions will reveal my true state. This may differ considerably from what I had imagined my true state to be while in my armchair! It is for this reason that Inigo advocates spiritual poverty, an attitude of mind and heart that will enable me to trust in God as my rock, my refuge and my fortress, whatever the circumstances in which I find myself. If I am able to do this, I shall be able to accept loss of health, or wealth, with comparative equanimity. That is why, in the Two Standards meditation, Inigo imagines Jesus telling his followers that they are to 'endeavour to help all people by attracting them first of all to the most perfect spiritual poverty', for spiritual poverty means a genuinely total trust in God, our rock, our refuge and our strength.

After attracting them to spiritual poverty, his followers are also to attract people to the practice of actual poverty. The 'actual poverty' of which Ignatius writes is the poverty embraced by members of religious orders and congregations who take vows of poverty, chastity and obedience. Poverty, in this context, does not mean destitution, which is an evil, and therefore to be resisted.

The poverty to which members of religious orders bind themselves is basically a renunciation of ownership, or private use of personal possessions, which now belong to the order/congregation they have joined. The religious body to which these people belong may possess wealth, but the money belongs to the whole congregation and must be used in serving the people to whom they are sent, not on their own self-aggrandisement. Like all the vows religious take, the ultimate object is not to set ourselves apart, as though we were some superior caste, but to enable us to be able to live the life to which every single being is called, living as the Spirit prompts us, not allowing anyone, any organisation, system or any power, whether religious or secular, to be the ultimate and dominating influence in our lives, so that when we act, we act freely and not out of fear.

Importance of the Practical Experience of Deprivation in Order to Attain Freedom

Sensitivity to the plight of the poor is usually directly related to personal experience of poverty in some form. It is very difficult for anyone to have true detachment from wealth and possessions who has not first had some experience, at least for a short period, of living as a poor person is forced to live, not knowing where the next meal is coming from, or being obliged to 'live rough', or to bring up a family on less than half the average national wage.

What a difference it would make to the governments of Britain and the Western world if the people responsible for legislation on housing, education, social welfare, health and transport were obliged to undertake experiential training before taking up ministerial responsibilities. Ministers responsible for housing would have to undertake a series of placements, taking their families with them. They would be required to live homeless for a couple of months and survive on state benefits. This would be followed by a further two months during which they would have to live in a rundown housing estate. When ministers eventually took up their responsibilities, they would do so on the under-standing that they and their families would be obliged to return to their placements for an indefinite period if the minister failed to make an appreciable difference to the housing situation during his/her term of office! Future Ministers of Education would be obliged to work as caretakers or teachers in a variety of schools. They, too, would be obliged to return to their placements if they failed to improve the schools for which they carried ministerial responsibility. Future health ministers would have to spend a few months working as nursing auxiliaries in a variety of hospitals. They would be banned for life from having recourse to private medical care. Transport ministers and their families would be forbidden the use of private transport during their tenure of office, with the threat of permanent withdrawal of their driving licences if they effected no improvement in public transport. Such measures would ensure radical change within a very short period! Without such experiences, the vision of the decision-makers is bound to be limited: the same failures will recur, and the gap between rich and poor will widen.

In writing this last paragraph, part of my mind has been thinking, 'Better avoid deliberate exaggeration if you hope to be taken seriously.' But I recognise the source of that thought: it lies in the part of me that wants to be accepted; which would like to consider itself well endowed with common sense. That part of my mind is not primarily dedicated to the truth of things and to openness to others. It is dedicated, instead, to my wish to be approved, recognised and accepted. This attitude is a final and formidable barrier to my own freedom and to the freedom of others. Inigo was well aware of this barrier in his own life, in the life of those around him, and in the life of the Church. It is for this reason that he imagines Jesus urging his servants and friends to try to help all peoples 'by attracting them to a desire of reproaches and contempt, since from these results humility'!

The Meaning and Value of 'Reproaches and Contempt'

My translation of the Spiritual Exercises refers to 'reproaches and contempt'. Another translation renders the phrase: 'insults, injury and abuse'. The words are to be understood in terms of any serious setback or significant loss that we experience. These can include loss of wealth, status and reputation; the onset of serious bodily or mental illness; and the loss of those we love. These things are obviously not desirable in themselves, and they can plunge us into a state of desolation that becomes destructive if we allow it to determine our decisions. If they were desirable in themselves, we should render the best possible service to one another by piling on 'insults, injury and contempt' as the quickest available release into freedom. If we were to find ourselves acting in this way, we should soon discover that our victims were imprisoned with us in a spiral of escalating violence. Any desire for 'insults, injury and contempt' for their own sake is a clear indication of psychological ill health.

What is Inigo conveying through his emphasis on the desirability of 'insult, injury and contempt'? We saw earlier that it was possible to react to the experience of desolation in such a way as to render it creative. In the same way, it is possible to react to 'insult, injury and contempt' in such a way that they too can become creative. An example is to be found in my response to a good dose of criticism, which can certainly help me to realise that I have become very dependent on false securities in terms of my own good opinion of myself. The criticism can plunge me into a state of misery and self-doubt, which can spill over into every area of my life. The source of my misery lies in my assumption that my security lies in my sense of self, not in God. If my security were really rooted in God, I could accept the criticism peacefully because the criticism of me would have lost its power to devastate. If my ultimate security does not lie in God, but in my own idea of myself, I am, as it were, reduced to nothingness if my idea of myself is threatened by criticism. This is an acutely painful state which is, of course, based on a lie. If I were really reduced to nothing, there would be nothing to worry about!

To be humble is to recognise the truth of things and to live accordingly. The humble are rooted in the earth, know their utter dependence on the rest of creation for every breath they breathe, every movement, every thought, every longing of the heart. Knowing this utter dependence and their own tininess in the face of the universe is not a cause of bitterness and resentment to the humble, but a cause of great wonder and delight.

In a previous chapter we considered the phrase: 'Wisdom is to know the harmony of things and joy is to dance to its rhythm.' The humble see things in perspective. They see themselves as part of a mysterious, yet benevolent and fascinating creation. They are aware of their own fragility, of their own failings and sinfulness, but they are not preoccupied with them. Such preoccupation would be an inverted form of pride, replacing God at the centre of our lives in favour of our rotten selves! Humble people surrender their ego to the goodness and greatness of God, and in so doing they experience a wonderful sense of freedom; the freedom of which St Paul writes in his second letter to the Corinthians: 'For our sake God made the sinless one into sin, so that in him we might become the goodness of God' (2 Cor. 5:21), and again to the Galatians: 'I live now not with my own life but with the life of Christ who lives in me' (Gal. 2:20). The humble catch glimpses of this truth. In losing life, in letting go of their own ego, they discover a much fuller life. Clinging to nothing, they possess all things; letting go of their own securities, they discover that God really is their rock, their refuge and their strength. Through humility, they catch a glimpse of the wisdom of the God who put aside his divinity and became one of us, so that we might find our true identity, which is to be at one with God and with all creation.

At the end of the Two Standards meditation, Inigo suggests a prayer that asks God to receive us under Christ's Standard, first in complete spiritual poverty, and even in actual poverty, if that is God's will for us; second, in bearing reproaches and injuries, so that through them I may learn humility and become more like Christ.

Inigo does not suggest that we should pray to desire reproaches and injuries, but for the grace to bear them. If reproaches and injuries come our way, we are invited to pray for the grace to bear them, but we do not have to go looking for them!

For the full text of the Two Standards meditation and some suggestions for praying it, see Appendix 4.

Three Different Ways of Approaching Decision-Making

After the Two Standards meditation, Inigo presents an exercise called the 'Three Classes'. This is an application of the message of the Two Standards to the making of an actual decision. The meditation considers three different ways of approaching decision-making. Two of the ways are, in fact, methods of avoiding the question to be faced. Many of us are familiar with these two methods in our everyday life, but we may not recognise them as ways of escape from decision-making.

Inigo imagines three people of goodwill who have each come into a vast fortune of ten thousand ducats, which has been honestly acquired. Each one has to decide what to do with the money. All three desire peace with God, and so their question is: 'What is to the greater glory of God? That I should keep the fortune, or relinquish it?' The question is not, 'What is the right thing to do?' but rather, 'What is for the greater glory of God?'

'The glory of God' is a very beautiful religious phrase that eludes definition. The first time I camped on a deserted island off the West Coast of Scotland, I awoke on the first morning to heavy mist and light drizzle, my mood matching the weather. As I sat having a porridge breakfast, a faint sun began to break through. One hour later sky, sea and the island were transformed. I spent another hour sitting and gawking at the beauty around me, then found myself walking around and singing to the seagulls, 'Gloria Dei'. Reflecting on this experience afterwards, I came to love the phrase 'The greater glory of God'. It was the sudden revelation of the island's beauty that had made me sing 'Gloria Dei'. Glory is about the revelation of the wonder and the beauty that underlie all our dull, grey experiences. When Inigo speaks of making a decision 'for the greater glory of God' he means making a decision which, as it were, allows God's goodness to flow into me more, and through me to flow out to others, revealing the goodness and beauty that always underlies the greyness.

The first method of decision-making – postponement

The first method of decision-making is represented by the person who wants to remain at peace with God, and wishes to be free of all acquisitiveness in terms of the ten thousand ducats. This person keeps postponing the decision about accepting or relinquishing 'until tomorrow', and dies still owning the fortune. Few of us have any difficulty in recognising this delaying tactic in ourselves and in others, with our deep-down resistance to change.

The second method of decision-making – determining God's will

The second method is represented by the person who wishes to be free of all acquisitiveness, but in such a way that they can still hold on to the cash! This method works on the will of God until it has been successfully aligned with my own will! Instead of acting out of our deepest desire, we stop halfway down at a more superficial desire – the wish to keep the money – and we call that superficial desire 'the will of God'. Instead of allowing God to be God to me and through me, I am primarily concerned that God should fall in with my decision!

This second method is very revealing. It raises many questions and we can find ourselves wondering whether we could possibly be so crass as to try to manipulate the will of God to our own predetermined ends. Take, for example, the wars of the twentieth century during which politicians and most church leaders assured their people that the war in question was being waged 'pro Deo et Patria', 'for God and country'. The 'will of God' was used to back up the call to arms, as though in our honest search to find the will of God, each side suddenly discovered that God was telling them to 'Go off and kill the enemy'. Another example is to be found in the existence of our divided Christian Church. Our Christian dividedness cannot be the will of the God who called us in Christ to be 'one flock and one shepherd' (John 10:16). Yet each denomination justifies its separate status by an appeal to the will of God. God is certainly the God of infinite variety, not the God of uniformity: but God is also the God of unity, not of division.

The third method of decision-making – acting against our acquisitiveness

The third method of decision-making is represented by the person who wants to be thoroughly open to God and to be swayed neither by desire to keep, nor the desire to get rid of the fortune. This person is open to either alternative and only wants to act in accordance with the way in which God is moving them, so that their decision is for the greater glory of God. In preparing for this decision, the person strives not to be influenced by any motive other than the greater service of God.

Having considered these three methods of approaching a decision, Ignatius recommends the retreatant to repeat the prayer already given at the end of the Two Standards meditation, and then he adds, as if it were an afterthought, a most important note about the way to deal with feelings and inclinations in reaching a decision.

In the context of the Three Classes meditation, the note concerns feelings of attraction or repulsion towards either acquiring, or relinquishing, the ten thousand ducats. If our feelings/inclinations are inclining us towards acquiring the ten thousand ducats, we should beg God to choose us for service in actual poverty, but the method can be used in any other context, in any serious decisions in our lives.

His advice is that whatever way our feelings/inclinations are drawing us to one decision rather than another, we should keep begging God earnestly to choose us for the opposite, however reluctant we may feel. This prayer protects us against unconscious influences in our decision-making. It is a way of detecting hidden agendas of which we may be unconscious, but that may, in fact, be determining our decisions and depriving us of our freedom. Inigo is not suggesting that we should always act against all our inclinations. He is suggesting a method of discernment that can enable us to distinguish our deeper desires from the more superficial ones, so that our actions and reactions become wholehearted and free. Although Inigo includes this note in the context of the Three Classes meditation, this method of begging God to choose us to follow a course that may oppose our inclinations can be applied to any serious and life-changing decisions.

Humility is a virtue that brings freedom and the ability to act confidently, because the source of our confidence is God, our ultimate identity. Lack of humility cuts us off from this source: lacking confidence in ourselves we become easy victims of controllers, whatever form the control may take.

Today, one of the most destructive controllers is the consumerist economy which relies on our subservience to the latest fads and fashions in clothing, hairstyles and furnishings, as well as our adherence to politically correct statements and 'acceptable' views. This form of totalitarianism that afflicts all of us, believers and unbelievers alike, is far more effective in achieving conformity than any external authority, whether political, economic or religious; far more effective than jack-booted armies, or the most powerful and repressive police presence.

Rich and poor, we are all vulnerable to the control of a consumerist economy because we all suffer from the lack of self-confidence that springs from a lack of true humility and results in a desperate scramble to become financially and socially secure. Much is said in Britain today about the millions of pounds being invested in inner-city regeneration and the importance of alleviating poverty in developing countries. Such concern for the poor is welcome, but it does not touch the root of the problem, which is the need to enable people who have been oppressed to build up confidence in themselves: their problems cannot be solved by money alone. Without this building-up of confidence, the millions of pounds that are poured into the work of regeneration are likely to be wasted, for such regeneration is only sustainable if people possess a measure of self-confidence.

The following chapter links up and develops the themes we have been considering in previous chapters by reflecting on the meaning of pilgrimage and on seeing life as a journey.

Exercises

1 In Appendices 2 and 4 you will find texts from Scripture, including a section on 'Texts to accompany the Two Standards meditation'. Some of these may be helpful in praying the Two Standards meditation.

2 Discover your own images of Christ and of Lucifer. Drawing, painting or working with clay may be helpful. Don't try too hard, just draw/shape whatever the imagination presents. Or you may prefer to borrow images from literature and films, such as *Lord of the Rings*.

3 What do you find attractive in the life and teaching of Jesus? Focus your heart on these things. An attraction is a sign that you are being called to live out those qualities in your own way, in your own circumstances.

4 Explore for yourself the relationship between freedom and humility: is it possible to be genuinely free without being humble, or humble without being genuinely free?

PILGRIMAGE

'Put on your travelling shoes and jump into the arms of God'
(Meister Eckhart)

Going on pilgrimage is a practice found not only in all the major
world religions, but also in the secular world. People flock to
Memphis, the birthplace of Elvis Presley. Pilgrims appear daily at
'The Cavern' in Liverpool, where the Beatles began their career.
People make annual pilgrimages to prehistoric monuments such
as Stonehenge. Has this universal phenomenon anything to teach
us about the nature of God, the nature of the Church, and the
nature of the human journey in which we are all engaged, believers
and unbelievers alike?

This chapter addresses these questions and develops some of
the themes of previous chapters in the context of pilgrimage. The
reflections that follow are based on my experience of two walking
pilgrimages. The first one started in the south of England, at
Weybridge in Surrey, and took me to Rome in 1975. The second
pilgrimage began on the west coast of Scotland, at Skelmorlie in
Ayrshire, and took me to Jerusalem in 1987.

The experience of going on pilgrimage is an act of trust that has
much to teach us about the meaning of faith. One of the earliest
epithets ascribed to the Church is 'pilgrim'. A pilgrim people are

on a journey, but have not yet reached their destination. Because they are on a journey, they do not know what is coming next: they do not have final answers. Pilgrims are constantly subject to surprises and have to take risks. They must not settle into any permanent resting place while on the journey: neither palace nor hovel! Nor must they ensconce themselves in the stronghold of unalterable opinions or seek ultimate refuge in any organisation, ideology or philosophy. None of these can provide them with a fixed and final resting place. The ultimate destination and security of pilgrims lies only in the trust that enables them to proceed confidently in their insecurity.

Why Go On Pilgrimage?

In the early centuries of Christianity, pilgrims began to go to Palestine where Jesus had lived, taught, worked, suffered, died and rose again, or to Rome, where the early Christians, including Peter and Paul, had suffered martyrdom. Christians set out on pilgrimage for a variety of reasons – not all of them virtuous. In medieval times, pilgrimage took the place of our modern tourism. Holy men and women who had died were now understood to be in heaven. Pilgrims believed that their relics would emit some kind of heavenly radiation that could be transmitted to the pilgrim who touched them; thus ensuring the pilgrim's earthly well-being and the continuing protection of the saint concerned. So strong was this belief that there are accounts of pious pilgrims trampling one another to death in the stampede to touch a relic. The possession of a saint's relic was key to the promotion of religious tourism: the relic could be an arm, a leg or even a piece of the saint's clothing. The theft of relics from rival pilgrimage centres was not uncommon; neither were false claims concerning the authenticity of specific relics. Pilgrimage was sometimes under-taken as a form of penance in the belief that it would shorten, or remit altogether, the time the pilgrim might otherwise have to spend in purgatory, a place of purification from sin after death, to prepare them for heaven! Some went on pilgrimage as a convenient way of escaping from home for a while; others found it a cheap way of enjoying a holiday while robbing fellow pilgrims!

Pilgrimage Mirrors the Journey of Life

Pilgrimage has been described as 'the poor person's substitute for mysticism'; for a direct experience of God. Underlying all our conscious reasons for going on pilgrimage, or for undertaking some long and arduous journey, there is the fundamental search for meaning, for an answer to the hunger and thirst of our being for some kind of fulfilment. We may not be conscious, at first, of this fundamental desire for meaning. The unconscious is much less restricted by constraints of time and space and it can prompt us to undertake things for reasons that may be concealed from us at first. We think that we are doing something for one reason, only to discover the true and unconscious reason very much later.

When I decided to walk to Rome in 1975, my conscious reason was the fact that I liked walking. I wanted to spend some months studying in Rome and was free to go there in June. I was, however, advised to postpone my arrival until September, because the summer weather would be oppressively hot in Rome; libraries would be closed and the people I wanted to meet would be away. I decided to try walking to Rome, leaving in mid-June and arriving in Rome in early September. It was only after the ten-week walk was over that I began to realise how valuable the experience had been. When I decided to walk because I like walking, I had no idea of what I was letting myself in for!

Pilgrimage is a way of projecting our inner and unmanageable hopes, longings, bewilderment, fears and confusions into an outer and more manageable form. We choose some objective that represents the unidentifiable longing of the inner self. For pilgrims, the objective is the holy place to which they have decided to go. We set out on our journey and subsequent decisions are ultimately determined by the desire to reach our destination. We may think that the sole purpose of the journey is to reach our chosen destination but, at a deeper level, we are also setting out in order to reach a better understanding of the inner journey that we embark on at conception and complete at the moment of death.

It is probable that explorers, climbers and sailors are inspired by a similar motivation to undertake new and risky ventures. It has been said that people who go on epic journeys 'are all slightly mad'. It is certainly true that the more intense the inner confusion, the more demanding the outer form in which it is likely to be manifested.

The lessons I learned from my two pilgrimages appear platitudinous when written down, but truths that come to us through the soles of our feet, communicate life and energy, as well as knowledge, in a way that is seldom possible through the medium of the printed page.

On both pilgrimages I learned much about the nature of desire and the importance of constantly returning to our basic desire. There were moments of doubt about the wisdom of undertaking both pilgrimages. Why subject myself to the discomfort and risks of such journeys? In both cases, the desire to reach my destination was very strong. Had this not been the case, I should have abandoned both pilgrimages at an early stage. It was not that I was continually saying to myself 'I want to reach Rome', 'I want to reach Jerusalem'. However, this desire determined the decisions of each day: the distance I walked; the route I followed; the things that I ate and drank; when, where and for how long I slept. At the end of each pilgrimage I realised that reaching my destination was of minor importance compared with the lessons I learned through the journey itself. One lesson was the value of listening to our basic desires and dreams, and the importance of allowing our lives to be shaped by them. I also learned the importance of distinguishing short-term, peremptory and superficial desires from those that are deeper and quieter. The superficial desires were shrill and peremptory, demanding an immediate end to the pilgrimage because my feet were painful! It was only when I attended to my feet and had a rest that the deeper desire to reach Rome or Jerusalem could enter my consciousness again. As we noted earlier, our desires are like shy children: they thrive on attention, but can cause havoc if ignored.

On both pilgrimages prayer became simpler. I most often prayed the prayer of the psalmist, 'Lord, show me your face', or 'Lord, show me your attractiveness, so that your attractiveness determines all my decisions'. Pilgrimage mirrors life in that it needs direction and purpose. The ultimate purpose of pilgrimage is to help us find direction in our lives; to enable us to discover our own basic desire, which will then determine all the decisions of our lives.

But it is not necessary to go on a walking pilgrimage in order to learn these lessons. It is possible to go on the lengthiest pilgrimage and fail to learn anything at all! The review of the day, which we explored in Chapter 4, pages 57–61, is especially valuable, because it can enable our more basic desires to surface from the turmoil of the day. A person who is confined to a wheelchair, but habitually returns to their basic desire, has learned more about the meaning of pilgrimage than the pilgrim who covers 1,500 miles on foot but is totally unreflective.

The Purpose of Luggage

When walking with a haversack, the weight of the luggage travels down to the heel and ball of the foot, where blisters can be excruciating. This obvious truth was borne in on me through every muscle after the first day's walking to Rome. It is easy to overload the haversack with goods that we consider vital for our health and safety. We can so easily be persuaded that we need to carry extra clothing, a spare pair of boots, a proper first-aid kit, a camp bed to ensure a proper night's sleep, a more spacious tent in which we can stand up straight, food containing the necessary vitamins and calories to keep us going, and a larger water flask to guard against dehydration. The more pious might be persuaded to carry a collapsible kneeling bench to ensure correct posture in prayer! Today's pilgrim might feel it unsafe to travel without a mobile phone and a laptop computer to provide daily maps and guidebooks. If we allow ourselves to be persuaded by all this prudent advice, we shall collapse under the weight of it. From this simple lesson on the need to travel light, there follows a platitude of profound wisdom:

Luggage is for the journey, not the journey for the luggage.

That truth is so clear that I feel embarrassed to mention it, yet forgetfulness of this fact is the cause of most human conflict. As individuals and as nations we find ourselves trapped in the belief that the point of our journey through life is the accumulation of luggage. I buy, therefore I am. I become what I possess. I cling to and defend my possessions with all the strength of my instinct for self-preservation, so that I am ready to kill for the sake of my belongings. My true self has disappeared beneath a heap of possessions. Countries go to war for the preservation/accumulation of their possessions, but this reality is concealed behind cunningly constructed webs of words about 'freedom', 'human rights', 'democratic values' and 'the preservation of civilisation'. Such rhetoric was in evidence during the 1991 Gulf War. In the words of one US commentator, 'If Kuwait had grown carrots, but was without oil wells, would the Gulf War ever have happened?'

After my pilgrimage to Rome, I reflected on the truth that luggage is for the journey, not the journey for the luggage:

> 'Those who profess faith in God, who experience his mysterious call within them, form a restless people in search of a way, the way of at-one-ness. They will be a joyful people who have found direction in life and want to communicate it, sing of it, tell everyone about it, because the unity they experience is a summons to greater unity. They will be a gentle people, tolerant, not preoccupied about possessions, because they are in search of the only possession that matters and that no one can take from them. They are not worried about social status and prestige, because they have found a security within themselves that nothing can destroy; nor are they afraid of being challenged, because they know how little knowledge they have, and welcome every challenge as an opportunity to learn.
>
> 'Ideally, the Church is a pilgrim people, blissfully happy in their indifference to wealth and possession, unworried by the insecurity of all systems and institutions because they know they have no abiding city here. They are en route, a learning people, always ready to admit their errors in the face of truth, welcoming the truth wherever it is found, and knowing that it can be found among all peoples, whether Christian or not.
>
> 'What a marvellous Church that would be! . . . [but] it is as though the pilgrim [Church has] . . . accumulated too many possessions on the way, found the weight too heavy to carry and so settled down to look after and protect the overloaded rucksack. The pilgrim Church became the settled Church, the static Church. The pilgrim people, unable to cope with marauding bands, settled down to protect themselves, threw up stockades, then high walls. The pilgrim Church became the parade ground Church, the beleaguered

garrison of Christ the King. Within its high walls the loyal troops performed their outmoded arms drill and manoeuvres in the parade ground, assured that as long as they kept up the drill and obeyed orders without question, they could be sure of ultimate victory' (Gerard W. Hughes, *In Search of a Way* (first edition), pp 125–6.)

If we really believed, in our various churches, that luggage is for the journey rather than the journey for the luggage, we would cease to be parade ground churches – all practising outmoded manoeuvres within our separate stockades. On a pilgrimage, it is the desire to reach the destination that unites the pilgrim people and enables them to travel light. In the journey of life it is the strength of our basic desire that enables us to keep going and saves us from a living death, entombing ourselves in securities that are of our own making and do not come from God. It is for this reason that we need to keep begging God, in the words of the psalmist, to: 'show me your face', 'show me your attractiveness'. It is for this reason that the Christian churches need to concentrate on manifesting the attractiveness of God here and now rather than assuring people that they can only experience the beauty and wonder of God after death.

Another consequence of our profoundly divided spirituality is the fact that while we can certainly recognise the importance of 'travelling light' and 'focusing on our basic desire' within the realm of the 'spiritual', we can fail to see that it is also vitally important to 'travel light' and 'focus our basic desire' in every area of human life, including our political and social structures.

The Preservation and Accumulation of Our Possessions: 'National Security'

The possessiveness that afflicts individuals, nations and Churches is rarely exposed as greed. It is justified by those in power as 'a prudent attitude that assures our personal and national security'. Security becomes the 'idol' to which we offer all that we have and all that we are. One of the most obvious examples lies in our trade in arms and in weapons of mass destruction. Every nation knows that their neighbour's 'defence' is, in fact, a means of aggression. Consequently, for their own defence, each nation must prepare for even more effective aggression. A small fraction of the money spent on weapons of death could transform the lives of millions, alleviating hunger, protecting and improving health and providing clothing, shelter and education.

Our consumerist culture fools us into thinking that joy, happiness and contentment are only to be found in the accumulation of possessions. It is this attitude that ravages the world's resources, divides the 'haves' from the 'have-nots', and leads to frustration on the part of the 'haves' because it distracts their attention from their deeper needs and desires. The hunger and thirst for oil, the resulting conflicts and further potential conflicts, have led to the US Star Wars project. Massive sums of money are spent on filling space with lethal weaponry, while millions of people die of starvation and many more are condemned to lives of destitution. As I walked the road to Jerusalem in 1987, the peace of the countryside was frequently shattered by the roar of fighter aircraft practising low-flying along the valleys and contributing to 'national security' with their screaming message of destruction.

The Idol of National Security: A Product of Our Fear

Why such universal madness? It is because we live in fear. The purpose of our journey through life is no longer the praising, reverencing and serving of God, but rather the self-preservation, at all costs, of the individual, the group and the nation. Our security-conscious, no-risk culture imprisons us in innumerable precautions. In most countries we profess freedom of speech, but it can be an expensive freedom that can cost one's livelihood in many professions, especially in politics and even within the Church. This security-conscious, no-risk culture is, in fact, highly dangerous. It undermines the very heart of the Christian message and endangers the survival of the human race, because individual and national security become an all-consuming idol that devours our humanity and compassion, allowing us to invest in and plan the death of our enemies, and the destruction of the earth that sustains us.

If we can open our eyes to what is happening in the Western world, the growing fear that fuels a booming arms trade which, in turn, fuels even greater fear, the Gospels can begin to strike us like a two-edged sword. Three of the Gospels describe the same event

– Jesus calming the storm – so it must have been a key passage for the early Christian Church:

> One day [Jesus] got into a boat with his disciples and said to them, 'Let us cross over to the other side of the lake'. So they put to sea, and as they sailed he fell asleep. When a squall came down on the lake the boat started taking in water and they found themselves in danger. So they went to rouse him saying, 'Master! Master! We are going down!' Then he woke up and rebuked the wind and the rough water; and they subsided and it was calm again. He said to them, 'Where is your faith?' They were awestruck and astonished and said to one another, 'Who can this be, that gives orders even to winds and waves and they obey him?' (Luke 8:22–5. Also in Matt. 8:23–7 and in Mark 4:35–41.)

When we read of the calming of the storm, our twenty-first century reaction tends to be, 'Did it really happen?' Then the doubts set in and we begin to wonder whether we have any faith. When a Hebrew heard such an account, the first question would not be, 'Did it really happen?' but 'What does it mean?' This is a much more important question, and one that would remain, even if the literal truth of the event were to be disproved beyond any question. The boat represents the Church, threatened both by external persecution and by internal dissension. For the Hebrew, a stormy sea is a manifestation of the power of evil and destructiveness. The calming of the storm vividly illustrates the central message running through the Jewish Scriptures and the New Testament: God alone is our rock, refuge and strength, our only ultimate security. It is only when the disciples call upon Christ that he wakes up and calms the storm. What does this calming of the storm say to us about the nature of faith?

Faith is not primarily about belief in religious formulations, church teachings and liturgies, however important these may be: faith is primarily faith in God. We can only experience God in our experience of life, so faith is faith in the facts in which we find ourselves, and God is in the facts, so the facts must be kind. That is why the phrase 'Do not be afraid' is constantly repeated in the Bible. Unless we constantly allow ourselves to listen to the words

144

'Do not be afraid' resonating in our inmost being, we are in danger of finding ourselves becoming the obedient servants of the idol, 'security', which squeezes the humanity and the life out of us.

Glimpses of Spiritual Freedom and its Cost

In walking long distances, I gradually became more accustomed to the weight of the haversack and no longer felt it a continuous burden. I often experienced an exhilarating sense of freedom and felt sorry for people passing by in cars, laden with luggage. This was an inkling of the joy we could experience if we really possessed the gift of freedom; if we had learned true detachment, which allows us to delight in the things of earth without being possessed and imprisoned by them. Through long-distance walking, I learned to delight in the gift of freedom, but I also began to understand the cost more clearly.

The unnecessary luggage that we carry in our own minds is much more burdensome than any haversack. One does not have to walk very far on pilgrimage before stumbling across another profound platitude:

The more attached we are to our own likes and dislikes, the greater our capacity for misery along the way.

If I am only happy when walking along level, grass-covered paths far from the roar of traffic, with clear skies above me, a gentle wind at my back, and the temperature in the mid-sixties, then I am doomed to be miserable in most places at most times of the year. If I am not content to sit in the open air and share my meals with ants and insects, but must instead find some sheltered, clean and hygienic place, then I am likely to collapse from malnutrition. Alternatively, I can reorganise my route, and perhaps double its length, in order to ensure that it includes sanitised resting places. The more fussy I am about where I sleep and for how long, the more impossible my journey will become. Reflecting on this as I walked, I began to see that the weight of the haversack was not the only burden to be carried. The invisible weight of our own disordered attachments is a much heavier burden, and it can force us to abandon our journey.

A less obvious burden is the weight of our conditioning: the burden of our inner attitudes and values to which we are so accustomed that we no longer notice them. This includes our religious beliefs and convictions, our attitudes to people of other cultures, of other faiths or of none, and our political leanings. As long as we remain in our familiar environment, we are unlikely to become aware of our conditioning and the extent to which it blinds and deafens us to what is going on around us. The more convinced I am that my own views are the criterion of all things, the less capable I become of appreciating, valuing and enjoying surroundings that are unfamiliar to me. Travel is said to broaden the mind, but I can travel the world, meet people of every class and nation, and return seething with anger, disapproval and condemnation, confirmed in the conviction that my particular perspective on the world is the only proper one.

I may, alternatively, spend a lifetime without moving more than five miles from my own front door and remain appreciative, tolerant, interested and curious. It is a question of inner attitude. Our 'certainties', in which we take such pride, can act as iron masks that provide us with only a very narrow slit for vision. The slit offers some very clear detail, but is unable to provide us with an overall picture. The strength of our personal convictions can be in inverse ratio to their breadth. We can go through life, strong in our certainties, disapproving of all that lies beyond our own very limited vision and learning nothing, because we do not feel the need to learn anything! This narrowness of vision can take many different forms. It is to be found in the religious believer, the atheist and in politicians of all parties from the diehard conservative to the anarchist. Such blinkered vision can result in most bitter controversy, often leading to physical violence, death and destruction. In its most extreme and ugly form it is to be found in racism, sexism and in every form of narrow nationalism. Religious belief can be communicated and fostered in such a way that it nurtures inhuman, divisive and destructive attitudes that make atheistic humanism a very understandable response, but atheistic humanism, too, can become tyrannical and intolerant.

Our Own Conditioning as a Key to Inner Freedom

In order to begin to understand the meaning of inner freedom, we need to explore our attachment to our conditioning a little more closely. It is impossible to grow up without conditioning, but some forms of conditioning are less open to life than others. We can be brought up to consider those who are not 'one of us' as 'the enemy' to be avoided, damaged or destroyed. The 'enemy' may be those who do not belong to 'my family', 'my village', 'my city' or 'my nation', or those who do not belong to 'my race' or 'my religion'. Such exclusion diminishes our capacity for enjoyment and delight in the diversity of life, in other people and in ourselves. It also increases the range and intensity of our destructive tendencies, and this brings us to the roots of peace and violence, creativity and destructiveness. The roots are to be found in our own minds and hearts.

Because we are individuals, we have differing ideas and opinions, likes and dislikes, many of which are the result of our conditioning. We also have particular ways of seeing and perceiving, some of which are, of their nature, divisive and destructive. We are unaware of our conditioning until we are freed from it. Before we are liberated, we live contentedly in our chains while protesting our freedom. It is comparatively easy to recognise the conditioning of past generations, who accepted slavery and child labour as integral to a well-ordered society. The death penalty was considered to be a just sentence for sheep stealing. The vote was restricted to men of the propertied classes. Women were not allowed to vote, whether propertied or not. Neither could they hold public office nor practise medicine, for example. Racism infected the social and political structures of many countries, and was divinised in South Africa as a manifestation of the will of God. It is good to ponder the destructive conditioning of previous generations and the destructive conditioning that we perceive in other individuals and other nations, provided it can help us to recognise our own present destructive conditioning, for example, the competitive nature of our educational system, which then permeates our inner thought patterns and so affects every area of life. We look at ourselves and others competitively and comparatively. It is of the nature of competition that only one individual or one group can actually 'win' or 'be first';

the majority must therefore jostle and struggle to get a place in front to avoid the perception of failure. One way of compensating for our constant perception of ourselves as failures is to try toppling the successful or the notorious by smearing their characters. 'If I can't be "first", neither can he!' This creates enormous wealth for tabloid newspapers and other branches of the media, while providing us with some compensation for the resentment we experience at our own perceived failure.

We are also the victims of a potentially destructive conditioning which leads us to believe that 'we' are in sole possession of the whole truth. 'My group', 'my political party', 'my religion', 'my nation' or 'my race' is therefore superior to others, and justified in exercising superiority over them. Such beliefs are inherently wrong, because they are exclusive, and therefore divisive and destructive. Some truths may be good in themselves, but the way in which I relate to them can be destructive of my own freedom and that of other people. I may, for example, be a staunch supporter of world peace and justice, but my strength derives not from my hunger for peace and justice, but from the fact that it is I who support the issue. If, in my pursuit of peace and justice, my views or plans on some particular issue are criticised or rejected, I shall refuse to give in because I have identified my very self with my views. I shall stick to my views and my ways, even if it leads to the break-up of the peace organisation to which I belong. Such tragedies can happen in any kind of group, not least in those dedicated to the promotion of Christian spirituality! My ego can become the source of my strength and the object of my worship. In traditional language, this is the sin of pride, the root of all evil. This leads us to the third platitude:

The burden does not lie in the goods we carry, but in the way we relate to them.

How are we to rid ourselves of the burden of our conditioning? How are we to lose those inner attitudes and ways of perceiving that blind and deafen us and can lead us to acts of destructive violence? The burden lies not in the things that we carry, but in the way in which we relate to them. It is possible, although difficult, for an individual to possess much, and yet to remain free. It is possible to own possessions, but not to be owned by them. If the possessions were to be stolen, confiscated or destroyed, the owner might regret the loss, but the core of their being would not be damaged, neither would they fall into a state of despondency, because they had never allowed their wealth to possess them. Such a person remains free whether they possess or do not possess. They have never assessed their true wealth in terms of their possessions.

Wealth can be a life-stifling burden for the individual and for the nation. It can act as an anaesthetic injected directly into the nervous system: thus restricting us more effectively than a pair of handcuffs, depriving us of freedom in the core of our being. But as we have already seen, the root problem is not wealth, but the way in which we relate to wealth. If we are to remain free in relation to our possessions and to our situation in life, then we must learn to be detached from all these things, which means that we shall be able to enjoy and appreciate possessing them and sharing them, but we are not devastated if they are taken from us. We have possessed them without being possessed by them.

To express this in religious language: we must not allow our possessions to become our idol, whether 'possessions' in the form of wealth, qualifications, achievements, or gifts of character. If we allow any of these things to possess us, we diminish ourselves, sacrificing our God-self to idols, the greatest desecration of which we are capable.

Religion can set us free from inner conditioning, but it can also imprison us. Religious sectarianism, bias and bigotry all arise from false attachments to 'my' way or 'our' way of understanding God, religion and life. We can use God to justify our own narrowness, describing our false allegiance as loyalty to God and to God's will. Religious belief has, in the past, been used to sanction oppression and exploitation of others – slavery, for example, was sanctioned for many centuries by Christians, and apartheid was, until recently, considered by the leadership of the Dutch Reformed Church of South Africa to be a divine command. Men are becoming increasingly aware of their past oppression and exploitation of women in society as a whole and across the world, but few are ready to acknowledge the continuing oppression and exploitation of women today, justifying the oppression on theological grounds. The Dutch Reformed Church has not been alone in its practice of 'apartheid'.

The Burden of Our Conditioning Gives Insight Into the Nature of Peace

When passing through the former Yugoslavia on my way to Jerusalem, many things irked me – the difficulty in finding accommodation, the shortage of food in the shops and its lack of variety, the way in which roadsides were littered with rubbish, the lack of any large-scale maps – and the unreliability of those maps I did find (the only detailed maps were for military use only). I noticed that these irritations could so prey upon my mind that I became unable to appreciate the beauty of the countryside through which I was passing. I could not give my full attention to the people I met, or to the thoughts and memories that came to me on the road. It was only much later that I came to understand the significance and implications of this. My conscious reason for the pilgrimage was to give myself time and space to think about peace. The trivial irritations I encountered on the way taught me an important lesson about the nature of peace and the roots of violence. The irritations had arisen because circumstances were not as I wanted them to be: I was glimpsing the tyranny of my own ego.

I began to see that the greatest danger to our individual and national freedom does not come from some enemy nation destroying or invading our country, nor from the possibility of a tyrannical form of government, whether secular or religious. The greatest danger threatening our freedom lies in our own increasing addiction to building up personal and national security. At an individual and group level this danger reveals itself in a spirit of 'me-centredness', which ignores the truth that our personal well-being is inextricably bound up with the well-being of others. At a national level, our desire for security expresses itself in our reliance on nuclear weaponry and military might as 'our rock, our refuge and our strength'. This is a form of national idolatry that can gradually destroy the humanity of a nation, leading that nation to threaten and to kill the innocent or, at the very least, to collude with those who are doing the threatening and the killing in the name of upholding peace, defending freedom, and preserving democracy. As an individual, my greatest danger is not the loss of those dear to me, sickness, an accident or loss of my job, but attachment to my own ego.

The Tyranny of the Ego

We are essentially 'persons in relationship' and can only discover our true identity in relation to other people and other things. It is for this reason that solitary confinement is so deeply dreaded. Only the very strong can withstand imposed solitude without suffering permanent psychological damage. Egoism is a form of self-imposed solitary confinement in the sense that the egoist can only relate to himself or herself and has no other point of reference. Instead of relating to other persons, the egoist relates to beliefs, convictions and principles. The beliefs, convictions and principles may, in themselves, be good and honourable and may earn the egoist all sorts of accolades and decorations for 'dedicated service' to the nation, the Church, or a particular professional body; but the root of the egoist's dedication lies in personal self-esteem: 'These things are worthwhile because *I* support them', rather than 'These things are worthwhile in themselves and therefore I shall dedicate myself to them'. The egoist is not primarily drawn to specific adherence or to a particular field of action by any concern for truth, justice or other inherent good.

Ego strength can be enormously powerful. The egoist can stimulate and inspire others with genuine dedication to an organisation or a cause. But the strength and dedication is ultimately directed towards personal or national self-aggrandisement. This may lead to the oppression of others and even to their death. As we saw in a previous chapter, Adolf Hitler was a tragic example of overwhelming egoism, sending his troops into the battle at the end of the Second World War when his armies had been defeated on all fronts and inevitable defeat was staring him in the face.

'Wisdom is to Know the Harmony of Things, and Joy is to Dance to its Rhythm'

Egoism is interested only in the harmony that egoism can impose and control. Nothing else is perceived to be of any worth or importance. Self-regard and personal aggrandisement lead to destruction of the true self, which finds its own ultimate identity in God. In Christian understanding, God's own 'Self' is, in fact, relationship: the relationship of three Divine Persons, Father, Son and Holy Spirit, in such a way that neither Father, Son nor Holy Spirit possess anything that does not belong equally to the other two persons. In Christian understanding, each human being is made in the image of the God who is three Divine Persons. Each one of us therefore lives within this Trinity, so my life is essentially a life of 'relatedness': a relatedness not only to the three Divine Persons, but to every human being and to the whole of creation.

As we saw earlier, egoism confines us within ourselves. Instead of being related to other persons and other things, I relate only to myself. I choose to have no other point of reference. The French existentialist philosopher Jean-Paul Sartre (1905–80) took the view that 'hell is other people': '*L'Enfer, c'est les autres*'. I prefer '*L'Enfer, c'est moi*' – 'Hell is me'. Full-blown egoism creates inner hell and I can think of nothing worse than to be permanently incarcerated within my own ego.

Pilgrimage Providing Glimpses of the Unity of All Things

There were moments on the road to Rome and on the road to Jerusalem when I experienced a momentary glimpse of our unity with all things. I had known in my head that there is unity within all creation, but I received my first glimpse of this reality in the Scottish Highlands while preparing for the pilgrimage to Rome. One evening while I was walking through hill country, I saw the fir trees swaying in the wind and suddenly felt that I was a part of them. Particle physics teaches us that subatomic particles can be at one moment a particle with a particular location. Through human observation, among other things, the particle can become a wave and the wave has no location. On that evening in the Scottish Highlands it was as though I had escaped from my 'particle' form; while watching the swaying fir trees I had been released momentarily from the confines of my own body to become one with the trees. It was as though I was experiencing my own soul as coterminous with the universe. The experience lasted for a split second. I can recall it, but I cannot place myself back into the wonder of the moment.

Many years later I met an elderly Aboriginal artist who appeared to live in constant awareness of his unity with all things. This ongoing experience was responsible for delivering him from incarceration in his own ego and had enabled him to rise above an experience of appalling brutality. He had endured a horrific upbringing on the land of a white farmer, where his people were treated like animals, whipped and beaten. On a particular occasion during the 1940s, the farmer lost one of his cows, suspected the Aborigines, and asked the culprit to come forward. No one moved, so he took thirty Aborigines – men, women and children – shot them, and then burned their bodies. Next day the stray cow returned to the farm. The murdered people belonged to the artist's own family group. I asked him how he managed to cope with the memory of this outrageous massacre. He turned to me, then began pointing, 'See sky', he said, 'see sun, cloud, birds and trees. See you, me? We all one'. When I heard him say this, I understood that my own assent to the truth of the unity of all things did not permeate my being in the way that it permeated his. I imagined that if I had been in his position I would never again find it possible to know peace. But I was also able to glimpse something of the man's inner world. He was so deeply aware; so 'at one' with the unity of all things, that in some mysterious way he was able to share this experience with the whole of creation, which absorbs the pain and the poison of this world, and counteracts it with its healing power.

The End of the Pilgrimage

On both pilgrimages, I found the moment of arrival at the final destination to be strangely flat, especially my arrival at the main bus station in Jerusalem! I had begun to walk from Nazareth to Jerusalem, but after two days through the West Bank in intense heat and towns swarming with Israeli troops, I made the rest of the pilgrimage by bus. Jerusalem bus station did *not* fill my soul with the psalmist's delight, 'And now our feet are standing in your gateways, Jerusalem' (Ps. 122:2).

Reflecting on this later, I found the momentary disappointment had been rich in meaning, for it taught me that the object of the journey was not so that I could find God at the end of it. Very slowly I have begun to see the significance of this truth. Christianity can so be taught that it leaves us with the impression that this life is not really important: the point of life in 'this vale of tears' is to stagger and struggle one's way through it, obeying God's will at all costs, so that we may reach heavenly bliss at the end of it. The truth that the pilgrimages taught me is that God is on the journey all the time, not just at the end of it. The point of the journey was to learn this truth rather than to reach a particular destination, however holy, and there is no end to the exploration!

As Christians we profess 'God is in all things: all things are in God'. In practice we deny this, because we separate God from ordinary life through our split spirituality. The collapse in church membership in so many industrialised countries is partly to be explained in terms of a deepening understanding that God is not to be relegated to the end of the journey. This life is not to be considered a punitive transit camp that we must endure before moving on to a better existence, in which we shall be with God for ever – provided, of course, that we have complied with the rules of the camp. If we have failed to abide by the rules, the understanding has been that we are doomed to be transferred to an even more unpleasant camp where we shall be tormented throughout eternity!

If God is with us in the reality of everyday life, it follows that every single human being is of infinite value here and now. 'God became a human being in order that human beings might become God.' It is in the 'ordinary' that we are to find God. God is in the facts, so the facts must somehow be kind. This is not to deny that the facts can often be horrific, cruel and murderous. When we say God is in these facts, we mean that there is no evil situation that God cannot transform into something creative. In Christian understanding, it is astonishing, but true, that God has chosen to be involved in horror, cruelty and murder, becoming, in Jesus, the victim of it. Jesus manifests not a 'Mister Fixit' God of pomp and majesty, but a God of wild, all-consuming love, who loves all that has been created. As the prophets wrote, God has married creation for better or for worse, and God is always faithful. Nothing, not even death, can extinguish the fire of God's love.

The journey of life is the journey towards this truth: the truth of our at-one-ness with the God of love and compassion; the God in whom all creation has its being. In life's journey, the destination is always the starting point and the starting point is the destination.

Consider these words with your head and they can sound like gibberish – a jangle of words. Consider them with your heart and they may begin to sound like the opening notes of a symphony that touches the very core of our being; a symphony that carries us out and beyond ourselves and then sets us back at our starting point, which we can now see in a different light. And the process is continuous. The object of pilgrimage and of any religious undertaking is not primarily to help us to reform the world: the object is to enable us to see and to know that we are all one, and that it is in God that we live and move and have our being.

In the next chapter we shall explore the themes 'We are all one' and 'We are a pilgrim people of God' in greater detail.

Exercises

1 Consider the three platitudes:
    (i) Luggage is for the journey, not the journey for the luggage (see page 140).
    (ii) The more attached we are to our own likes and dislikes, the greater our capacity for misery along the way (see page 145).
    (iii) The burden does not lie in the goods we carry, but in the way we relate to them (see page 148).

    Have they anything to say to you about your own experience of life's journey so far?

2 If any reader is interested in a pilgrimage on foot, there are many beautiful and ancient routes through France and Spain to the Cathedral of St James of Compostella in Santiago, one of the oldest pilgrimage places in Europe. For details, contact:

    Confraternity of St James,
    First Floor,
    1 Talbot Yard,
    Borough High St,
    London SE1 1YP
    Tel.: 020 7928 9988

REFLECTIONS ON CHRISTIAN UNITY

O N THE PATH TOWARDS Christian unity, a most useful question was posed by Mahatma Gandhi (d.1948): 'Consider the poorest person you know and ask whether the next step you take will be of any use to them.'

The split nature of our spirituality expresses itself in the divided state of the Christian churches; divided both from one another and within themselves. When Christians pray for unity with other Christians, what is it that they are praying for? And if unity is achieved, what form will it take? What effect, if any, would unity between Christians have on individuals and nations who do not subscribe to Christian beliefs?

The word 'church' means very different things to different people. Men and women in the industrialised countries of the world are leaving the churches in large numbers. What is it that they are leaving? Are they abandoning 'Church' because they are rejecting the deepest longings of their hearts, or are they leaving because they no longer find an answer to their spiritual hunger in 'Church' as they now experience it?

Christians have inherited the term 'People of God' from Judaism, and the term 'pilgrim people of God' is central to

Christianity. When I use the word 'Church' in this chapter I am referring specifically to the 'pilgrim people of God' unless otherwise stated. The 'pilgrim people of God' are a people on a journey of discovery: a people who allow God to be the God of love and compassion to them and through them. This pilgrim people exists for the good of the entire human race and, like their Lord, they are called to embrace all peoples, all races and all classes. All the churches are called to become pilgrim people.

We cannot come to God individually: if we respond to God's Spirit we are drawn into unity; into the communion of God, Father, Son and Holy Spirit. The Latin word for Church, *ecclesia*, means 'called out', and so Christians are 'called out' into unity with one another and with all creation. We have to become more perceptive and responsive to the Spirit of God if we are to find the unity to which Christians, and all peoples, are called. It is for this reason that a spirit of prayer must lie at the heart of all work for unity. The precise form that Christian unity will take, we cannot foretell.

The following reflections are drawn from my experience as a member of the Roman Catholic Church. I am most grateful for all that I have received from the Catholic Church – not least for the vision of what the Church is called to become, a vision that enables me to see why the Catholic Church and all other Christian denominations are in constant need of reform if they are to be true to their calling to allow God's kingdom to come; a kingdom that is inclusive of peoples of all faiths and of no faith.

My reflections are presented in the form of seven steps or experiences that have helped me to discover a more life-giving understanding of Church. They are presented to encourage readers to reflect on their own experience of Church and their own understanding of the unity to which all Christians are called. These seven steps have helped me to see that most of the controversies that divide churches within themselves, and from one another, arise because members take their stand on one particular step, as though it were the only one. They then denounce those who are not standing on exactly the same step! This was my own attitude for the first twenty-five years of my life!

Until the age of twenty-five, I understood Christian unity in terms of all Christians uniting together in the one Roman Catholic

Church. At some point the 'other Christians' would be followed into the Roman Catholic Church by people of differing religious faiths or of no faith! I took my first steps away from this exclusive notion of the kingdom of God during the four years I spent at Oxford studying Classics. This was my first experience of being taught by people who were not Roman Catholics. I was very impressed by the openness, friendliness, learning and intelligence of the tutors and lecturers. The fact that they were so learned and intelligent led me to wonder why they had not become Catholics! After Oxford, I embarked on four years of theology, and the subject in which I took the greatest interest was ecumenism. After one year in England, I was sent to Germany, where the Reformation had begun, and spent the remaining three years at the Jesuit college, Sankt Georgen, Frankfurt/Main. In the mid-1950s, ecumenical relations were very much further advanced in Germany than in Britain.

The First Step

The 'Una Sancta' movement

In Frankfurt I learned of a new movement called 'Una Sancta', the Latin term for 'One Holy'; Una Sancta had been started by a German Roman Catholic priest, Max Joseph Metzger (1887–1944). He was executed by the Nazis in 1944 because he was caught attempting to send a message to his friend, the Protestant Archbishop of Upsala, outlining proposals for post-war Germany. Metzger had served as a military chaplain during the First World War and had subsequently become a pacifist. He had begun to see very clearly that the Roman Catholic Church could only be effective in promoting world peace to the extent that she was able to promote peace among fellow Christians.

The aim of Una Sancta was not that all Christians should become Roman Catholics, but rather that Lutherans should become better Lutherans by being more open and faithful to the demands of Scripture and to their own tradition. Similarly, Evangelicals were to become better Evangelicals, Roman Catholics better Roman Catholics, etc. The thinking behind the Una Sancta movement was very simple: if we are open to God's Spirit, then God will bring Christians into unity.

The discovery of Una Sancta was an enormous relief to me: I no longer had to convert everyone who was not a Roman Catholic! I could also start learning about God and the nature of the Church from Christians of other denominations.

In Germany, too, I received my first introduction to the writings of the Jesuit theologian Karl Rahner (1904–84). Rahner's writings helped me to notice and question the dualism of my inherited spirituality. Instead of being remote and apart from all human experience, God is, in fact, present in all things. Creation itself is a sacrament or sign of God's presence – and an effective sign. Reality is not two-layered, as though the supernatural hovers above and apart from the natural; as though grace is to be found apart from nature, and the sacred is only to be found in what we call 'sacred places'. In the whole of creation, there is nothing *to* which we can point and say, 'This is exclusively natural', meaning that 'God is not present in this'. God is *in* all peoples, pervades and permeates all things, all circumstances, and is the living spirit at the heart of all that exists. In reading Rahner I discovered that God had escaped from my spiritual cocoon and was now running free! God was no longer the colossal, remote and immutable 'statue of bronze' of my early education. God was more like a spring of everlasting life welling up within me.

Steps two to seven that follow are based upon events that helped me to see more clearly some of the practical implications of the truth that God dwells in all peoples and in all things.

The Second Step

The connection between Christian unity and our attitudes to peace and war

When my Jesuit training was completed in 1960, I was sent to Stonyhurst, a Jesuit public school in Lancashire, where I began to teach Latin, Greek and Religion. Being a 'public school', which in Britain means a private school, it was obliged to have a Combined Cadet Force (CCF) which all boys had to join, parading twice a week, usually in military uniform. Easter fell early in 1961 and for this reason the boys remained at school during Holy Week, their vacation beginning on Easter Monday. The Holy Week services ended with High Mass on Easter Sunday, attended by the students in military uniform. Immediately after Mass, the CCF paraded in the school playground, performing a march past with bugle and drum accompaniment. The Rector, as overall Superior of the College, stood on a dais and took the salute. Early on Easter Sunday morning, I met an enraged colonel, in charge of the CCF. He pointed to the wall in the middle of the school playground. On it someone had painted the unilateral disarmament logo of the Campaign for Nuclear Disarmament (CND) and had written below in large, clear letters, 'MARCH BEGINS HERE (NO CHILDREN PLEASE)'. The dais on which the Rector was to take the salute was now floating on a nearby pond, adorned with a bed sheet for a sail! I was put in charge of the criminal investigation. My heart was not in the job. The boys' prank had raised very disturbing questions. Was it not in fact blasphemous to encourage children to celebrate the feast of the resurrection with a military parade? Was this not in fact a far greater crime than painting slogans on walls and floating a saluting base on the pond? This prank began to shake some of my hitherto unquestioned beliefs, including the belief that war can be just – a belief that had been held by the Roman Catholic Church for more than fifteen hundred years. Who was I to doubt such teaching? Once I had allowed the question of the justness of war into my mind, a torrent of other questions followed. What was the relationship between our essential Christian beliefs and the way in which we ran the school? Could we be using religion as a way of justifying worldly values, persuading ourselves, for example, that it was God's will that we should obey a country's call to arms? This brings me to the third step, and it was this step that opened my original questions about the justness of war into a much wider arena in which questions were raised about every other aspect of life.

The Third Step

The Second Vatican Council and Albert Camus

The third step in my understanding of ecumenism came about through the decrees of the Second Vatican Council (1962–5), and also through my reading of some humanist writers, notably the French existentialist atheist Albert Camus (d.1960). The Council recognised and acknowledged the fact that God is at work in

Christians who are not members of the Roman Catholic Church, also in people of other faiths and in those of no faith who nevertheless seek the truth. The Council also made formal acknowledgment of the fact that God is at work in the world and not only within the Roman Catholic Church. Its teaching proclaimed the fact that God's kingdom of truth, justice, love, peace, reconciliation and forgiveness is to be expressed through the social, political, economic and legal structures of society. No other Church Council had ever engaged so explicitly with the everyday life of the peoples of the world as opposed to members of the Roman Catholic Church. It was made very clear that ecumenism concerned the way in which we all relate to one another in every aspect of life. Consequently, ecumenical concerns would henceforth include all the ways in which we relate to each other as human beings.

It was the writings of Camus that encouraged me to re-read the Hebrew prophets. Although he was an atheist, Camus expressed his hunger and thirst for justice with all the passion of a prophet. At the end of the Second World War he was invited to lecture to a group of French Dominican priests. Camus begged them to live in fidelity to the call of Jesus as expressed in the Sermon on the Mount, so that atheists and Christians could join together in the struggle to promote world peace and justice.

In re-reading the prophets, especially Amos, Jeremiah and Isaiah, I discovered a God of passionate love and compassion for all peoples and for all creation, especially for the poor and the powerless. This was no longer the God of the catechism! In response to the classic question 'Who is God?', Roman Catholic children had long been required to learn by rote the catechism answer that 'God is the Supreme Spirit who alone exists of himself and is infinite in all perfection'. In the prophets I was discovering a God who did not merely 'exist of himself', but was passionately involved with every aspect of creation.

My eyes were being opened and I was discovering that the ultimate test of true faith was no longer conformity to a specific creed, to Church teaching and to Church discipline. I was becoming aware that the test of true faith lay in the extent to which we allow God to be the God of love and compassion to us and, through us, to everyone we encounter.

The unity we seek is the unity of a life lived together in love and in compassion. Christians who exercise compassion are thus more likely to experience a sense of unity with compassionate people of whatever belief or disbelief than with members of their own denomination who fail to live compassionately. God is not a set of doctrines, nor a form of worship, but the source of all life and all love. The teachings of our churches, our forms of worship and our laws are important, but they are means to an end, not ends in themselves. They are means to enable us to allow God to be the God of love and compassion to us, and through us, both collectively and individually.

Most of our ecumenical problems arise because we mistake means for ends. If I insist that the teaching, the form of worship and the laws of 'my' Church are superior to those of 'your' Church, I may be aglow with righteousness, but totally unaware that my very 'orthodoxy' has become an idol. I am taking the view that 'It is the truth because I subscribe to it' rather than 'I subscribe to it because I believe it to be the truth'. By insisting on the superiority of 'my' Church, I may well be failing in love and compassion and thus closing myself off not only from those who do not agree with me, but also from God.

These perceptions began to set me free from the spiritual dualism that I had previously taken for granted. I was no longer thinking in terms of 'spirit-good, matter-bad' – I was instead becoming more aware of the bonds that bind Christians together, regardless of denomination; the bonds that bind each one to every other, regardless of religious faith or lack of it. Christians are called to recognise, delight in and learn from 'that which is of God in everyone'. They are certainly not called to live in a state of constant religious paranoia, seeing everyone who is not 'one of us' as 'the enemy'. This was a welcome and deeply attractive vision of the mission of the Church. I was discovering that Jesus could be liberated from my private cupboard and released into the world for which he came, taking me with him!

The Fourth Step

In September 1967 I left Stonyhurst to become chaplain to Catholics at Glasgow University, a city not famed for its ecumenical spirit. I was to spend eight years there. In Glasgow I experienced the truth of Martin Buber's observation: 'Nothing so masks the face of God as religion.' I came to understand that Christ's religion of love and compassion can become the religion of hate and inhumanity when Christians give more attention to their differences than to the Sermon on the Mount, practising a Christless Catholicism, a Christless Protestantism.

Prayer lies at the heart of ecumenism

Many students at Glasgow during those years had rejected their Christian faith, or they were seriously considering doing so. I spent many hours in conversation with such students, talking about the God they had rejected, or were about to reject. This experience helped me to understand the importance of examining our images of God. What a liberation it was to realise that all our ideas of God are inadequate, that God alone can teach us who God is, and that unless God prays in us, we cannot pray. To what kind of God are we praying? And to what extent do the Churches train their members in prayer; as distinct from summoning them to services at which prayers are recited? As far as I can see, the answer is 'Hardly at all'. Even in theological colleges and seminaries where future ministers/priests are trained, the students seem to be given very little encouragement and help in the practice and exploration of their prayer.

GLIMPSES OF THE WIDER ECUMENISM

Two occasions in Glasgow gave me practical glimpses of the universality of the mission of the Church to all peoples.

One day I received a visit from a near neighbour to the chaplaincy, a Polish woman, who worked in the university department of Soviet studies. She was Catholic, her husband atheist, and they wanted to have their child baptised in our chapel. She told me that most of the friends and relatives attending the baptism would be agnostic/atheist. Before the ceremony, I wondered how to present this sacrament of Christian initiation to an unbelieving congregation, and began to question myself. What did I think I was doing in performing the ceremony? I knew the theological answers: through this sacrament the child would be incorporated into the very life of God, Father, Son and Holy Spirit; the child would be cleansed from original sin and filled with the grace of God. But how was I to communicate this truth to people who did not believe in any of it? What did I believe myself? Did I think that through baptism God bestowed all these favours on this particular child, but not on the children of the atheists and agnostics in the congregation? This was an extremely important question. The answer I arrived at helped me to appreciate the value and importance of sacraments as outward and effective signs of God's action in our world, but it also helped me to glimpse something of the limitless and continuous love of God for all peoples, at all times and in all places.

The sacraments are signs, and effective signs of God's continuous action in this world. The God whom the sacraments signify is a God who loves and calls all people to share in the life of God, a God who makes a Covenant with all creation. The initiative is always God's initiative. No human being, no human organisation, can control God, thank God! Therefore, in administering the sacraments we are not controlling God and must never act as though we were: instead we are celebrating our awareness of who God is; of what God is like for all peoples, of all times and places. In the ceremony of the baptism I've just mentioned we were celebrating our awareness of the mysterious dignity of this baby, called to share in the very life of God. But God calls every child, loves every individual, is giver of breath, bread and life to each one. It is very important that Christians should celebrate their awareness in solemn liturgies and other forms of worship, but the form of worship should always remind us that God is not exclusive, that God's love and compassion include every human being without exception. The object of all formal worship is to bring about in us a change of mind and heart, so that in every aspect of life we act as channels of God's mercy and compassion to all those we encounter.

The funeral of a Church of Scotland deaconess was the second occasion on which I received a practical glimpse of the universality of the mission of the Church. Stella Reekie's funeral was attended by people of all faiths and of none. A Sikh gave the address. 'Stella', he said, 'was like water. She cleansed, refreshed, gave life and always assumed the shape of the person she was with, so that

I thought of her as a Sikh, my Muslim friends thought of her as a Muslim.'

As a Red Cross nurse at the end of the Second World War, Stella had been among the first to enter a Nazi concentration camp. This had been a transforming moment for her – comparable to the experience of St Paul on the road to Damascus when he fell to the ground and heard the voice of Jesus. After the war, Stella worked with displaced persons in Germany and in Britain for many years. She then decided to become a missionary in Pakistan, where she remained until reaching the normal age for retirement. When she returned to Glasgow, a local Council of Churches appointed her as a liaison person between Christians and immigrants, many of whom had arrived from Pakistan. Stella's small flat, which she called 'The International Flat', was usually thronged with people from a number of countries. She always gave her guests her full attention, knew each one by name, and made a point of feeding them.

During her funeral, the Sikh who gave the address paid this remarkable tribute: 'I never understood what Christians meant when they said, "Jesus died for our sins". But I know that Stella gave her life for us.'

Stella's funeral helped me to understand that ecumenism is not an optional extra for the more socially minded. Ecumenism should permeate all our activities and everything we do. It is essential to an understanding of the meaning of the Christian faith; an understanding of the significance of Christ, who described himself as 'the way, the truth and the life'. This phrase can be used by Christians to underline the fact that 'we possess the truth'! It can also serve as an escape from the obligation of having anything to do with those who disagree with us, whether Christians of a different denomination, or people of other faiths or of none. As a Christian I believe Jesus Christ to be 'the Way, the Truth and the Life', but I also believe that it is only through openness to peoples of differing denominations, of other faiths and of no faith that we can come to know the breadth and depth of the presence of Jesus in all peoples and in all things. We need to note the difference between saying – or thinking – 'Jesus is the Way, the Truth and the Life: I believe that this is true', and saying – or thinking – 'Jesus is the Way, the Truth and the Life *because* it is I who believe that this is true'.

It was these and similar experiences in Glasgow that prompted me to ask if, after leaving Glasgow, I might work on spirituality. I have never liked the word 'spirituality', but it is a convenient shorthand word for lengthier phrases and questions such as: 'What is God like?', 'What is a human being?', 'What is the meaning of life?', 'Who am I?', 'How am I related to other human beings; to the rest of creation?', 'What is it that gives life its value?', 'What is happiness and how am I to find it?'

This leads to another step that helped me to see more clearly the essential inclusivity of God's kingdom.

The Fifth Step

The Holy Spirit does not belong exclusively to any one particular denomination

I began my study of spirituality with my already-mentioned ten-week walk to Rome in 1975, followed by three months' study there on the Spiritual Exercises of the founder of the Jesuits, Inigo of Loyola, the spirituality on which Jesuit life is based. In Rome I came across a phrase uttered by a contemporary of Inigo, Jerome Nadal, in response to the question: 'For whom are these Spiritual Exercises suited?' Nadal, in the sixteenth century, had replied, 'For Catholics, for Protestants and for pagans!' This phrase delighted me, and when I was later asked in 1978 to develop St Beuno's, a Jesuit house in North Wales, as a spiritual centre, I tried to ensure that it would always serve 'Catholics, Protestants and pagans'! Inigo wrote his book of the Spiritual Exercises assuming that this type of retreat would be given individually and not to groups. Every individual is different and the Exercises were designed to enable individuals to discover for themselves out of their own personal experience. The Spiritual Exercises became the victim of their sixteenth-century success: demand outran the supply of retreat-givers, and soon the individually given retreat gave way to the preached retreat, which then became the norm for almost three hundred years! Besides being open to 'Catholics, Protestants and pagans', St Beuno's also specialised in the individually given retreat, a practice that still continues.

It was a great privilege to accompany people on these retreats. It soon became very clear that the Holy Spirit does not 'belong' to any particular Christian denomination, and operates freely outside what we may consider to be the boundaries of Christianity.

After I had left St Beuno's at the end of 1983, I gave a retreat in daily life, over a period of six weeks, to one particular pilgrim, who prayed faithfully and fruitfully throughout the retreat. A few months after the retreat I received an invitation to the pilgrim's baptism! I had assumed the pilgrim was already baptised. The more I engaged in this work, the less conscious I became of the denomination or religious faith of any pilgrim. This particular retreatant is now an Anglican deacon and will be ordained priest next year, having, after the retreat, spent three years working with Voluntary Service Overseas in Uganda, followed by a three-year theology degree in Edinburgh leading to theological college.

After leaving St Beuno's, I asked if I might work on spirituality with people, of any Christian denomination or none, who were engaged in some form of work for peace and justice, and this has occupied me ever since. It is this work that has led me to a sixth step in my understanding of Christian unity.

The Sixth Step

The marks of the one true Church

1. 'SHE IS ONE'
The justice/peace groups with which I worked were composed of people belonging to differing Christian denominations, sometimes to other faiths, and frequently subscribing to no formal belief. After two years in this work, I found the words of an old catechism question constantly coming to mind: 'What are the marks of the one true Church?' The catechism answer was: 'She is one, holy, catholic and apostolic'. In the catechism, this neat answer was followed by further questions. The answers to these were designed to prove that the only Church in which all four marks were to be found was the Roman Catholic Church. Why was this question about the marks of the Church constantly coming to mind while I was working on justice/peace issues with people of differing denominations, differing faiths and of no formal belief? I soon began to realise that I was experiencing the four marks of 'the one true Church' within the groups of people I was meeting.

There was a unity, an at-one-ness, among the members of these justice/peace groups. I was discovering that issues of peace and justice were drawing people together in harmony across the divisions and boundaries of religions and across the generations, races and classes. One small but significant example of unity was the custom of sharing food. At one-day justice/peace workshops, participants would be invited to bring a packed lunch. The food would be laid out on a common table so that each one could help themselves as they wished. This custom was less frequently followed during one-day prayer workshops, at which participants were more likely to keep their packed lunch for personal consumption!

We also held eight-day, individually given, residential retreats for people active in some form of justice/peace work, whatever their religion or lack of belief. Every evening the retreatants met for a half-hour period of silent prayer together, during which time we could pray silently for one another: for families and friends, and for oppressed people and their oppressors throughout the world. In evaluating these retreats, people frequently wrote of the power of these silent half-hours; the sense of the presence of God felt in our unity. The experience of giving retreats to such very mixed groups provided me with a most encouraging insight. Unity is not something that we are called upon to 'create' among Christians, and between Christians, and those of differing faiths or of none: the unity already exists and we are invited to discover it.

Prayer enables us to reach deeper levels of ourselves where we begin to discover that at-one-ness with God is also the source of at-one-ness within ourselves and with others. In prayer, and in listening to other people's prayer experiences, it becomes clear that our religious divisions are primarily cultural rather than theological. They are the result of specific conditioning rather than the fruit of mature conviction. Our religious education can lead us to emphasise our differences rather than the reality that unites us: in this way we lose sight of the fact that our unity lies in God, not in specific forms and structures.

2. 'SHE IS HOLY'

Most people active in work for peace and justice would never consider themselves to be holy. As we have seen in earlier chapters, the word 'holiness' is a victim of our split spirituality, so that many people who are committed to justice/peace issues would consider the epithet 'holy' to be an insult! Some people active in justice and peace work can be acting out of unresolved past hurts, which can cause them to become aggressive and unjust in the campaigning for justice. Misplaced enthusiasm for a cause can destroy the cause itself, no matter how worthy. It is important to take the time to reflect and consider, and to begin to make connections between external manifestations of violence and one's own inner violence. The hardest task for anyone involved in work for justice and peace is the development of 'inner justice', 'inner peace'. It is frequently through personal engagement in work for peace and justice that we become aware of our own lack of inner peace and inner justice.

The most admirable and effective activists in the fields of peace and justice are those who have a strong sense of compassion, a sure sign of holiness – although rarely recognised as such. People with a powerful sense of compassion react with their whole being when individuals or groups are threatened, exploited or oppressed; a compassion that flows from their awareness of the dignity and the sacredness of every human being.

3. 'SHE IS CATHOLIC'

In its literal sense, the word 'catholic' means universal, embracing all creation. One of the marks of genuine holiness, of allowing God to be God to us and through us, is a growing sense of at-one-ness with other people, regardless of race, religion or nationality. Such people cannot subscribe to measures that threaten the lives of their brothers and sisters. Such measures may include a national defence policy that threatens mass destruction, or trade practices endangering the lives and well-being of millions through depriving them of adequate water supply, food, shelter, basic health care or education. True 'catholicism' is the catholicism of the Hebrew prophets, the catholicism of Jesus, who taught that our relationship with God is to be tested by our behaviour to those who are hungry, thirsty, imprisoned, etc. While it is right and good that we should have different methods of expressing our beliefs, different ways of worshipping God and organising our Christian communities, the test of the ways and means of all our Churches is the extent to which they make us more compassionate, make us more truly 'catholic'.

4. 'SHE IS APOSTOLIC'

The English word 'apostolic' comes from a Greek word *apostellein*, meaning 'to send', so the apostle is 'the one who is sent'. The Latin word for one who is sent is *missus*, so to be apostolic is to have a mission. There is a passage in the prophet Jeremiah in which the prophet is complaining to God about God!

> You have seduced me, Yahweh, and I have let myself be seduced;
> you have overpowered me: you were the stronger.
> I am a daily laughing-stock,
> everybody's butt.
> Each time I speak the word, I have to howl
> and proclaim: 'Violence and ruin!'
> The word of Yahweh has meant for me
> insult, derision, all day long.
> I used to say, 'I will not think about him,
> I will not speak in his name any more'.
> Then there seemed to be a fire burning in my heart,
> imprisoned in my bones.
> The effort to restrain it wearied me,
> I could not bear it (Jer. 20:7–9).

I have heard many people who live compassionate lives echo Jeremiah's complaint. Many discover that the commitment is far more demanding than they anticipated. The causes in which they engage can become emotionally exhausting; and the extent of their commitment may disrupt personal relationships, even within the immediate family. Under the strain, many people feel tempted to abandon their undertaking, but they find, like Jeremiah, that they are unable to pull out. It is at this point that it can be helpful to look at the pain and suffering and then ask: 'If I gave it all up, where would I prefer to be and what would I rather be doing?

Would I prefer to give it all up and live quietly and without commitment, or do I choose to continue as I am despite the pain and suffering?' It is at this point that people generally realise that they want to continue as they are, despite the pain. They experience a sense of mission: a sense of being 'sent out'. This is the true meaning of 'apostolic'. We are being seized by the Spirit and 'sent out' into situations that threaten our securities.

Whenever I met with justice/peace groups, I used, at first, to ask those who were Christian whether they found support for their work from their own church or parish community. More often than not the answer was negative. Many churches are generous in collecting money for the Third World, but few enquire into the deeper reasons that lie behind the need for food, water, clothing and medical care. In the words of the Brazilian Roman Catholic Archbishop Helder Camara (1909–99), 'When I give food to the poor they call me a saint: when I ask why the poor have no food they call me a communist.' I have asked many priests and ministers why they fail to mention issues of peace/justice from the pulpit. The most frequent answer is either: 'Because the pulpit is not the place for politics' or 'Because the subject causes conflict in the parish'. We should try and avoid confrontation and conflict whenever possible, and we should certainly try to win people over by persuasion, but our primary commitment must be to truth and justice rather than to being nice to one another. If we regard absence of conflict as the highest good, we are rejecting the gospel of Christ, who warned that his followers would be brought 'before kings and governors' (Luke 21:12) and betrayed by family and friends.

It is important and desirable that church leaders and theologians of differing Christian denominations should try to produce agreed statements about doctrine and policy, but unity among the Churches does not depend foremost upon doctrinal agreement. God is not primarily a doctrinal statement, but the compassionate source of all life. If we are living in God, then we are living in compassion. When local churches act together in compassionate concern for those in their immediate vicinity and also for those further afield, the members of those Churches will inevitably be drawn into a closer unity.

May the day come soon when all Christian Churches can

gather together in an Ecumenical Council that focuses primarily on a compassionate concern for issues of justice, peace and reconciliation!

The Seventh Step

For the first few years after leaving St Beuno's, I tried to work almost exclusively with people active in justice/peace. At first, I thought that I was dealing with a specific aspect of spirituality. Slowly, it dawned on me that there is no such thing as an isolated and particular 'spirituality of peace/justice'. Spirituality is a matter of becoming more attentive and responsive to the Holy Spirit dwelling within us and among us: the Spirit of love and compassion, forgiveness and reconciliation, peace and justice. If we think of it in terms of an isolated and specific 'spirituality of peace/justice', it could imply that other forms of spirituality do *not* engage with peace/justice! Any spirituality that fails to develop an appreciation of the unity of all things and of all peoples, and that leaves us without any hunger or thirst for social justice, must inevitably prove to be a false spirituality. It will not be drawing us closer to the living God who hungers and thirsts after justice, as we read in the Hebrew prophets. It is a sign of the split in our spirituality that in too many churches, people who are active in justice/peace issues feel themselves to be on the margins.

A Non-Ministerial Ecumenical Ministry

Christians discover the unity that exists within themselves and with others through learning to pray in an 'earthed' way and having the opportunity to talk about this experience of prayer across denominational boundaries. Many such groups are active in Britain and Ireland today. In writing this book, I began with one chapter that described the development and spread of this work in Britain, Ireland and abroad. It soon became two chapters, then three, until I realised that the topic required a book of its own. It will be a book about the enormous spiritual wealth within every one of us, ways of accessing this wealth for ourselves and of enabling others to do the same. In most cases, our religious training has been such that few of us believe that we possess this wealth.

Fewer still know how to begin to access it, and even fewer know how to enable others to discover this wealth for themselves.

The process of introducing people to ways of praying in an earthed way is not complicated, as we saw in Chapter 4. The experience of learning about prayer does not come from books, but from our own experience of praying. Provided people are learning to pray through praying themselves, they can also be trained to introduce others to these methods if they appear to have the aptitude and inclination. They can be trained to accompany others in their prayer, encouraging them to learn how to discover for themselves without being intrusive or trying to 'advise' or 'sort people out'. Such training can be made accessible for people who are unable to find the time or the money to go on residential courses.

A Hidden Fear of Ecumenism: Fear of Losing Identity

Economics can influence ecumenism for better and for worse. Financial considerations can oblige denominations to share a common place of worship. Such sharing might appear to be a desirable method of promoting Christian unity. It can, however, serve to accentuate the differences between denominations. Clergy, afraid of losing their specific denominational identity, may begin to stress the areas in which they differ rather than to emphasise points of unity. Resistance to ecumenism can arise from fear of losing our identity.

Beneath the fear of losing denominational identity lies the fear of losing control. If we promote forms of prayer that encourage people to pray freely in the Spirit with members of other Christian denominations, we risk losing control – the Spirit might take over! These forms of resistance are subtle, and would not be expressed in this way. A minister or priest would be unlikely to declare publicly: 'I am opposed to ecumenism and I do not believe in encouraging the laity to pray with members of other denominations. Nor do I approve of teaching them methods of prayer that might allow the Spirit to take over and lead them to question their place in the Church. The role of the laity is to obey, pray and pay!'

While rarely expressed overtly, such opinions can still be found in many parishes. The desire to control, to dominate, is a major obstacle not only to ecumenism, but to any spiritual growth. Immense pain is caused by attempts to stifle the Spirit by the exercise of tight control, and by the refusal to act as Churches together if we can possibly manage to get by on our own. Such attitudes can lead to a massive exodus, not just from church membership, but from the visions and dreams of God within us – and that is far more serious.

When people are encouraged in prayer to distinguish the creative from the destructive and to follow the creative, they come to life. They long to share their experience with others, and that longing is at the heart of the mission of the Church. We need the support and teaching of the Christian community transmitted through our Churches in order to nurture and develop, promote and uncover the wealth that is in us: to enable people in parishes to be trained in prayer and then to listen to others and help to train them also.

Jesus is risen! The Church of Christ exists for the sake of our world and there can be no salvation for any of us outside that world. The unity we seek as Christians is a unity that binds us to all peoples and to all creation. In the words of St Paul to the Colossians: 'God wanted . . . all things to be reconciled through him and for him, everything in heaven and everything on earth, when he made peace by his death on the cross' (Col. 1:19–20).

God, in Jesus, made peace by his death on the cross. In the next chapter we shall look more closely at this peace of Christ that comes to us through the cross.

Exercises

1 Take the seven steps mentioned in this chapter and ask yourself the following questions at each step: 'What was my felt reaction in reading it: Attraction? Repulsion? Or another feeling?' As far as you can tell, what are the reasons for your reaction?

2 Write out your own steps towards ecumenism. What step, or steps, have you already taken? What steps would you like to be able to take?

3 What are the essential features you would like to see in a Church that draws all Christians into unity?

REFLECTION ON HUMAN SUFFERING, DEATH AND CHRISTIAN FAITH

PAIN, SUFFERING AND DEATH raise questions for every human being. The question preoccupied the ancient civilisations of the Middle East who offered accounts of creation which converged in essentials while differing in detail. A common factor was the assertion that human beings were created from the carcass of a slain goddess of chaos. As a result, men and women became the puppets of warring gods and goddesses. The aim of human life was to keep on the right side of the warring deities, placating them by religious rituals. The creation myths were very patriarchal. Woman was considered to be the chattel of man, a possession with no more rights than his camels, sheep and oxen.

According to these myths, any failure to appease the gods and goddesses would result in suffering! There is a modern parallel: any failure to appease 'the gods' of contemporary fashion and political correctness also results in suffering! We can begin to see the relevance of these ancient myths to life in the twenty-first century!

The book of Genesis thunders against these myths, asserting that in place of throngs of warring deities there is only one God whose very word is creative: '"Let there be light", and there was light' (Gen. 1:3).

In the Genesis account of creation man and woman are made in the image of God, not from the carcass of a goddess of chaos. According to the first chapter of Genesis, 'God saw all he had made, and indeed it was very good' (Gen. 1:31).

The Source of Evil?

If God's creation is 'very good', where does evil come from? The book of Genesis tells us that evil results from specific human choices and that pain and suffering are the punishment for these choices. Such statements do not satisfy the biblical writers, let alone the reader of the twenty-first century! The biblical writers are constantly asking: 'Why do the innocent suffer?' This question is particularly in evidence in the Psalms and also in the book of Job, where the patient and exemplary Job is tried by dire and undeserved misfortune. The biblical writers offer a variety of reasons for the suffering of the innocent, and Jews and Christians have been struggling with their suggestions ever since. There is a school of thought that presents suffering as a gift from God, who piles on the pain in order to prepare us for a life of bliss hereafter! The 'why' of suffering became increasingly urgent during the twentieth century when more than a hundred million people died in wars – the majority of the dead being innocent civilians, including the six million Jews killed in the Holocaust.

Perhaps the problem can never be solved, but attempted explanations can deepen our understanding and help us to respond to suffering in a way that is creative. During the first evening of a workshop on mental pain, participants were invited to share their experiences and their expectations for the workshop. One woman, who was well acquainted with severe mental and physical pain, commented: 'I believe the answer is somehow to be found in the pain itself.' This answer struck me at the time and has become increasingly intelligible and helpful. God is in all things. God must, in some way, be in the facts. Therefore the facts must somehow be kind, including the facts of pain and suffering.

The Answer to Pain and Suffering Lies Somehow in the Pain Itself

According to the third chapter of Genesis, evil came into the world through the mistaken choices of Adam and Eve. Before criticising the inadequacy of such an explanation, it may be helpful to reflect on the truth it contains in terms of our own experience. In Chapter 4 we looked at moods and feelings in the 'Review of the Day'. We traced our moods and feelings back to the desire which gave rise to them and then asked the question, 'What is the object of that desire? Is it for the advancement of my own private kingdom, or for the advancement of the kingdom of God?' These are searching questions and they can reveal the source of much of our pain.

We all have to find some purpose in life whether or not we are religious believers. I may decide that my purpose is to eat, drink and be merry. I may, on the other hand, decide that my purpose is the accumulation of as much wealth and power as possible. Alternatively, I may experience a religious conversion and decide that the object of my life is to know, love and serve God. Whatever my purpose, I shall soon discover that facts and circumstances are continually thwarting me. If I am dedicated to eating, drinking and making merry, I shall be thwarted by indigestion, hangovers and headaches! If I am committed to accumulating wealth and power, I may well find that the stock market collapses and that I am ruined. If I am dedicated to knowing, loving and serving God I am likely to discover that God is not comfortable to live with! God seems to be most unreasonable, uncaring and deaf to the appeals of his faithful followers. The Israelites were very familiar with this experience!

We try to alter circumstances to escape our woes. If I am suffering as a result of 'eating, drinking and making merry', I try to improve matters by dieting, visiting a health farm or undergoing surgery. I become increasingly frustrated! If I have been accumulating wealth and power and the stock market has crashed I may try to 'bend' the rules and end up in prison. If I have been trying to know, love and serve God and am finding the experience uncomfortable, I may follow the example of the Israelites in the desert and try to discover other gods who are more to my liking!

Whichever way I turn, I crash against the obduracy of the facts and join the majority of human beings who, in Thoreau's words, 'live lives of quiet desperation'!

Much of Our Pain Comes from Our Own Choices

The source of much of our pain is to be found in the choices we make. Christians believe that God has created men and women to be at one with God and with all creation. Our hearts are restless because we keep trying and failing to create our own peace, our own happiness. We are trying to do this in our own strength; independently of God and of the rest of the human race. The pain of frustration can be excruciating when our carefully built securities break down. We can feel torn apart – an accurate description, because in my search for security I can hand myself over to the accumulation of wealth, which then becomes the purpose of my life. To lose my wealth will then be to me like a loss of life itself. More difficult to survive than the loss of possessions is the loss of our status, our ability to control other people. Having identified ourselves with possessions or status, their loss can lead us to take our own lives in desperation, or to take other people's lives to preserve what we believe to be our security. This happens to us as individuals, as groups, as nations and as churches.

If I belong to a Christian denomination that provides me with a clear identity as a Roman Catholic, an Anglican, a Presbyterian or whatever, there is a danger that my denominational identity will take the place of God for me and become my idol. There can be many forms of religious idolatry!

Belief in God – Liberation or Imprisonment?

The pain we suffer ourselves and inflict on others when we try to create our own peace and happiness independently of other people's welfare and of the deepest desire of our own hearts is not to be attributed to God. We scapegoat all kinds of individuals and groups in order to escape blaming ourselves. God is frequently the most popular scapegoat. Many people blame religion for the ills of the world and claim that it would be a happier, safer and more peaceful planet if religion was banned. But Soviet Russia and her satellites did not become a paradise on earth when religion was banned for seventy years.

Can belief in God lead us to a deeper understanding of pain and suffering? Can religious belief enable us to bear suffering and, through suffering, to grow into a renewed appreciation of life and a new sense of freedom? Belief in God can certainly transform us in this way, but God can also be presented in such a way that belief in God fails to set us free. Christian faith can be turned into a form of bondage for ourselves and for others and we can become so enamoured of our invisible 'chains' that we prefer death to freedom.

Faith can be taught in such a way that it adds to pain and suffering rather than alleviates it! Conscientious Christians may become so accustomed to pain and anxiety that they feel bad about feeling good! The cross of Christ is certainly central to the life of a Christian and Jesus tells us that 'Unless you take up your cross daily and follow me, you cannot be my disciple.' The cross was the most painful form of death that the Romans could devise, but Jesus is not telling us that 'Unless you undergo intense pain and suffering you cannot be my disciple.' Nevertheless, his words have been interpreted, preached and communicated in precisely this way in some Christian writing and teaching. Jesus came to bear witness to the truth, to show us in his life and in his teaching what God is like, a God of unconditional love. This witness threatened both the religious and the secular authorities of his time. Taking up the cross does not mean 'delight in the sufferings that befall you and add on more of your own making', but 'delight in God and God's creation and do not allow the threat of punishment to deter you'. Pain and suffering can be glorified and divinised as though they were God's gift to the chosen. When St Teresa of Avila (1515–1582) was travelling one stormy night the coach overturned, landing herself and her Sisters in the mud. She is said to have prayed, 'If this is the way you treat your friends, Lord, it is no wonder you have so few'!

Suffering can certainly purify, ennoble and bring us to our senses. It can provide insight and help us to grow in wisdom. But suffering can also brutalise. Those who abuse children have frequently suffered abuse themselves, and professional torturers can be most effectively trained in their craft by undergoing torture themselves. In many biographies of saints, their holiness appears to be in direct proportion to their capacity for enduring self-inflicted austerities such as flagellation, fasting and reciting their prayers while standing in freezing water – not to mention their endurance of suffering at the hands of others. This could lead us to believe that God is best pleased when our suffering is at its most acute!

In our Christian enthusiasm we can literally divinise suffering, presenting God as the 'divine punisher'; a God with a voracious appetite for blood, whose murderous inclinations can only be assuaged by the precious blood of his own Son. If this last sentence seems to be an outrageous exaggeration, reflect on the following statements – each one of unimpeachable orthodoxy:

- I thank God for the gift of Jesus Christ and beg to be like him.
- Jesus obeyed God's will in everything, even to accepting death, death on a cross.
- I must be ready to do God's will, even if it leads me to death on a cross.
- How are we to know this will of God for us? By obeying those whom God has put in authority over us.
- If we are to live always in this readiness to obey God's will, no matter what it may cost, we must constantly practise self-denial.

If these statements are acted upon without reflection, they can be utterly destructive of human freedom and human life. They can be so interpreted that they present an image of a God whose will appears to be our suffering and death. This is the antithesis of the God whom Jesus presents in his life and his teaching.

The uncritical glorification of suffering can lead to a very unholy rivalry among Christians about our relative sufferings; we boast of our afflictions, as though life's journey was a kind of Olympic sufferathon. Wallowing in our brokenness can become a subtle form of pride, leading us to pay more attention to our pain and woundedness than to God's goodness. We are so absorbed in our own inner agonies that we have no energy to notice the pain of anybody else – let alone react to it!

The Attitude of Jesus to Pain and Suffering

After his baptism and the temptations in the desert, Jesus returns home, goes to the synagogue and quotes from the prophet Isaiah (61:1–2):

> The Spirit of the Lord has been given to me,
> for he has anointed me.
> He has sent me to bring the good news to the poor,
> to proclaim liberty to captives
> and to the blind new sight,
> to set the downtrodden free,
> to proclaim the Lord's year of favour.

He then declares that the text he has just read 'is being fulfilled today even as you listen' (Luke 4:18–20).

In the Gospel accounts, apart from teaching and praying, the main activity of Jesus is healing and sharing meals! When the Pharisees complain that Jesus heals even on the Sabbath, he tells them that 'The Son of Man is master of the Sabbath' (Luke 6:5).

Jesus came to heal, to comfort and to give life, not to inflict suffering on us. His disciples were still attached to a punishing God and failed to grasp his message at first. When they try to arrange for Jesus to stay in a Samaritan village, the Samaritans refuse to receive him because he is on his way to Jerusalem. 'Seeing this, the disciples James and John said, "Lord, do you want us to call down fire from heaven to burn them up?" But he turned and rebuked them, and they went off to another village' (Luke 9:54–6). The God of Jesus is not the 'punishing God' of James and John! When Jesus instructs his disciples on their mission, he tells them they are to bring peace wherever they visit: 'Cure those who are sick, and say, "The kingdom of God is very near to you"' (Luke 10:9).

In his parables of the kingdom, God is presented as the God of love and compassion, whose kingdom is open to all peoples, wicked and good alike, and especially open to the poor, the weak and the powerless: a God who rescues from pain and suffering and who brings us back to life. The Good Samaritan acts in a Godlike way; the father of the Prodigal Son, who also welcomes the self-righteous elder brother, is a central image of God. Jesus is the Good Shepherd sent by God, who leaves ninety-nine sheep to rescue the one that is lost. God is the father at the wedding feast (Matt. 22:1–14) who sends the servants out into the highways and byways to bring in as many people as possible to the feast, 'anyone you find'. The servants gather all the people, both good and bad.

Jesus presents the core of his teaching in the Sermon on the Mount, which begins with the words, 'How happy are you who are poor; yours is the kingdom of God.'

How Can the Utterly Destitute be Blissfully Happy?

The original text of the Beatitudes uses the Greek word *makarioi* for 'happy'. A person who is *makarios* is blissfully happy, with a happiness nothing can disturb, not even death itself. The text also uses the Greek word *ptochos* for 'poor', meaning 'utterly destitute'. To be utterly destitute is to be without food, water, clothing and shelter, and deprived of friendship, of all support.

There have been Christians who have taken the view that if the *ptochoi*, the utterly destitute, are in fact the 'blissfully happy', then the people who should be rewarded at the final judgment are those who ensure that the destitute remain in grinding poverty! Conversely, it is those who have tried to alleviate their sufferings who should, in fact, be damned! Such teaching has been preached in the name of the gospel; its supporters claiming that it is wrong to interfere with the divine plan by trying to improve the lot of the poor. Prosperity is a mark of God's favour, and poverty a sign of God's disfavour! The gospel of prosperity is being preached in many countries today, especially in Africa, and in North, Central and South America. Such teaching is very consoling for the affluent, and it is for this reason that many dictatorships and totalitarian governments have encouraged religious movements, provided their attention is focussed on the next world and not on issues of social justice in this world.

What, then, does Jesus mean when he says, 'How happy are you who are poor, yours is the kingdom of God'? Jesus came to rescue us from destitution, not to commend grinding poverty. The use of the Greek word *ptochoi*, the destitute, is the graphic expression for an attitude of complete and total trust in God who is at work in every detail of our lives. In this context 'the poor' are those who find their ultimate security in God and who share the attitude of St Paul: 'With God on our side who can be against us?' (Rom. 8:31). 'Nothing, therefore, can come between ourselves and the love of Christ, no matter whether we are troubled or worried, lacking food or clothes, being persecuted, threatened or even attacked. For I am certain of this: neither death nor life, no angel, no prince, nothing that exists, nothing still to come, can ever come between us and the love of God made visible in Christ Jesus our Lord' (Rom. 8:38–9).

The *ptochoi* are utterly dependent on God; they have no ultimate security apart from God. For this reason they can allow God to express Godself in all their thinking and acting. As a result, they live in practice what Jesus teaches in the Sermon on the Mount: 'Love your enemies, do good to those who hate you, bless those who curse you, pray for those who treat you badly' (Matt. 5:44). Why are they to live in this way? Because 'in this way you will be children of your Father in heaven, for he causes his sun to rise on bad people as well as good, and his rain to fall on honest and dishonest alike' (Matt. 5:45). God is not a God who sends pain, suffering and death, but a God who has such love and compassion for creation that God becomes one of us and enters into the pain and suffering of the world.

How God, in Jesus, Reacts to Pain and Suffering

God does not inflict pain on people and God does not act violently. God, in Jesus, absorbs the violence of his enemies in his own body, without retaliating violently, as we shall see when we look at the Passion of Jesus later in this chapter. Those who have surrendered their whole being to God are therefore surrendering their power to retaliate against attack with physical violence. They follow the instruction of Jesus: 'To the person who slaps you on one cheek, present the other cheek too; to the person who takes your cloak from you, do not refuse your tunic. Give to everyone who asks you, and do not ask for your property back from the one who robs you' (Luke 6:29–30).

The Sermon on the Mount is the core of the teaching of Jesus. It has been preached since the foundation of Christianity. It has also been ignored, even in the highest circles! God is still presented as a punishing God, and the theory of a Just War has allowed us to practise retaliatory violence with a good conscience, rewarding practitioners of the Just War with honours and titles and condemning those who oppose retaliatory violence for failing in their national and Christian duty! It is astonishing, and wonderful, that perhaps the most famous and successful exponent of the teaching of Jesus on non-violence was a Hindu – Mahatma Gandhi!

There are sound objections to the common interpretation that is often placed upon the teaching of Jesus about turning the other cheek. Are we to become God's doormats, trampled over by violent, ruthless, greedy aggressors? Are cowards to be considered the 'happy', the *makarioi*? Are those who risk their lives in defence of the poor and vulnerable to be considered criminal?

Jesus does not preach non-resistance to evil: he preaches resistance to evil, resistance to the aggressor, but without the infliction of deliberate physical violence. This form of resistance benefits both aggressor and victim and is based upon the truth emphasised by the Society of Friends, the Quakers: 'there is that which is of God in everyone'. Non-violent resistance can bring that which is of God into the consciousness of the aggressor and can prove very effective in stopping aggressors in their tracks.

'Do not resist an evil person. If someone strikes you on the right cheek, turn to him the other also' (Matt. 5:39). For Jews in Jesus's time it was a mark of utter contempt to strike someone on the cheek with the back of the hand (in order not to defile the palm!) A right-handed person would strike with the back of the right hand upon the right cheek of the victim. If the victim now turns the left cheek the aggressor has a problem. It is going to be difficult to strike the left cheek with the back of the right hand. In failing to retaliate violently the victim has deprived the aggressor of fear, which is the fuel of violence. In turning 'the other cheek' the victim presents an unexpected problem to the aggressor which distracts concentration from the act of violence!

'If someone wants to sue you and take your tunic, let him have your cloak as well' (Matt. 5:40). In a court of law a debtor could be ordered to hand over his cloak during the day. Normally, people would wear only a tunic under their cloak, so that when Jesus says, 'Give your tunic as well', he is advising the debtor to strip naked, a shock tactic to make creditors realise what they are doing to their debtors.

'If someone forces you to go one mile, go with him two miles' (Matt. 5:41). A Roman soldier had the right to command anyone to carry his pack for a distance of up to one mile. It was a punishable offence to compel the person to carry the pack for a greater distance. Jesus gives the advice to 'go with him two miles' as an example of the way to disarm an aggressor by the gift of generous service.

How might such shock tactics be translated into the world of today? Would it not be possible for all the anti-capitalist globalisation protesters to contribute the money they would have spent in going to the next G8 summit to raising funds to enable eight developing countries to invite a G8 head of government to spend a week living destitute alongside the destitute? As an agent of change this would surely be far more effective in terms of heightening the awareness of world leaders than the present arrangement whereby the G8 leaders live in luxury at enormous cost – tight security does not come cheap! Protesters, meanwhile, travel across the world to the edge of the security cordon around the leaders – violent conflict frequently follows with a consequent hardening of attitudes on both sides and no significant change.

The Meaning of the Cross

The motivation for non-violent resistance is not 'winning' or 'getting the better of' an aggressor, but rather a loving concern for the aggressor as well as for the victim. Such tactics require courage, steady nerves and great generosity of spirit. In following Jesus I am not being asked to embrace suffering and inflict extra suffering on myself, but rather to allow my whole being to reflect the compassion of God without being deterred by fear of suffering. Gandhi advised anyone tempted to non-resistance through cowardice to undertake violent resistance!

The teaching of Jesus on active non-violent resistance has been extraordinarily neglected by the official teaching of the Church. Christianity has consistently taught the centrality of the cross in the life of the Christian, but 'the cross' is generally interpreted in terms of pain and suffering, whether self-imposed or inflicted by others. In the same way, the Church has consistently taught the necessity of mortification and self-denial, but without stating clearly what it is that has to be mortified, or the identity of the 'self' which has to be denied. Those who are particularly observant or scrupulous may interpret this teaching to mean that we should never do what we like doing; adding the corollary that if we do, in fact, find ourselves liking anything that we are doing, we must be doing something wrong!

The Need for Self-Denial to Find Freedom and Our True Identity

There is a sense in which the practice of mortification and self-denial are essential, not only in the life of the Christian, but in every human life. The practice of self-denial is, in fact, our surest guarantee of mental, physical and spiritual health. We saw this in Chapter 4 when we considered our deepest desire and the words of St Augustine: 'Lord, you created me for yourself, and my heart is restless until it rests in you'. In reviewing his life, Augustine realised that his restless searching had been governed by superficial desires which left him sad and restless when they had been fulfilled. When Augustine experienced and responded to the love of God, he recognised that this love had been the unrecognised longing of his heart throughout his life.

Self-denial is life-giving and a doorway to freedom when it is understood in terms of denying superficial desires the right to dominate our lives and determine our actions. The self we are asked to deny is, in fact, the false self, the self of superficial desires which has the power to frustrate and dominate our true self, which is drawing us into the life and love of God. This true self must never be denied. It is only within the true self that we can discover unity within ourselves, with other people and with all creation. It is only within the true self that we can discover our true identity; an identity which our minds are unable to contain because it is rooted in the very life of the God in whom all creation has its being.

If we sincerely try to live out of our true self, which allows God to be God to us and through us, we are very likely to be hated, driven out, abused and denounced. Jesus warns us about this in his Sermon on the Mount. As I write these lines the Israelis are occupying Palestinian territory. Some courageous Israeli soldiers refuse to fight in Palestinian territory and there are some remarkable peace activists from many different nations, who are acting as human shields in order to prevent Israelis shooting at Palestinians and demolishing their homes. The Israeli soldiers who refuse to fight in Palestinian territory may be court-martialled; the peace activists who are acting as human shields have already been shot at. Soldiers and activists will be hated, abused and denounced. They do not risk their lives because they want to suffer: their actions are not praiseworthy because they have suffered, or are likely to suffer. They are praiseworthy because the actions flow from a delight in and respect for human life; from love and compassion and from a love that is greater than the love of self-preservation. This leads them to face danger and to risk their lives: this is acceptance of the cross.

Our Destructive Belief in Redemptive Violence

Supporters of active non-violent resistance are generally considered to be romantic idealists, who are out of touch with the realities of a violent world in which the weak and the oppressed will be trampled on by the ruthless unless the ruthless are deterred by violence. Is it not true that Christians in Western countries have a stronger faith in the efficacy of nuclear deterrence than in the Sermon on the Mount? Those among us who are the most vociferous upholders of the letter of the law are often the most deeply wedded to the doctrine of redemptive violence, supporters of 'zero tolerance' for criminal offenders, advocates of capital punishment, and supporters of a policy of nuclear deterrence. Our advocacy of violence is not seen as being in conflict with fundamental Christian belief. If we believe in redemptive violence, we may find ourselves in strange company; in agreement with tyrants, dictators, totalitarian regimes and terrorists throughout the ages.

Non-violent resistance has been practised for centuries by people of differing faiths and by people of no religious faith. The American theologian and peace activist, Walter Wink, underlines the unprecedented success of non-violent revolution during the twentieth century: 'In 1989 alone, thirteen nations comprising 1.7 billion people – over thirty two percent of humanity –

experienced non-violent revolutions. They succeeded beyond anyone's wildest expectations in every case but China. And they were completely peaceful (on the part of the protesters) in every case but Romania and parts of the southern U.S.S.R. If we add all the countries touched by non-violent actions in this century, the figure reaches almost 3 billion – a staggering sixty four percent of humanity!' (Walter Wink, *Powers That Be*, Doubleday, 1998, pages 116–17).

Active non-violence is not an escape from conflict: it can only be effective in so far as the conflict is faced and hatred and anger acknowledged. Only when anger is acknowledged can the energy of anger be redirected towards a creative response that is beneficial to both victim and aggressor. The bloodless fall of the dictatorial regime of Ferdinand Marcos in the Philippines in 1986 appeared to come about suddenly, but it had been preceded by a year's training of half a million people in the practice of non-violence. The 1991 collapse of apartheid in South Africa also appeared to come about with extraordinary swiftness. This, again, had been prepared for decades by black-led protest marches and demonstrations, the vast majority of them being non-violent. The African National Congress (ANC) had been founded in 1912 with the aim of securing racial equality and black parliamentary representation by peaceful means. It was only in 1960, when its members were banned by the South African government, that they turned to sabotage and guerrilla warfare.

If non-violent protest is to be effective, the motivation must be love for the enemy who is imposing violence upon us. Active non-violence does not preclude the use of restraining force. It does, however, prohibit the deliberate imposition of physical violence upon those who are subjected to restraint. However well the action may be prepared, there can be no guarantee that participants will come out of it alive, or unhurt. Those who engage in active non-violence have to be prepared to absorb the violence of the aggressor in their own bodies.

There are risks in non-violence, but its casualties need to be compared with the casualties of violent resistance. Violence, of its nature, breeds violence. Walter Wink includes a table indicating the enormous increase in war casualties over the centuries:

1500s	1.6 million
1600s	6.1 million
1700s	7 million
1800s	19.4 million
1900s	109 million

Civilian casualties are reckoned to have been 50 per cent of the total since the 1700s, with a sharp rise in the 1900s, and reckoned to be 74 per cent in the 1980s (Wink, *Powers That Be*, page 137).

Primitive Peoples' Superior Insight into the Nature of Violence

Ancient peoples did not possess the technology that makes it possible to destroy human life on earth within minutes. They did, however, possess a much clearer insight into the nature of violence and its dangers. René Girard (b. 1923), a native of Avignon, originally a specialist in medieval studies, became a lecturer in French literature at Indiana University, USA. Through his study of literature, he became interested in the relationship between religion and violence. It was through the study of religion and violence that he returned to Christianity, discovering in the Bible and in the life and teaching of Christ the only means of saving the human race from destructive violence. Girard's work on the interrelationship between violence and religion has been hailed as one of the major intellectual achievements of the twentieth century and he offers fresh and disturbing insights into the way in which Jesus lived out his teaching through his life, passion and death.

Girard claims that human conflict arises from our natural tendency to imitate, which is also the way in which we learn. For imitation he uses the word *mimesis*, because it is desire which gives rise to imitation, and the object of mimesis is not just to imitate, but to possess what the model, i.e. the person whom we are imitating, possesses. If the model whom we are imitating stretches out for something, for example, then we shall imitate that action. If we are both then stretching out for the same thing, there will inevitably be conflict, leading to violence. The next few paragraphs draw substantially upon the insights of Girard on the nature of violence.

The Scapegoat Mechanism for Quelling Violence

Ancient societies were very aware of the destructiveness of violence and therefore they established taboos, in order to prevent conflict erupting into uncontrollable violence. When taboos fail, there is another way of stemming violence and it is found among all peoples, both ancient and modern, namely, the scapegoat mechanism. In the biblical narrative the scapegoat was sent out into the desert to carry upon itself the wickedness and rebellion of the people (Lev. 16:21–22). Through this action, enemies are reconciled, and peace and order are restored for the time being. The scapegoat can be an animal, as in Leviticus, or a human being, or group of people. We see a striking example of this in the account of the Passion of Jesus in the Gospel of Luke. The Roman governor, Pontius Pilate, hears that Jesus is a Galilean and therefore under the jurisdiction of Herod. He passes him over to Herod who was in Jerusalem. Herod mocks Jesus and sends him back to Pilate, 'And though Herod and Pilate had been enemies before, they were reconciled that same day' (Luke 23:12).

Scapegoating can bring about a certain peace – but it is a peace which is founded on murder and on a deception. Scapegoating is a projection of our own guilt onto an animal, or an individual or group, whom we blame for our ills, and then set out to damage or destroy. But the death or moral destruction of the victim cannot remove our personal guilt. Scapegoating merely enables us to hide from our guilt and provides a brief respite from raging violence – but it cannot bring lasting peace. Violence inflicted upon a scapegoat or anyone else can only breed further violence. Another scapegoat will eventually be required. The scapegoat may be an individual, a group, a particular class or a nation. In past centuries, countless witches became the scapegoat for particular communities and they were burned, in the belief that they were the cause of ills befalling the community, such as infant mortality. In Christian Europe the Jewish people were scapegoats throughout the centuries during which they were persecuted, driven out and killed; a persecution culminating in the deaths of six million Jews in Nazi concentration camps during the 1939–45 war. For decades Communism was the scapegoat for capitalist countries, and since the collapse of Communism the West has transferred the 'evil empire' scapegoat to other states.

The scapegoat mechanism operates within each one of us. It tends to be unconscious, but is nonetheless murderous and enables us to feel righteous as we transfer our own anger onto another individual, group or nation. We see this in the people who cheer outside prisons when an accused person has been killed or has died, feeling that the world is now a better place. The pillorying of individuals and groups in the tabloid press feeds our voracious appetite for scapegoating, which is an indication of repressed and unacknowledged guilt. We cannot face our own sense of guilt so we project that guilt onto others and thus experience relief – 'It is their fault so it cannot be my fault!'

The public hounding of people who have been accused of sex offences is an alarming indication of our own repressed and unacknowledged guilt. The scapegoat reflex can be detected by noting our inner reactions to the news of the death of any individual or group. Do we feel sadness and compassion, no matter who has died? Or does the news of particular deaths come as a relief and leave us with a sense of well-being?

The Biblical Perception of the Scapegoat

In his studies on violence in literature, Girard found the biblical attitude to the scapegoat to be unique.

Violence and conflict are found in the Bible, but the Bible is unique in ancient literature because the writers always spring to the defence of the victim.

The Biblical Writers Defend the Scapegoats

The story of Cain and Abel is presented in classic fashion. Cain kills Abel, and out of the murder the Cainite community is founded. God condemns the murder, but when Cain says, 'Whoever comes across me will kill me', God answers, 'If anyone kills Cain, vengeance will be taken on him sevenfold'. The murder founds a new civilisation, as in many ancient communities, but God declares a law against murder: 'And the Lord put a mark on Cain to prevent anyone from striking him down.' Girard sees in this the establishment by God of a different system that opposes scapegoating. In the story of Cain, we perceive the establishment of a new system that discourages conflict and discourages the rivalry that is provoked by conflicting desires. Cain's murder of Abel leads, ultimately, to the creation of a city and the first cultural development of the human race. This does not, however, serve to excuse the murder of Abel: in contrast to the pagan myth of Rome's foundation in which Romulus murders his brother Remus and the murder is considered to be justified because it leads to the foundation of the city of Rome. The biblical myths assert that a culture founded on murder retains a murderous character which, in the end, becomes self-destructive.

In the Song of the Suffering Servant in Isaiah, the servant is presented as a scapegoat (Isa. 53:3–8):

> A thing despised and rejected by men,
> a man of sorrows and familiar with suffering . . .
> For our faults struck down in death.

The most striking characteristic of the Suffering Servant narrative is the innocence of the victim. This is in contrast to the mythical accounts of scapegoating in which the scapegoat is perceived as 'guilty'. What is the role of Yahweh in the death of the innocent servant?

Does God Inflict Suffering?

The Old Testament demonstrates a developing understanding of God, which is hardly surprising when one reflects that the Hebrew Scriptures were written over a period of many centuries. The notion of divine retribution is very much alive in the early books such as Genesis and Exodus, but in the later prophetic books God has been increasingly divested of the violence that is characteristic of primitive deities. In the Gospels, a picture emerges of a God who is no longer a God of retribution.

In the New Testament, Satan is identified with violence, with our imprisonment in cultural systems that bind us to violence. Satan is the source not merely of rivalry and disorder, but of all the forms of lying, whether explicit or implicit. Our culture is based upon a process of distancing ourselves from violence by projecting it endlessly upon new victims, new scapegoats.

Jesus reveals the murderous intentions of the scapegoaters: 'Alas for you, scribes and Pharisees, you hypocrites! You who are like whitewashed tombs that look handsome on the outside' (Matt. 23:27). The whitewashed tombs are hidden underground. They look most respectable from the outside, which gives a false sense of peace and security. Within, they conceal murder and every kind of evil. Jesus is telling the truth about violence, and it is at this point that it becomes clear to the authorities that he is going to have to go! The truth about violence must be expelled with violence.

In the Passion Jesus is presented as the innocent victim of the Jewish crowd, the religious authorities, the Roman political authorities, and even of the disciples: those who do not betray or deny Jesus nevertheless flee or remain as passive spectators. Together they form a group which is in a state of crisis and is temporarily united against Jesus.

If scapegoating is to be effective, the victim must take onto his or her own shoulders all the guilt from which the community needs to be liberated. If the scapegoating community is to be freed from guilt, the victim has to be guilty. In the narrative of the Passion it is demonstrably clear that the 'victim' is not in fact guilty, so the guilt is inevitably thrown back upon the scapegoating community and they find this intolerable. Their deceit and their murderous intentions are exposed and this exposition must be covered up. In the Acts of the Apostles the death of Stephen is a clear example of this. Stephen addresses his accusers in words which offer no quarter:

'You stubborn people, with your pagan hearts and pagan ears. You are always resisting the Holy Spirit, just as your ancestors used to do. Can you name a single prophet your ancestors never persecuted? In the past they killed those who foretold the coming of the Just One, and now you have become his betrayers, his murderers. You who had the law brought to you by angels are the very ones who have not kept it'. They were infuriated when they heard this, and ground their teeth at him. But Stephen, filled with the Holy Spirit, gazed into heaven and saw the glory of God, and Jesus standing at God's right hand. 'I can see heaven thrown open' he said, 'and the Son of Man standing at the right hand of God.' At this all the members of the council shouted out and stopped their ears with their hands; then they all rushed at him, sent him out of the city and stoned him (Acts 7:51–8).

The members of the Council cannot tolerate their own crimes being thrown in their faces. They stop their ears and kill Stephen to cast off the intolerable knowledge of cold-blooded murder.

The Death of Jesus: A New Foundation for the Temple of Humanity

'It was the stone rejected by the builders which became the keystone' (Luke 20:17). Jesus, the innocent victim, has undermined the ancient view of sacrifice, based on the belief that the guilt of a people can be taken away through the death of the scapegoat, the victim who is presumed to be guilty. Through the death of Jesus, the stone which had been rejected becomes a new foundation stone for the building of the temple of humanity; a temple that is no longer based on the scapegoating of victims who are sacrificed in order to allow murderers to escape their own guilt and their own violence.

Jesus Reveals a Non-Violent God

In the Gospels, the death of Jesus is presented as an act that brings salvation to all humanity, but at no point is it presented as an act that brings salvation precisely because the victim is murdered.

In the past, some theologians have produced explanations of the death of Jesus that correspond exactly with ancient mythical accounts of sacrifice in which a victim is killed and through the killing, enemies are reconciled and peace restored. But such reconciliation and peace in the ancient world are founded on murder and the peace and the reconciliation will not be permanent. In some theologies, God is presented as the murderer; a God of retribution, who can only be satisfied with the blood of his Son who, by shedding it, makes up for our sins and expiates them.

Jesus is the image of the unseen God, the expression of God in human form. Jesus lives and preaches a God of non-violence, who

lets his sun shine on the just and the unjust alike, who is represented in the parable of the wedding feast as inviting everyone to
his son's feast, 'wicked and good alike'. To live the life of God is to
love our enemies, do good to those who hate us, bless those who
persecute us. Jesus was a threat to those whose security lay in their
power to control, dominate and oppress precisely because he
manifested a God who did none of those things; a God who calls
us instead to love our enemies and do good to those who hate us.
Jesus opposed the misuse of power by civil and religious authorities. Jesus opposed such exercise of authority, a resistance that
brought him to arrest and crucifixion, but even in his final
moments he manifests the God of compassion: 'Father, forgive
them for they know not what they do' (Luke 23:34).

In the passion and death of Jesus it is as though the concentrated
evil and perversity of humankind is hurled at God through his
son, Jesus, and Jesus fails to respond with 'redemptive violence'.
We see this clearly when he is arrested in Gethsemane: 'One of the
followers of Jesus grasped his sword and drew it; he struck out at
the high priest's servant and cut off his ear. Jesus then said, "Put
your sword back, for all who draw the sword will die by the
sword. Or do you think that I cannot appeal to my Father who
would promptly send more than twelve legions of angels to my
defence?"' (Matt. 26:52–3).

Some Conclusions About the Nature of Pain and Suffering

1 Benevolent pain

In itself, suffering is an evil to be avoided. I do not believe God
inflicts suffering as a punishment for sin. Much of the pain we
suffer in our bodies can be seen subsequently as a necessary form
of self-protection: the pain is a symptom of a disorder that needs
attention. Torn ligaments are very painful and compel us to rest:
without the pain we could do permanent damage to ourselves.
The pain is unpleasant, but benevolent.

2 Ego pain – self-inflicted

Much of our bodily and mental pain is self-inflicted. Our
frustrations, our losses, whether of health, wealth, status or

relationships can lead to bitterness, resentment, an inner withering of the spirit, an inability to love and to forgive. This torment of mind and spirit can manifest itself in physical ailments. I referred earlier to Sartre's dictum, 'L'enfer, c'est les autres' – 'hell is other people'. He might subsequently have made the discovery that 'L'enfer, c'est moi!' – hell is me! I shall discover this particular 'hell' if I allow my choices to be entirely governed by my whims and inclinations, regardless of the long-term consequences for myself and others. I can lock myself into solitary confinement, my only companions being the darkness and my own unforgiving hatred of myself. The pain will be the more intense the more generous and loving others have been to me, the more attractive the life that was offered and rejected. It is the goodness of others and of God that torments me, not their punishment.

Why Do the Innocent Suffer?

The poor and innocent suffer for the greed and ambition of the powerful. We see this clearly in the poverty of the Third World, which could be alleviated by a little more justice on the part of so-called 'developed' countries. But rich and poor are linked in ways that we are only just beginning to understand. 'When a baby throws its rattle out of the cradle, the planets rock'. Nuclear physicists are discovering the extent to which the movement of subatomic particles can be affected by human observation, and how a change of direction in one particle has an immediate effect thousands of miles away. Is it not, therefore, possible that the positive or negative thoughts and desires of our minds and hearts can reverberate throughout creation? The major religions of the world believe that prayer can make a difference; that we can strengthen, encourage and provide hope and comfort to distant people of whose existence we may be completely unaware. There is a unity between us, because it is in God that we live and move and have our being. The Christian creed declares a belief in 'the communion of saints'. We may extend the meaning to include the totality of humankind, living and dead.

There is a long tradition in Judaism that the world is upheld at any given time by the presence of thirty-six Just People, known as the *Lamed-wah*. Through no fault of their own, the *Lamed-wah* bear the burden of the sin and guilt of the world; a burden which leads them from one disaster to another. They are not necessarily aware of their destiny as *Lamed-wah*, 'The Just', but they endure their intolerable burdens while retaining their trust in God, their love for themselves and for their neighbour. According to the legend, the world would die of its own corruption without the incorruptible fidelity of 'the Just'. In the book of Isaiah, the suffering servant is described in terms that could apply to one of 'the Just'.

> A man of sorrows and familiar with suffering . . .
> And yet ours were the sufferings he bore,
> ours the sorrows he carried . . .
> For our faults struck down in death (Isa. 53:3–8).

The Song of the Suffering Servant prefigures Jesus, the image of the unseen God. Like Jesus, we are called to allow God to be God, to us and through us. In the words of St Paul: 'I live now not with my own life, but with the life of Christ who lives in me' (Gal. 2:20). Jesus is called to bring life and to bring it more abundantly. We are called to do likewise. The lifestyle and teaching of Jesus was a threat to the authorities of Church and State who had him put to death. But death itself cannot conquer the love and goodness of God that continues to manifest itself today through ourselves. Jesus came to a point in his life when he was powerless and unable to escape the pain that engulfed him. On the eve of his death he prayed, 'My Father, if it is not possible for this cup to be taken away unless I drink it, may your will be done' (Matt. 26:42). Like Jesus, we too arrive at points in our lives when we are powerless and unable to escape the pain that engulfs us. It is at these moments that our lives can be most effective, if we will surrender ourselves to the transforming power of God; that transforming power which is at its greatest in our weakness and which brings life for the world out of death.

Whatever the suffering we endure, we can know that God is with us in our pain; God does not inflict suffering, but shares it with us. The transforming power of God is constantly available to us if we can surrender ourselves to God, as Jesus surrendered himself, for the life of the world.

Exercises

'I believe the answer is somehow to be found in the pain itself' (page 176). The exercises that follow are ways of meeting God in our own suffering – using the last words of Jesus on the cross for our prayers.

A simple way of praying these last words, taking one for each period of prayer, is to begin with the usual preparatory prayer, 'Lord, let everything within me be directed totally to your service and praise'. Be aware of your own pain, grief, anxiety, without any attempt to analyse it.

1 'Father, forgive them; they do not know what they are doing' (Luke 23:33–4).
2 Jesus' words to the repentant thief being crucified with him: 'I promise you, today you will be with me in paradise' (Luke 23:35–43).
3 Jesus said to his mother, 'Woman, this is your son.' Then to the disciple he said, 'This is your mother', and from that moment the disciple made a place for her in his home (John 19:25–7).
4 'I thirst' (John 19:28–9).
5 'My God, my God, why have you abandoned me?' (Matt. 27:45–6)
6 'Father, into your hands I commend my spirit' (Luke 23:44–6).
7 'It is accomplished' (John 19:29–30).

Imagine Jesus on the cross. He is there for you. He is with you now in your own pain. Hear him cry out the word you are contemplating. And hear the word being spoken now from deep within you. What do you want to say/do in reply? If, while you are putting yourself in the scene, watching, and listening, distracting thoughts come to mind such as 'How can I know Jesus spoke those words?', 'Should I be trying to pray like this when I am full of doubts about my own faith?', etc., acknowledge these as interesting questions that you can look at later, then continue watching/listening.

You can try praying imaginatively (as described on pages 65–8) on any scene from the Gospel accounts of Jesus' Passion and death.

UNLESS YOU LOSE
YOUR LIFE...

P ILGRIMAGE REFLECTS LIFE, AND the experience of going on
pilgrimage can help us to a better understanding of our own
lives. As I wrote in Chapter 8, on the road to Rome and then later
to Jerusalem I expected to be elated on arrival at my destination
after so many weeks travelling. In both cases there was a strange
sense of anti-climax. I began to understand the words of Robert
Louis Stevenson (d. 1894): 'To travel hopefully is a better thing
than to arrive'.

The feeling of anti-climax on arrival at both destinations
was full of wisdom. We can spend our days so looking forward to tomorrow, or in a state of regret or nostalgia for yesterday,
that we fail to notice the present. For Christians, a split spirituality can encourage us to pay minimal attention to this temporal
world of matter so that we keep our attention fixed on the
heavenly life to come. I am grateful for the two pilgrimages,
not primarily because I reached Rome and Jerusalem, but because
I was taught a much more valuable lesson, namely that God
is continuously and intimately present to each of us, whether
we go away on pilgrimage or not. We are very adept at locking
Jesus in the cupboard, or relegating God to a remote future that

does not yet exist, while ignoring God's presence at the present moment, in the circumstances in which we find ourselves.

Did the feeling of anti-climax at the end of each pilgrimage point to a further truth, which is that there can be no final destination at the end of life? Is death, in fact, a staging post upon a continuing journey? God alone knows the form that any further journeying may take, but it will be an exploration into the mystery of the God, who is love. In God all creation has its existence and is constantly being renewed, so we shall be journeying with one another as well as with God. Whatever happens after the experience that we describe as 'death', I cannot believe that we shall enter into some static state – that would set limits to the God who is infinite.

Ageing and Death – Stages in the Journey

There are few certainties in life, but there is one that unites all of us. We shall all die, and most of us will experience the process of ageing which, I understand, begins very shortly after birth! This chapter gathers the themes we have been considering and applies them to death and the process of ageing – subjects we usually prefer to ignore for fear of blighting the present. They are in fact a source of blessing and reassurance, because our fears become our allies when they are faced.

I was once invited to address a movement of Roman Catholic origin called 'Ascent', which aims to help older people to deepen or recover their faith and to have a complete confidence in God. As I read more about Ascent, I realised that reflection upon ageing and death is a most effective way of recognising and acknowledging our own transcendence; for ageing and the thought of death are tangential points with our present experience which can transform our understanding of life.

In preparing to address Ascent, I had to find a politically correct title for the lecture: 'Prepare to meet Thy Maker', 'On Persevering to the End', 'The Last Lap'. 'The Last Gasp'? And how was I to address the audience? 'Elderly', 'ageing', 'youth impaired', or with the latest politically correct form from the US, 'chronologically gifted'!?

We live in an extraordinary culture of virtual reality in which the lives of soap opera characters frequently provoke greater emotional response than the real people around us – let alone the plight of starving millions across the world. Are we perhaps like the characters in Plato's myth of the cave who mistake shadows for reality. Ageing, with its inevitable concomitants of reduced physical strength, failing energy and health worries can feel like a descent into nothingness – which adds depression to our problems. In today's enterprise culture, full of images of young, healthy, clever, economically successful people, those as young as fifty can have difficulty in finding employment and can feel that their life is behind them!

Can faith provide us only with the assurance that all will be well in the end, provided we turn back to God and say our prayers? What about here and now? How are we to cope with present fears and regrets, not to mention the remorse and guilt generated by past failures; what about our fears of becoming useless and a burden to our families and friends; and how are we to deal with the fear and pain of loneliness and the horror of possible oblivion? How do we cope when we discover our past certainties crumbling, including our faith in God? Do we just 'hang on' and refuse to listen to our fears? Should we try to ignore what is happening and pretend that all is well – put a brave face on it! Reality has an implacable quality, like an advancing steam roller that cannot be stopped by gossamer-like thoughts or pious assurances. How are we to cope?

Facing Our Fears

There is no permanent escape from our fears until we turn round and face them, as we saw in Chapter 6. God is in all things, therefore in some way God is in the fears that haunt us, so it is safe to look at them, even if we only do so in order to acknowledge that we do not feel strong enough to face them at the moment. God is not just aware of our fears: God is in them, sharing the fears with us.

Inner freedom is only to be found to the extent that we become able to face our fears. If younger people were also able to learn to face the fears that haunt them, our frenetic, individualistic and competitive society might be transformed into a society that cooperates instead of competing; one that cares for the earth instead of plundering it.

For some religious people, the worst fear that can beset them is the fear of God – especially in later life. Conscientious parents as well as unreflecting preachers and teachers can communicate to a child the image of a monstrous, capricious God, whose primary interest lies in our sins, and whose main preoccupation is the preparation of appropriate punishment that can last for ever. This false image of God can grow in the human psyche like a malignant tumour and blight our lives. I may know intellectually that such an image is deformed, but if it has taken root at an early age it cannot be eradicated merely by reading or hearing about a different sort of God – the God whom Jesus presents through his own life, his parables and his teaching in the Sermon on the Mount.

Ageing and 'The Dark Night of the Soul'

A very different fear of God comes from an awareness that the worst possible scenario is eternal separation from the God who is my all and for whom I long with every fibre of my being. This fear can afflict people who have been seized by the love of God; the intensity of their pain is proportionate to the depth of their love. Such torment is well attested in the lives of saints such as Thérèse of Lisieux, who became a contemplative nun in a French Carmelite monastery at the age of fifteen, died at the age of twenty-four in 1897 and was declared a saint in 1925. Thérèse suffered inner darkness throughout the final eighteen months of her life. Spiritual writers refer to such experiences as 'The Dark Night of the Soul' – an experience of inner purification that normally precedes a deeper and more intense awareness of the presence of God. In the case of Thérèse of Lisieux, that deeper and more intense awareness came only in the final moments of her life: ' "My God, I love you". [Thérèse] had barely uttered these words in the "night of faith", when she collapsed; then suddenly as though hearing a voice from heaven, she sat up in ecstasy, her look radiant, gazing above her. It was the rending of the cloud, the skies opening, illumination; and in that illumination she died' (Thérèse of Lisieux, Epilogue to *Collected Letters*, Sheed and Ward, London, 1949).

The split nature of our spirituality can lead us to conclude that the experience of the 'Dark Night' is reserved for high-powered contemplatives, but it is, I believe, far more common than we think. When we come across the Dark Night in ourselves, or in others, we can misdiagnose the symptoms as indicative of wavering faith, or as the manifestation of long-buried guilt. We all have to undergo an experience of purification, or diminishment, as part of the process of ageing. The Dark Night is an intense form of purification, but all of us undergo a process of purification through the experience of ageing, when we experience diminishment of everything that formerly gave us a sense of worth and value, including our religious convictions, so that we can become prey to all manner of doubts about God and an afterlife.

In the experience of the Dark Night, the sufferer can be stripped, like Job, of everything that formerly sustained him or her: possessions, family, reputation, health of body, religious certainties. Job's health of mind is also assailed by the assurances of his friends that his present afflictions must be the punishment of God for the evil for which Job is, obviously, responsible! When we have been stripped of our supports and the mind is plunged into the darkness of doubt, we are faced with the alternatives of despair, or surrender to apparent nothingness. But the heart nevertheless recognises that the 'nothingness' is of God; that it is in a mysterious way the heart's desire.

In the poem 'The Hound of Heaven', Francis Thompson compares God to a hound pursuing us as we flee down 'the arches of the years'. We try to hide, to escape, until eventually God corners us: this is the moment of enlightenment:

> All which I took from thee I did but take,
>   Not for thy harms,
> But just that thou might'st seek it in my arms.
>   All which thy child's mistake
> Fancies as lost, I have stored for thee at home:
>   Rise, clasp my hand and come!'
>
> Halts by me that footfall:
> Is my gloom, after all,
> Shade of His hand, outstretched caressingly?
> 'Ah, fondest, blindest, weakest,

I am He Whom thou seekest!
Thou dravest love from thee, who dravest Me.'

In fleeing from God, in driving God away, I am driving love out of my own heart.

On Learning How to Gaze and Let God Become Our Teacher

During the final nine months of his life I had the privilege of meeting every week with the historian and writer Donald Nicholl. Donald was an inveterate thinker. In his youth, he overheard some older people say of him, 'That poor young man thinks too much'. When I first visited him after the diagnosis of terminal cancer, he announced, 'I have given up thinking since hearing the news, I now spend my days in gazing. I think that thinking is a result of the Fall'! About eight months later, Donald handed me thirty-two close-typed A4 sheets which were headed, 'Thoughts on Death and Dying by Donald Nicholl'. I remarked, 'But I thought you had given up thinking, Donald', to which he replied, 'Yes, I have given up thinking, but these thoughts have come to me from gazing'!

As we grow older we usually have more time for gazing – a most useful, enjoyable and profitable occupation that is so often considered to be a waste of time. 'Gazing' is a matter of becoming still, of closing down our thoughts and simply observing, but without engaging with what we see in front of us, or with whatever comes to mind. The Indian spiritual writer, Anthony de Mello, compared the experience of gazing to standing on a bridge over a river and watching the barges pass to and fro below us – but without jumping off the bridge on to any one of the barges. Methods of becoming still were offered in Chapter 4, and these exercises can help to free us from the bonds of our conditioning and from our distorted images of God, of ourselves and of other people. 'Being' rather than 'doing' can free the mind of its obsessions and allow God to pray in us and to become our teacher.

In observing that 'thinking is the result of the Fall' Donald Nicholl was perhaps making a similar point to the Jewish philosopher Martin Buber (d.1965), whom I quoted earlier: 'Nothing so masks the face of God as religion'. The greatest obstacle to meeting God in our lives and in prayer is our store of false images and ideas about God. When we focus on God, we can focus on these false images, instead of allowing God to focus on us and to become our teacher. In the words of the prophet Isaiah: 'He who is your teacher will hide no longer, and you will see your teacher with your own eyes. Whether you go to right or to left, your ears will hear these words behind you, "This is the way, follow it".' (Isa. 30:20–1).

Handing Over Our Fears

The practice of stillness can enable us to look at our fears, anxieties, guilt, regrets and hurts without being overwhelmed by them. In imagination we can come before God and hand over our anxieties, our fears and our hurts, one by one. This exercise is not a denial of fears and anxieties, guilt and sinfulness: it is rather an acknowledgment that they exist, but that they can be handed over to the goodness of God; handed over in the belief that God, the divine alchemist, who is constantly transforming us in our weakness, can also transform our fears and anxieties, guilt and sinfulness into his own goodness. Christians celebrate this transformation when they celebrate the Eucharist; they celebrate the reality of the self-giving God who is continuously renewing us.

In the stillness we can present to God our fear of death and beg to be delivered from it. In stillness we become more receptive to the gift of wonder that comes naturally to most of us when we are children and before the ego begins to restrict our vision. This gift of wonder can return as we grow older. Out of the stillness I can gaze at the mystery that I am: billions of cells, each one unique to me and each one containing an intelligence that surpasses the capacity of my conscious mind. Each cell bears within it the design of the whole body, and the cells together form a communication system and a nourishing 'transport' system that science is still struggling to grasp. The more we grasp of this astonishing infrastructure, the more aware we become of our inability to understand the totality. However weak and ailing I may be, my body is interconnected with everything in the universe; it is intimately interwoven with everything that exists.

'In God we live and move and have our being' (Acts 17:28). 'Before the world was made, he chose us, chose us in Christ, to be holy and spotless, and to live through love in his presence' (Eph. 1:4). 'I live now not with my own life but with the life of Christ who lives in me' (Gal. 2:20). These words should fill us with a sense of wonder and delight. We can, however, hear them in such a way as to focus upon our personal failure to live a life of love in the presence of God. We do not have to deny our own lamentable performance, but if we acknowledge it in the presence of God, we can begin to see that the root of our failure lies in our innate tendency to focus upon ourselves and our own performance rather than upon God. It is as though God does not exist. Our undoing is our lack of faith. It is impossible for us to live lives that are holy and spotless. God alone is holy and spotless. Jesus told us that God alone is good. We can only be 'holy and spotless and live through love in God's presence' to the extent that we are prepared to surrender our lives to God. A sense of wonder can free us from the grip of our self-centred preoccupations and help us to grow into a fuller appreciation of life.

Enjoying Life, Befriending Death

When a Scottish friend, Ursula Burton, was diagnosed with cancer for the third time, she rang to tell me the news, giving me the essential facts and then talking at length about her return home through Edinburgh's Botanic Gardens which she had never seen looking so beautiful! If I had been the one to receive such a diagnosis, I would not have noticed the beauty of the gardens; my mind would have been too full of operating theatres and funeral services! Ursula had already befriended death, and had discovered such inner peace that she was able to appreciate the present moment to the full. If we are going to enjoy life to the full, we need to practise detachment: if we are to appreciate every moment of life, we need to befriend death. What a paradox! It is the wisdom of God.

I met with Ursula for the last time a few weeks before she died. She told me not to let 'them' put 'May she rest in peace' on her tombstone. 'I have no intention of resting in peace!' 'What do you intend doing?' I asked. 'I want to be with people who are crossing from this stage of life to the next.' During the weeks preceding his death Donald Nicholl had also spoken of his conviction that he would continue to work after his death by helping those who were dying to move into their new life.

Earlier in this chapter I mentioned the lecture I had been invited to give to 'Ascent', which helps older people to deepen or recover their faith and to acquire an absolute confidence in God. In drafting my talk I decided to include the story of Ursula and her desire to help those who were 'crossing over'. I had just typed the paragraph when I received a telephone call from a complete stranger who wanted to tell me about the help she had received through reading Ursula's book *Vicky: A Bridge Between Two Worlds*. This book is an account of Ursula's daughter, Vicky, who never recovered consciousness after a minor operation and remained completely paralysed for almost two years until her death. Along with her other friends, I think her wish is being granted!

A third friend, whom I only met as a friend a few years ago, but who died in 1897, is St Thérèse of Lisieux. When I first read her 'Story of a Soul' over fifty years ago, I was put off by her pious style. Reading her again recently, I recognised her diamond-like quality. The spirituality of her 'Little Way' is so simple but, in the words of T.S. Eliot, it 'costs not less than everything'. It is a spirituality that is available to anybody at any time and is a matter of doing the smallest and most ordinary things for the love of God. During the final months of her life Thérèse spoke frequently of the work she intended to undertake after her death. Two months before her death she observed, 'I feel . . . that my mission is about to begin. I can't rest as long as there are souls to be saved.' And the following day she remarked, 'God would not have given me the desire of doing good on earth after my death, if he did not will to realise it.'

The Christian creed includes the words: 'We believe . . . in the communion of saints'. In Greek and Russian Orthodoxy, in Roman Catholicism and in Anglo-Catholicism this belief is emphasised by the practice of honouring and praying to the men and women who are officially recognised as outstandingly holy. The feast of All Saints on 1 November is immediately followed by the Feast of All Souls, which includes all those who have died, but

are not 'Saints' in the sense of having been officially acknowledged as outstandingly holy. We pray that they may pass through
any necessary state of purification before they join those who are
already in heaven.

Being at Home with Those Who Have Died

I can see the value of having saints who are officially and formally
recognised, but I wish we could return to the custom of the early
Church when men and women were canonised by popular acclaim,
not by lengthy canonisation processes which involve years of work
and cost vast sums of money. These processes also give the impression that it is only the clergy and members of religious congregations
who are likely to be numbered among the saints, because the vast
majority of canonised saints fall into these categories.

In one of his Spiritual Exercises, Inigo of Loyola advises the
retreatant to see themselves as 'standing before God, our Lord,
and also before the angels and saints, who are interceding for me'.
When I first attempted to do this I found it too artificial and soon
grew bored of imagining myself in the presence of haloed saints
and harp-playing angels as portrayed in pious pictures. The phrase
took on a more real and homely meaning during my walk to
Jerusalem in 1987, when I was making my way through German
snowstorms one bitterly cold day. My thoughts had turned to
members of my own family who had died, and I found myself
talking with them. That evening I found a lodging and had a meal
with the landlady, who talked about her husband who had died
twenty years earlier. She told me that she was aware of her
husband's presence, spoke to him frequently and drew great
strength and comfort from doing so. She had not dared to tell her
family or friends about this, in case they thought her mad. Since
then I have met many other people who have had this same
experience, which feels perfectly natural, comforting, reassuring
and in no way 'spooky'. The dead are like shy guests at a party:
they will not intrude and can easily go unnoticed. If, however, we
give them attention, we can become increasingly aware of their
comforting presence. Those who have died remain alive in the
God in whom all creation has its being. It would seem to follow
that they must still be in contact with us in some way.

On Becoming Reconciled with Those Who Have Died

In old age we can be haunted by memories of wrongs we have suffered or wrongs we have inflicted on people who are now dead. We feel the need to forgive or to be forgiven. There is a helpful imaginative exercise, which can also be useful in the case of wrongs suffered at the hands of people who are still alive. I imagine myself entering a room in which Jesus is present alongside the person who has offended me. I tell my enemy of my hurt, anger and bitterness at what has been done to me. Then I pause, and allow the enemy to speak. Finally, I allow Jesus to speak to us both. In this exercise, as in all methods of prayer, it is important to be thoroughly honest in all that I say and not to force anything. If I find that I am unable to forgive, then I should say so to the enemy and to Jesus.

If I am finding it impossible to forgive, then I need to become still, and in the stillness to ask myself: 'In the depth of my heart, do I really want to do permanent harm to this person? Is that how I would like to be remembered – as a person who never forgave an injury? In spite of the anger I feel, can I find a depth in my heart at which I do not want ultimate harm to be done to this person? Can I even pray for their ultimate good?

If I feel the need to be forgiven by people who are now dead and whom I have wronged, I can do a similar imaginative exercise. I imagine myself entering the room in which Jesus is present with the person I have wronged. I ask that person to tell me how I have wronged them and the way that they felt. Then I pause and ask forgiveness. Finally I ask Jesus to speak to both of us. This is, in fact, what we do in a general way at the beginning of the Eucharist in the words, 'I confess to almighty God, and to you, my brothers and sisters, that I have sinned . . .'. It is a confession to those present and also to the whole people of God whom we have offended by our destructiveness. It is also a request for their forgiveness.

These exercises are not magic: they do not necessarily 'work' at the first attempt and bring us an instant sense of reconciliation and blessed relief from resentful anger and lingering guilt. If we keep doing the exercises we shall, however, find that whenever the anger or guilt threatens to swamp us, we are more able to deal with them; we are becoming more peaceful and are increasingly capable of delighting in the presence of God. We can become grateful for the existence of the person who offended us, or to whom we have given offence.

There are, however, instances in which people have been so badly seared by trauma that they dare not recall it in any shape or form. In such cases we may perhaps be able to pray to God without attempting to recall details, but asking that we may one day be able to want to forgive. In some cases the difficulty lies in forgiving ourselves – this is perhaps the greatest difficulty. If God gives us this gift of being able to forgive ourselves, we shall no longer have difficulty in forgiving other people.

Our Personal Struggles with Our Fears Have Cosmic Repercussions

We are no longer strangers on this earth: we are surrounded by hosts of supporters. Our minds cannot prove this, but our hearts can come to know it is true. What goes on in our hearts has repercussions throughout creation. The mystics have been saying this for centuries. In the sixteenth century, St John of the Cross said that one act of pure love was more effective than any amount of activity. With the diminishing mental and physical capacities of old age we can still pray for and long for the well-being of all peoples. Nuclear physicists are now asserting that human observation, for example, can affect the behaviour of sub-atomic particles, and that change in one part of the universe effects immediate change in other parts, separated by thousands of miles. Prayer, which is wrung from us in weakness and helplessness, may one day prove to have been the most valuable moment of our lives, preparing us for the next stage of the journey when we can more effectively work for the well-being of all peoples and of all creation.

Exercises

Some Scripture passages to be prayed imaginatively as described on pages 65–8.

1 The raising of Lazarus (John 11:1–44)
   Imagine yourself entombed like Lazarus. Hear the stone being
   moved from the mouth of the tomb, then keep hearing the
   voice of Jesus calling you by your name and saying to you,
   'Arise, come forth'. How do you want to react, and what do
   you want to say in response?

2 Jesus appearing to the disciples in the upper room (John 20:19–
   21)
   Imagine the scene, the people in the room, and what they are
   doing and saying. Ask them why they are so terrified. Talk to
   them about your own fears and terrors. See the risen Jesus
   appear in this room of fears. Hear him say to the disciples and
   to you, 'Peace be to you' and watch as he shows you his
   wounded hands and side. What do you want to say in reply?
   Then hear him say to you, 'As the Father sent me, I am now
   sending you?' How do you reply? Always speak to him honestly,
   from your heart, trusting that he loves you far more than you
   can love yourself.

3 Jesus appearing to Mary of Magdala (John 20:11–18)
   Imagine the event as John describes it and enter into it. If
   'distracting' questions occur to you, such as 'How can I know
   this really happened?', 'Do I really believe in the resurrection?',
   etc., recognise these as interesting questions to be looked at
   later, and continue putting yourself in the scene: watching,
   listening, responding to Jesus and to Mary of Magdala.

LIGHT IN THE DARKNESS

THE TITLE OF THE first chapter of this book was 'Split Spirituality', a spirituality which can allow us to show great reverence towards God and the things of God, while taking care not to allow God to interfere in ordinary everyday matters. The intervening chapters reflected on different aspects of human life, showing how the split can impoverish us, separating us from ourselves, from each other and from God. When we speak of spirituality we are talking of ways and means which enable us to become more aware of the Holy One in every aspect of our lives, 'closer to us than we are to ourselves', and so exploring the wealth that is within us.

The Split Nature of Our Spirituality Seen in the Split Between Spirituality and Church

We have examined the split nature of our spirituality, which affects every aspect of human life and is reflected in the divisions and conflicts within and between ourselves, our Christian Churches, between nations. The split is like a cancer afflicting the body of the human race. Cancerous cells split off from the rest of the human body and begin to multiply independently of it, finally killing the body before perishing themselves. Such cancerous cells are 'fearfully and wonderfully made'. If they could speak they might describe themselves: 'We are a vigorous new life, determined to overthrow all those oppressive powers which bind humankind with the chains of capitalism/terrorism. In order to safeguard ourselves we must root out those who oppress us with their financial imperialism and military might/threaten our Western values of freedom, democracy.' The call of the cancer cells may sound familiar! My 'individualist' spirituality can focus attention upon 'me', 'my group', 'my church', 'my national interests' to the exclusion of all other concerns. Just as the cancerous cells, pursuing their own agenda, devour the whole body before perishing themselves, so in human life groups which, if small, are called terrorist groups, and if large, called nations, can become so intent on achieving their own aims that they threaten the existence of the rest of the human race before perishing themselves.

One of the clearest signs of the split in our spirituality today is also the least noticed: it is the split between churchgoing and spirituality. Spirituality is becoming increasingly popular, church-going increasingly unpopular. Prophets of gloom predict empty churches by the end of the twenty-first century. Modern media can pick up such predictions and keep repeating them – 'The Church is finished', 'Christianity is outdated' – until they are assumed to be dogmatic truths.

Spirituality Needs Church: Church without Spirituality Becomes an Idol

Spirituality cannot flourish without Church: Church without spirit-uality becomes an idol. By spirituality I mean all that can enable us to become more aware of the Spirit of God, the Holy One in whom we all live. By 'Church' I mean 'the pilgrim people of God', a united, inclusive body which, in faith and with hope, continuously strives to let the unity of the God of love and compassion for all peoples and for all creation become the passion of their lives. Such a Church requires organisation and structures of some kind, but the structures and organisation are at the service of the Spirit.

All Christians are being called to a radical conversion and to a new understanding of Church. No Church and no religion can set definitive boundaries for the Spirit of God who is in all things. That call to conversion is coming both from those who are still regular church members, including church leaders and also from the millions of Christian people who have become disaffected, and have either drifted away or departed in anger because of their negative experience of Church. The Chinese character for crisis includes one figure signifying danger, and another signifying opportunity. The crises of Christianity in recent decades contain both danger and opportunity. The more we can focus on the hope, the more likely we are to detect the real dangers. The real danger is the neglect of spirituality in the Church, that we become so preoccupied with the institutional elements of the Church, its structures, forms and manner of organisation that we lose touch with the Church's essence, the presence of the Holy One, who embraces and draws into unity all peoples and all creation.

I have spent the last eighteen years working ecumenically on spirituality in the UK and overseas with people who are active in some form of work for justice, peace and reconciliation. Despite all the difficulties and scandals in the Roman Catholic Church, and the gloomy prophecies of recent years, I feel very encouraged by the hope, generosity, compassion and depth of faith I find among Catholics.

Those who are most deeply committed to work for justice and peace are frequently the most critical of Church as they experience it. Such criticism is often amply justified, but their understanding of Church is such that they fear that they are cut off from God because, although they try to live according to the Spirit during the week, they find themselves unable to tolerate dull, impersonal and uninspiring forms of worship on a Sunday!

In the following paragraphs I write of the split between 'spirituality' and 'Church' as I now experience it within the Roman Catholic Church, with which I am most familiar, leaving it to readers to judge whether what I write has any relevance to their own Church, or to the culture in which they live. I am very grateful for everything that I continue to receive from the Roman Catholic Church; for the richness of her tradition, her wisdom, the universality of her membership, living and dead, and her essential homeliness. Consequently, I feel free to speak from within it, to express my own experience as honestly as I can. I shall be touching on subjects that are complex, sensitive and likely to give offence. It might be more prudent to say nothing, but I cannot be silent and remain at peace. One of the dangers of our age is the assumption that only the experts are competent to speak on any particular issue: this can reduce the vast majority of us to submissive silence. I ask questions: I do not know the answers: but we must face the questions.

The Understanding and Exercise of Authority

The Second Vatican Council (1962–5) was the most radical assembly of Roman Catholic bishops in the two thousand-year history of the Church. The decrees of the Council were very carefully drafted in order to obtain the assent of a largely conservative assembly of bishops, yet they caused uproar in many parts of the Church and it still re-echoes today.

When the bishops convened for the Council, one of the first decrees they considered was on the nature of the Church. The preliminary draft of this document was prepared by Vatican officials and its first chapter was on the hierarchical nature of the Church. The assembled bishops rejected this draft. In the final decree, the first chapter was entitled 'The Mystery of the Church'. The mystery must be expressed in visible forms, but everything in the Church, its organisation, manner of teaching, its style and manner of worship must be provisional, and must never be considered to be of the essence of the Church, otherwise we fall into religious idolatry, replacing the living God of love, compassion and surprises with irreplaceable structures and utter predictability.

The Original Meaning of Authority

The nature and practice of authority is a question that exercises not only every Christian body, but every human organisation. Many of the post-Reformation Churches, struggling to free themselves from the domination of Rome, have ended with far more authoritarian structures than ever afflicted the Church they left. One important element in the understanding and exercise of any authority lies in the nature of human fear.

Fear is a healthy instinct and essential for our survival, but it is also a most paralysing and dangerous instinct. Our fears, not necessarily conscious, of extinction, of meaninglessness, lead us to build up defences and securities that allow us to remain in control. Power struggles arise from this fear and they can vary from the building up of nuclear arsenals with more than enough to ensure the destruction of all life on the planet, to petty jealousies over trivialities.

The root meaning of 'Authority' is the Latin word *augeo* meaning 'I increase'. Authority is that which preserves and nurtures life and encourages those over whom it is exercised to develop into the people they were created to become. This is a very different meaning of authority from the imposition of control, coercion and power, whether by physical or psychological means. In the Gospels, Jesus gives very little detail about the form the Reign of God is to take in the world, but on one topic he is unmistakably clear, namely on the subject of authority. 'The greatest among you must become the least of all, and the greatest among you the servant of all, because the Son of Man came, not to be served, but to serve, and give his life as a ransom for many' (Mark 10:42–5).

The manner in which authority is exercised within the Church can help us to grow in freedom to become the people we are called to be, trusting one another and living for one another, or it can become a form of control, intensifying fear and stunting our growth. Good structures can limit the damage of power struggles within an organisation and can encourage the growth of peoples into freedom, but structures alone, no matter how good in themselves, can never eliminate the misuse of authority within the Church, or any other body. Ecumenical deliberations about Church structures, forms of worship, expressions of belief will only be fruitful in so far as all those concerned have put on 'the heart and mind of Christ' as St Paul advises, a heart and mind which is inclusive of all people, especially the poor, and dedicated to the well-being of all.

The Importance of Spirituality

If we fail to nurture spirituality, that is, awareness of the Holy One in whom we all live and who cherishes every person, the misunderstanding and misuse of authority will continue. There are countless individual Christians and Christian groups today who live out gospel values, who appreciate and cherish human life, are moved by a spirit of compassion, yet feel alienated from the Church to which they belong or once belonged. The Church needs their enthusiasm, a word which means, literally, 'the presence of God within'; they need the life-giving tradition that the Church has to offer. The nurturing of spirituality is a far more fundamental problem, not only for church members but for all human society, than questions about the ordination of women, married Roman Catholic clergy, doctrinal formulations, or problems about the exercise of authority within the Church.

To explore this assertion that spirituality must be taken more seriously within the Churches, Christian readers might look at the following questions. Readers who belong to other faiths, or to no particular faith, may wish to pass over some questions, but a number of them are applicable to all beliefs.

- Has your Christian education left you with a strong belief in the Spirit of God present and at work within you and within all creation? Has it enabled you to learn to trust yourself and your own inner promptings? Have you been encouraged to allow God to become your teacher and to consult your teacher within your own heart?
- Have you ever been taught ways of praying on your own? Have you been taught ways of meditating, contemplating and learning to allow your everyday experience to become the substance of your prayer?
- Have you ever been encouraged to talk about your own felt experience in prayer and helped to see the connection between your prayer experience and everyday life?
- In the theological training of Christian clergy, do you know how much time and attention is given to the nurturing of the spiritual life of students, as distinct from academic, administrative and pastoral aspects?
- In your experience, is criticism of the Church welcome? Is it listened to and acted upon?
- Within your own Church, have you ever had the opportunity to speak freely and without fear about your questions or doubts concerning faith, church doctrine, worship, church discipline?
- Does your experience of Church encourage you to collaborate

and to contribute your skills to the running of the parish – as distinct from cooperating in work already decided upon and controlled by the clergy?

- To what extent has your Christian education encouraged you to live reflectively in the light of the Gospel and to regard the questioning of Church and State as integral to true faith?
- Have you ever been taught about the importance of desire, its relation to God's will and encouraged to search for your own deepest desire?

There must be enormous spiritual wealth in every individual because the Spirit of God dwells in each one: spiritual wealth is not the preserve of any particular religion, Christian denomination, or class of people. Why is this spiritual wealth not bringing clearer signs of life to Christian churches in the Western world? Is part of the reason that the spiritual life of church members has been badly neglected, including the spiritual lives of the clergy? Have we been nurtured in a spirituality that helps us to learn to trust our own judgment; a spirituality that encourages us to discover for ourselves and to make connections between prayer and daily life? If we have been nurtured on a split spirituality, it is not surprising if we have not learned to trust our own judgment in religious matters. We can remain spiritually infantile while becoming high earners or respected leaders in our own professions. Such spiritual immaturity ensures that the gospel does not interfere with ordinary, everyday events and transactions, a split that has enabled us to enjoy the affluence that capitalism offers while failing to notice the connection between our wealth and the starvation of millions. The parable of Dives and Lazarus is for Sundays, not for weekdays in the City. This spiritual immaturity has allowed high-ranking clergy to bless nuclear submarines and a Catholic chaplain to bless the plane that dropped the atomic bomb on Hiroshima in 1945.

A Spirit of Fear and Timidity

A lack of confidence in our own judgment about religious matters can leave us afraid to ask questions, in case the answers should lead us to conclusions that conflict with those of the religious authorities. Such a lack of confidence would be especially damaging if it afflicts church leaders, because it can prevent them from speaking out as they should, or from encouraging local initiatives in case they run out of control. If any of us lacks confidence in our own judgment – which does not mean we consider our judgment infallible – then the approval/disapproval of those in authority can become the most important consideration in all our decision-making. Much of this behaviour is unconscious and can appear under the guise of 'concern for the best interests of the Church/organisation'. Such fearful servility can be labelled 'outstanding obedience, utter loyalty', when in fact it can be a sign that the person has lost touch with their inner self, where we communicate with God. The Spirit of God is a Spirit of truth, of courage and of freedom, a Spirit whose vision is all-encompassing and not limited to any particular section of the human race.

In all our Christian Churches we need spiritual leadership rather than the leadership of control and management: a spiritual leadership that exercises authority by drawing us to search for the face of God, for that for which we most long, encouraging us to grow into the people we are called to become. The true exercise of authority will always encourage us to discover for ourselves, lead us into freedom, encourage us to take initiatives and act upon them. True authority enables us to become increasingly perceptive and responsive to God's promptings and frees us from all manner of servile fear.

What kind of authority do we experience in our Church? If our experience of authority is negative and our fear is great, we may be able to declare this only to God in the silence of our hearts – but that is an important beginning.

Obedience to Whom?

As an 'authority figure', however minor, have you ever found yourself saying, 'I am very sorry to have to do this/say this, but as a priest/bishop I am obliged to do so'? Do you ever feel caught in the struggle between role and person, between authenticity and what we describe as 'obedience'? The word 'obedience' comes from the Latin *obaudire*, meaning 'to listen carefully'. To listen to whom? To God? If we are to listen to God we need other people to help us in our listening. It is for this reason that we need leaders and teachers in the Church. We need leaders who can help us to listen, and to respond to the promptings of God in our experience of life and become more responsive to it. Those who do not listen cannot help us to practise true obedience.

True obedience enables us to listen to the promptings of the Spirit and to respond to them. Without true obedience we cannot live a Christian life. If we ignore the promptings of God and hand over responsibility for our lives to those in authority whom we obey without question, we are failing in true obedience. No human being can ever exempt us from our personal responsibility. 'I was only obeying orders!' cannot excuse our conduct.

In the book of Ezekiel God has stern words for the shepherds who fail in their trust. These are shepherds whom the flock is not called to obey and from whom God has taken the mantle of authority: 'Woe to the shepherds of Israel who only take care of themselves. Should not shepherds take care of the flock?' (Ezek. 34:2). And the prophet continues: 'I will rescue my flock from their mouths, and it will no longer be food for them. For this is what the Sovereign Lord says: I myself will search for my sheep and look after them. As a shepherd looks after his scattered flock when he is with them, so will I look after my sheep' (Ezek. 34:10–12). 'I will search for the lost and bring back the strays. I will bind up the injured and strengthen the weak, but the sleek and the strong I will destroy. I will shepherd the flock with justice' (Ezek. 34:16).

In the Gospel of Matthew Jesus underlines the importance of listening to God: 'You are not to be called "Rabbi" for you have only one Master and you are all brothers. And do not call anyone on earth "father", for you have one Father and he is in heaven. Nor are you to be called "teacher" for you have one Teacher, the Christ' (Matt. 23:8–10).

The function of authority in the Church is to enable us to become more aware of Christ, our teacher, always at work within us and around us. In order to do this we have to learn discernment, to become more conscious of our own capacity for self-deception, to listen to the teaching of the Church and the advice of those we can trust. If, on some particular occasion, it is unclear to us how we must act, then it is wise and prudent to obey orders. But we can hide from our own responsibilities and use obedience as our justification. We have to ask ourselves ,'Do I really dare to be free? Do I really dare take responsibility for my own life? Do I dare to face my own fears?' If the answer is 'No', and I just obey orders from without, then there can be no end to my self-deceptions, for I have betrayed my very self, my soul. If, on the other hand, I can acknowledge my fears to myself and to God, and pray, like the tax gatherer in the Temple, 'God, have mercy on me, a sinner', then, like him, I shall be in a right relationship with God.

The Paralysing Power of Fear

Our fears, if not confronted, sap our emotional as well as our physical energy, imprisoning us within the narrow confines of our own concerns, diminishing us and those around us.

Fear can contribute to our divided state as Christians, for we can come to consider people of other Christian denominations, or of other faiths, to be threats to our own security in the faith we hold. Such security cannot be of God, because the security of God would make us want to break down the walls that divide us and lead us to rejoice in our differences. Fear of insecurity can blind us to the prison we build for ourselves. Dorothy Rowe, a psychologist, in her book *Depression*, claims that at the root of depression is an unwillingness of the victim to face some fear, of which we may not be conscious at first. On a national scale, lurking beneath our nuclear deterrence policy, is the fear of radical change in our lives. We are so enamoured of what we call our national security that for its sake we are willing to risk not only the lives of our enemies, the majority of whom will be innocent civilians, but our own lives too, and possibly all human life on the planet.

Fear of rejection can paralyse us and prevent us from speaking the truth as we perceive it. A constant concern to please the powerful may ultimately prevent us even from being able to perceive the truth at all. This fear can afflict the leaders of churches, who may justify their silence by an appeal to the split spirituality that separates the things of the spirit from everyday life, so that they can justify their silence on matters of life and death by claiming that they have no brief to interfere or speak on matters of state policy. The Hebrew prophets suffered no such qualms! Neither did they care whether or not they suffered rejection.

In the Catholic Church, bishops are expected to make authoritative statements within their own diocese and to speak as an episcopal body for the nation. Because 'authoritative' is generally understood as 'binding', a statement to which the loyal Catholic must agree, or accept quietly, it is not surprising that the majority of bishops are reluctant to speak publicly on complex issues. Because, as a body of bishops, they are expected to produce unanimous and definitive statements on the most complex matters at very short notice, it is not surprising that they may have nothing to say immediately. Once they have spoken, it takes a very courageous bishop to voice any disagreement. On momentous events like, for example, the Falklands War in 1982, the 1991 Gulf War, and the recent war in Afghanistan, there were no immediate and clear protests from the episcopal body. This is not a reflection on individual bishops, but on structures and assumptions within which they have to work.

If church leaders are to exercise an authority that is to encourage their people to grow in freedom, to think and to discover for themselves, to learn to have faith in God at work in all circumstances, then they must speak freely and truthfully, without hiding their own doubts, misgivings, questions. This does not undermine their authority, but wins the love and respect of their people, encouraging them to meet God in their own doubts and questioning. Individual bishops and bishops as a body should not feel that they can only communicate with their people through authoritative statements.

In the statements that not only bishops but any Christian makes, whether individually or as a body, the spirituality that underlies our statements needs to take account of the fourfold grid described in Chapter 4 (page 43), by which I mean that our concerns must never be limited exclusively to the welfare of the Christian community, because the Spirit, the Holy One, is God of all creation. Just as in the testing of our spirituality, our spiritual health does not depend simply on our prayer life and our relationships within our own immediate circle, but must influence our attitude to all human beings, whatever their faith or lack of it, their race, class etc., and also affect our attitude to the environment, so too, every Christian Church's spirituality must be tested.

In January 2002, one Catholic newspaper had a leading article hailing President Bush as the leader of most eminent moral stature of our time. The reason for the fulsome praise of George W. Bush was a speech he had given condemning abortion, declaring, 'Unborn children should be welcomed in life and protected by law', a welcome statement in itself, but given at a time when the US were attacking Afghanistan. The richest country in the world was pounding one of the poorest with bombs, including cluster bombs, which act like personnel landmines: they can lie around for years afterwards, maiming and killing innocent people. A split spirituality leads to a selective morality. This is a problem for every Christian denomination and for all society, not just for the Catholic Church. Where is the focus of our attention and interest? Does it go beyond our own ego, our own group, whether secular or religious, beyond our own nation? Our Christian belief is that every human life is sacred both in the womb and outside it. If we really believed this, the whole Christian body would rise up in protest at all the world's arms trade and at all the propaganda that justifies terrifying violence as a means of overcoming terrorism when, in fact, it spreads and intensifies it.

Our Split Spirituality Impoverishes Our Understanding of the Sacraments

Our split spirituality diminishes God, confining God to the cupboard, as mentioned in Chapter 1. Another illustration of the split is in the way we can come to understand and to administer the sacraments in general and the Eucharist in particular, inclining us to think that God's grace is limited to the sacraments we confer and receive.

In Chapter 9, I mentioned the Polish woman who wanted to have her baby baptised at a ceremony which would be attended mostly by atheists, including the child's father. What did I really believe I was doing in baptising the child? Was I bringing this child into the very life of God, Father, Son and Holy Spirit and so freeing her from original sin? And what did this action say about the children of the atheist congregation? Were their children to remain outside the life of God and to be doomed to separation from God forever, either in limbo or hell? The phrase which helped me then and which helps me still is, 'Sacraments are celebrations of our awareness'. In baptism, what is the awareness that we celebrate? We celebrate the nature of God's life and of all human life, that, in fact, all of us, no matter who we are – our beliefs or lack of belief, whether virtuous or vicious, whether we are successes or failures, rich or poor, sick or healthy – are being called to be at one with God whose living Spirit is in each of us.

It is necessary for Christian believers to celebrate this truth, not because God demands it, but because we need to celebrate because it is such good news. By celebrating this truth it can seep into every cell of our being, be shared with all our friends, help us to see life with new vision. The celebration is an act of thanksgiving to God for this awesome gift and a pledge to bring up this child to know the love and compassion of God, not just in catechism classes, but in every experience of its life. That is why the baptism ceremony should be public, joyful and sensitively adapted to the needs of those present, the music, language and symbols all designed to create a sense of awe, mystery and longing in the participants. Unfortunately, our split spirituality can lead us to think that provided the words 'I baptise you in the name of the Father and of the Son and of the Holy Spirit' are uttered and water poured over the child's head, that is enough.

How Our Split Spirituality Affects Our Understanding of the Eucharist

The clearest sign of the depth of the division separating us as Christians is seen in our attitude towards the Eucharist. Because the Eucharist is at the centre of Christian life, exclusion from the Eucharist is a cause of profound pain to some and of spiritual impoverishment for all.

In 1998 the Roman Catholic Hierarchies of England and Wales, Ireland and Scotland produced a joint teaching document on the Eucharist in the life of the Church called 'One Bread One Body', establishing general norms on sacramental sharing. Who may receive the Eucharist and who may not receive?

When I first read the document I felt uneasy, for I could not see how the norms laid down for sacramental sharing followed from the teaching passages that preceded them. When I read the document again later, I tried a new method: I noticed the sounds that each paragraph suggested. Some passages sang to me; others screeched at me. Those that sang were mostly Scripture quotations, but here are some other passages that sang:

God wills 'to draw humanity into communion with himself and with one another, so as to share God's life, the life of the Holy Trinity'. [13]

'It is ultimately the conversion of human hearts that is God's loving will . . . We receive the sacrament of God's body and blood so that we might more powerfully *be* the sacrament of Christ and his salvation in the world.' [53]

'To receive in truth the Body and Blood of Christ given up for us, we must recognise Christ in the poorest, his brothers and sisters.' [67]

'As St Augustine of Hippo reminded us, at the Eucharist "we receive what we are, and we become what we receive".' [94]

When I reflected on these and on other Scripture quotations in the document that sang to me, they were all to do with the universality of God's call, the essential inclusivity of God's kingdom, which excludes no one and no thing.

The screeching sounds all came from the norms determining who may and who may not receive the Eucharist at a Roman Catholic celebration. The general ruling is that Christians not in full communion with the Catholic Church may not receive the Eucharist at a Catholic celebration, except 'if there is danger of death, or if there is some other grave and pressing need'. When two Christians wed and celebrate their wedding in a Eucharistic celebration, 'the spouse who is not a Catholic (but who has received special permission to share in the Catholic Eucharist on the occasion of the wedding) remains, however, someone who is not in full communion with the Catholic Church', and for this reason the directory stresses that 'Eucharistic sharing can only be exceptional'. Even when the bride, or groom, is admitted to Holy Communion at a Nuptial Mass, it is not envisaged that this be extended to relatives and other guests not in full communion with the Catholic Church (s111). '. . . Exceptional sacramental sharing between the Catholic Church and those faith communities which have their roots in the Reformation cannot be reciprocal' (s.117). In other words, Catholics may not receive Holy Communion with those communities.

When I read these lines I could 'hear' the distress of the many couples I know who have been excluded from sharing together in the Eucharist – members of inter-church families; people who have been divorced and remarried; those who hunger for the Eucharist, but do not feel able to become members of the Roman Catholic Church. The pain of inter-church families continues throughout the marriage and becomes acute whenever they celebrate the Eucharist in a Roman Catholic church. Their children are not permitted to receive the Eucharist in the Roman Catholic church if they also receive in a Church of the Reformed tradition. Deeply committed Christians in inter-church marriages suffer most profoundly from these regulations.

The norms or regulations of the latter part of the document are not in tune with the beauty and mystery of the earlier sections. The norms come across as cold, legalistic and divisive. In giving these personal reactions, I am asking questions, not giving answers, nor advocating Eucharist all round, nor eliminating all meaning from the phrase 'to belong to the Church'.

What is the Reality That the Eucharist Celebrates?

Is the Eucharist simply a remembrance of the Last Supper when Jesus took the bread, blessed it, broke it and gave it to his disciples saying, 'This is me, given for you. Do this in my memory'? It is far more than the commemoration of a past event. It is celebrating a reality which was revealed at the Last Supper, but which is as present to us now as it was two thousand years ago. The Eucharist is a sign of the reality of God's nature, a God who, in Jesus, took a piece of bread, broke it and gave it to his disciples saying, 'This is me, given for you. Do this in my memory.' This is a declaration of the nature of God in whom we all live and move and have our being; therefore it is also a declaration of the truth of our own existence. The God of Jesus is the God of you and of me. God's existence is a giving, so that we, all of us, might live. Jesus tells us, 'Do this in my memory'. He is not simply saying, 'Repeat this ritual regularly'. He is saying something far more important: 'Let this be the pattern of your lives, too, so that you live to give life to one another, so that your lives become Eucharist.' We need to celebrate the Eucharist together: it deepens our awareness of who we are, that our ultimate identity is in God, the God of mercy and compassion. This awareness leads us to live what we celebrate, allowing God to be God to us and through us.

It is right that the Catholic Church should celebrate the Eucharist in her own way, true to the Scriptures and to tradition, adapting the words and the form to the needs and the culture of the congregation. If, in the Eucharist, we are celebrating the limitless and continuous love of Christ for all creation, can it be right to refuse the Eucharist to someone who approaches in good faith? If we do consider such a refusal to be right, do we not imply that we can control and put limits on God's love? The person refused has no doubt about the answer: I have met many of them. Can we not welcome people of other Christian denominations who come to receive the Eucharist in good faith, so witnessing to the unconditional hospitality and love of God for all creation, leaving it to God to lead that individual, it may be to full membership in the Catholic Church, or not so to lead them? Can we say, 'You may not celebrate the reality of God's loving presence among us, because you are not one of us'? But is that not the message we give to other Christians by these norms?

The final paragraph of the bishops' document strikes a hopeful note: 'We hope that the common study of these difficult questions may lead to a deeper understanding of the nature of the Church, and bring nearer the day when we can come together united in faith in the Eucharist' (s.121). The final paragraph sings and I hope that what I have written can be one of many contributions that can contribute to the day when we can, officially, celebrate together.

Facing Our Fears – The Sexual Abuse Scandals

In recent years the Roman Catholic Church has been rocked by scandals of sexual abuse by members of the clergy. The shock waves are discouraging candidates from entering into training for the priesthood: they are demoralising clergy and shaking Catholic congregations in many countries. What measures are we to take to protect children from such abuse, to help those who have been abused, and how are we to ensure that offenders are prevented from re-offending? Has our Christian spirituality anything to offer victims, their families and offenders?

This is an enormously complex issue and such a highly sensitive one that any comment on it can act like a spark on dry tinder. It will probably take us decades to unravel the complexities and to understand more clearly the underlying reasons for the crimes, for the nature of the public reaction to them, to learn how to protect children without afflicting them with paranoia, and to know how to act justly and effectively with the offenders so that they do not offend again and are offered hope for the future.

In Chapter 10 we looked at Girard's analysis of the nature of human violence and the key role of scapegoating as a means of defusing violence between opposing factions by uniting them in hatred for and expulsion of the scapegoat, which may be an animal, a human being, or a group of people. The mechanism can defuse violence in the short term, but the violence, like an underground fire, will erupt again and more intensely. How is our Christian spirituality to guide us in this matter, or is it so split that we cannot apply it to those accused or condemned of paedophilia? Do we have to amend Jesus' instructions in the Sermon on the Mount: 'Love your enemies, and pray for those who persecute you' [adding, 'Unless, of course, they are accused or condemned of paedophilia]? Has our Christian spirituality anything helpful to say to us in the sexual abuse crisis, or is it, in practice, utterly impractical and dangerously soft on crime?

The only effective answer to violence is non-violent resistance. Has this anything to say to us on the paedophilia crisis?

Children must be protected from abusers, but in such a way that they are not encouraged to distrust all older people, or to live in fear of their own sexuality. Children who have been victims of abuse must be given every possible help to enable them, as far as possible, to recover from the trauma of the abuse and its after effects. Vital for their recovery is that they should be freed from the infection of the violence done to them, so that they do not live lives of bitterness and resentment against those who have wronged them. The spiritual aftercare of the victims is of far greater importance and value than any financial compensation. This is not to deny the need for financial compensation in particular cases. It is possible for people who have suffered appalling violence to live later at peace with themselves, with forgiveness for their aggressor, without denying, in any way, the seriousness and hurtfulness of what they suffered. We live in a culture in which many do not consider forgiveness to be a virtue. They encourage victims in their bitterness and resentment at the offence, and this can blight the victim for life. Children, and their parents, must be rescued from this fate.

What of the offenders? They must make recompense, in so far as they can, for their crime. How are they to be helped to genuine repentance? They cannot be coerced by imprisonment or by any other means into repentance. It is only in God's light that we can begin to see light. The more humanely the guilty are treated, the more likely they are to recognise the goodness of God at work in them, and so acknowledge the seriousness of their offence. In the case of child abusers, one form of treatment, both in prison and outside of it, is aversion therapy, where people have to keep admitting to themselves 'I am a child abuser/alcoholic/drug addict/ etc.'. This may prove effective, in some cases, in curing a particular obsession, but I wonder at what cost to the person. As we have seen in earlier chapters, for the Christian, the ultimate reference point when we say 'I' is God, 'my rock, my refuge, my strength and my hope'. To keep convincing myself that I am an abuser, alcoholic, etc. is itself a form of abuse because it is to deny my true identity and deprives me of all hope. To say, 'I have been guilty of sexual abuse/drug addiction/etc. and I am in danger of handing myself over to these tendencies' is a truer statement and one which offers hope.

What has our Christian spirituality to say about the present day scapegoating of paedophiles?

National scapegoating of a particular group denotes some kind of illness in the nation's psyche, a national neurosis, which needs to be investigated. We live in a blame culture. It can be very comforting to blame others, and the more we blame, the more righteous we feel and the more blind we can become to our own destructiveness. Jesus said, 'Do not judge, and you will not be judged yourselves; do not condemn and you will not be condemned yourselves' (Luke 6:36–7).

St Seraphim of Sarov (1759–1830), a Russian Orthodox monk, who spent much of his life as a hermit in the woods, where he befriended bears and wolves, once said, 'Never condemn each other. We condemn others only because we shun knowing ourselves.'

There are thousands of people whose lives have been ruined by accusations of child sex abuse besides the vast numbers who have served or are serving prison sentences. The worst torment for many who are guilty of any criminal offence is not the confinement of prison, nor the vilification they have suffered through their trial and the prospect of more when their prison term is over, but their own inability to forgive themselves, the darkness and hopelessness in which they feel enveloped. They are the outcasts of society today. Who is to minister to them? What hope can our Christian spirituality hold out for them in practice? There are Catholic priests who have been accused of paedophilia and their future is bleak, especially for those who have served prison sentences: they are banned not only from any future priestly ministry, but also from any form of pastoral work. Do we really believe that God's mercy and compassion can stretch to those guilty of paedophilia? If those priests are willing, why should they not be allowed to do pastoral work with any adult who, knowing their past, wants their ministry? Do we believe that God's grace can be strongest in our powerlessness and in the possibility of the wounded healer? Such priests could have a vast ministry, not only with people accused of paedophilia, but with any who feel lost, rejected and worthless. Are they to be forever banned from doing Jesus' work among his friends, 'the outcasts and the sinners'?

The Need for Spiritual Renewal

We are in desperate need of spiritual renewal; not great drum-beating campaigns with thousands gathered in football stadiums to listen to massed bands, pious pop groups and 'well-known' speakers, but rather the quiet sowing of mustard seeds. In the rest of this chapter I describe one form of spiritual renewal which is happening in various parts of the world. It is simple, can engage anyone who is willing to take part, and does not require committees, fund raisers or massive buildings! This kind of renewal encourages people to pray simply to God out of their own experience. It encourages those who show the aptitude and interest the elementary principles of accompanying others in prayer, so that people can get in touch with the spiritual wealth that is in them and learn to minister to each other, without thinking such important work must be the preserve of the clergy.

Such renewal includes what is called 'individually given retreats' – sometimes residential, but much more commonly in daily life, so that those making the retreat carry on with normal life, but reserve a period of time daily for private prayer. Regularly during the retreat they meet daily with a prayer accompanier, with whom they talk about their felt experience within their prayer time and afterwards. Especially when organised ecumenically, such retreats can be amazingly helpful for individuals, for the life of a locality, college, university or prison. This type of retreat can be held anywhere and its length can be adapted to the needs of those making it. For the last seven years this type of retreat has been offered at Westminster, not only to members of the House of Lords and House of Commons, but to anyone who is employed in the building.

Such retreats do not require endless committee meetings to organise, nor vast sums of money to launch, and it is possible to offer them both to very busy people and to those with little or no money to spare. In a later book I am hoping to write about these retreats, their origins, method, how they connect with everyday life, and how people who have made these retreats and found them helpful can be trained in the elementary rules of retreat-giving and spiritual accompaniment. Here is one example to illustrate the fact that there is a great hunger for spiritual renewal in Britain, and great spiritual wealth in us, but it has rarely been tapped. Few people are aware of the spiritual wealth within them, still fewer know how to help others to discover their own spiritual wealth, and hardly any know how to get started on this kind of work.

A Millennium Prayer Journey

In preparation for the millennium year, well over a thousand people in the midlands of England took part in a Millennium Journey of Prayer over the space of one year, and there were many other groups in other parts of the country. The people came from many Christian denominations and a few were from none. Those joining the Millennium Journey undertook to pray on their own every day, and to meet once a month in groups of six to talk about their own experience of prayer during the previous month, and to listen to the experience of other members of the group. The guidelines for the group meetings emphasised that these meetings were for listening to one another. They were not for discussion, or for sorting out the problems of members or of the world! Group members took turns in chairing the meetings. The task of the chair was to ensure that the group guidelines were adhered to, so that everyone had an opportunity to speak; nobody was allowed to theorise, but each was to speak from their own experience. Anybody who seemed to be trying to sort out others was firmly but gently restrained! Group meetings had a time limit of one and a half to two hours. Meetings were held in one another's houses and hospitality, if offered, was to be limited to tea, coffee and biscuits! Groups were organised geographically so that no member had too far to travel.

The Journey of Prayer began with a one-day regional meeting, to introduce the concept and to describe some of the methods of prayer mentioned in Chapter 4. The regional meeting included time for participants to comment on their reactions to the methods of prayer and to ask questions about them. In the course of the year there were further regional meetings every three months to which all groups within the region were invited. This enabled the different groups in the region to pray together, to listen to very brief progress reports from each group, and to deal with various difficulties and questions. Most participants were very faithful to daily prayer and to the monthly group meetings. During the closing regional meetings at the end of the year many groups spoke of their intention of continuing to meet and of forming new groups. The groups that had flourished were those which kept to the guidelines offered for their monthly meetings and had listened faithfully to one another. Many of the groups were asking for retreats in daily life during the following year and demand far exceeded the number of trained retreat-givers available.

Readers do not have to wait for a blare of trumpets declaring that spiritual renewal has begun. If you can gather one or two people who are interested in practising some of the prayer methods described in Chapter 4, invite them to meet for a set time once a fortnight or once a month. At the meeting, listen to each other as you describe your felt experience during the prayer and in its after-effects. You can follow the guidelines given in Appendix 1, then see how the Spirit moves you! Where two or three are gathered in Jesus's name, he really is in the midst of them!

Working over the past eighteen years with people of differing Christian denominations or of none has deepened my faith in God, a God of surprises and of compassion for all people and for all of creation. But these years of insight, joy and delight have also been years of pain and disappointment, because I see the hunger of people for an answer to the emptiness and restlessness within them and they do not usually hear it in their churches. I see their spiritual wealth, their unpretentious generosity and spontaneous compassion, yet so many think of themselves as 'outside the Church', because they do not necessarily attend Sunday worship. Their sense of rejection is deepened by those church people who regard them as 'outside', or at the very least as 'on the edge'! Regular churchgoers need to pray for the grace and the wisdom to recognise the Spirit of God at work in those whom they consider, and who often consider themselves, to be 'outsiders'. Some belong to a differing religious faith, others profess no formal belief, many are in a love/hate relationship with the Church to which they belong, or once belonged

The Christian Church has so much to offer, but the message is frequently presented in a style that fails to speak to the cries of those who are suffering, or to assuage the thirst of those who are parched. Specific cultural values become idols and the misuse and misunderstanding of authority can stifle the life, spontaneity and creativity of people in the name of God. We become so enamoured of our particular ways of doing things that we fail to lift up our eyes to see the glory of God all around us. Locked in our religious and denominational certainties, we can remain blind and deaf to the beckoning of God.

All Manner of Things Will be Well

In spite of all this, I feel confident in the future of the Church because I know that God is always greater, and that no one of us can predict what forms the Church may take in future. Any Church structures can only be justified in so far as they enable all of us to become more aware and more responsive to the reality of our existence, that we live enfolded within the goodness of God, our ultimate identity, and that each of us has a unique role to play in the life of the world, to let God be the God of love and compassion to us and through us, whatever our circumstances. In your moments of joy and delight, know that God is delighting in you and for you: in your moments of darkness and pain, hear that voice in the depth of your being, calling you by your name and saying, 'Don't be afraid. I am with you. You and I are one undivided person.'

I end with a prayer which I have found very helpful and which provides the essence of what I have been struggling to express. When you make the prayer, remember me, and I shall remember all readers:

> Take, Lord, unto Thyself,
> My sense of self; and let it vanish utterly:
> Take, Lord, my life.
> Live Thou Thy life through me:
> I live no longer, Lord.
> But in me now
> Thou livest:
> Aye, between Thee and me, my God,
> There is no longer room for 'I' and 'mine'.
> (Tukaram – Indian Peasant Mystic 1608–49,
> from *The Oxford Book of Prayers*, OUP, 1985)

I am hoping to write a book of suggestions for ecumenical prayer groups and on the organisation and running of training courses to teach people the elementary principles of prayer accompaniment and prayer guiding. I have set up a website for people interested in learning more about differing ways of developing a spirituality that enables us to meet God in all things. I hope this will develop as a participative website rather than an instructional one. I am particularly interested in hearing of the experience of other people in the development of methods of training which are available to all and which do not require financial outlay on the part of participants. The website address is www.gerardwhughes.com.

For readers who are interested in learning more of spirituality centres, retreat houses, spirituality networks, training courses, etc. in the UK, the annual magazine *Retreats* offers the programmes and events of over 200 retreat centres, besides articles, book reviews, general information and a map of all the centres. Contact:

The Retreat Association
The Central Hall
256 Bermondsey Street
London
SE1 3UJ

Tel: 020 7357 7736
Internet: www.retreats.org.uk
Email: info@retreats.org.uk

The Irish Jesuits have a website offering daily help with prayer: www.sacredspace.ie.

GUIDELINES FOR USING THE BOOK IN GROUPS

THE SUBJECT MATTER FOR group meetings may be a chapter, or part of a chapter, or to share your felt experience after doing one of the exercises at the end of each chapter.

General Guidelines

For this kind of meeting, six is a good number, but thriving groups often begin with two or three people. How often to meet, where and for how long is for the group to decide. Always have a fixed length of time for your group meetings, e.g. one and a half hours. If you decide to meet in one another's houses and the host wishes to offer hospitality, then let it be very simple, e.g. tea, coffee, biscuits, not an elaborate party!

The purpose of this book is to encourage people to discover for themselves, so in your meetings, the primary object is to listen to each other, not to discuss, argue, theorise, advise, or sort each other out!

Let each person in the group share, in so far as they are willing, their own felt experience in reading a chapter, or doing an exercise, and let the others listen, but without interruption or comment.

After each has spoken it is good to have a few moments of silence before the next person speaks. This is a mark of respect, but is also gives time for reflection on what has been said.

After each has spoken, there may be more from your own felt experience that you would like to share, and so the conversation continues, but it is rooted in felt experience.

When all have spoken, the chairperson can then invite people to say what, if anything, has struck them during the meeting. Finally, the chairperson can invite members to ask, 'Where would you like to go from here?' and also the particular question, 'What topic for our next meeting?'

It is important that you should agree beforehand that whatever is shared in these groups should be treated in confidence.

Guidelines for the Chairperson

Invite each member of the group to assist in ensuring that the guidelines are kept. It is good to let each member of the group chair the meeting in turn, if they are willing.

Ensure that anyone who wants to speak has the chance to do so. Allow a short pause after each has spoken. This is both a mark of respect for the speaker and also offers time to reflect on what has been said.

Gently restrain anyone who theorises, lectures, argues, advises, or seems to be trying to sort out the rest of the group, or any individual within it!

Ensure that the formal part of the meeting ends at the time agreed beforehand.

Ensure that everyone knows the date, place, time and topic for the next meeting.

SOME SCRIPTURE PASSAGES FOR PRAYER

(THESE ARE JUST A few passages to get you started. You can then find your own texts!)

On God's Love for Us

Psalms 8, 23, 91, 130, 136, 139, 145
Isaiah 43:1–7, 46:3–4, 49:14–16, 54:4–10, 55:1–11
Wisdom 11:21–12:2
Hosea 11:1–9
Luke 1:46–55,67–79, 11:1–13, 12:22–32, 15:1–32
John 14:18–23, 15:1–15
Ephesians 1:3–14, 2:1–10, 3:14–21
Romans 5:1–11, 8:31–9
2 Corinthians 4:7–16, 5:16–21

On Desire

Psalms 27, 42, 43, 63
Romans 8:36–9
John 1:35–9
Mark 10:17–27

God's Desire to Forgive Us

Matthew 9:10–13
Luke 7:36–50, 15:11–32, 18:9–14, 19:1–10
John 8:1–11

On God's Healing

Mark 1:40–5, 5:1–20,25–34, 7:31–7, 10:46–52
Luke 5:12–16, 7:36–50

On Forgiving Others

Matthew 5:20–6, 5:43–8, 6:7–16, 7:1–5
Luke 6:20–45
1 Corinthians 13:4–13

On Trust

Matthew 6:24–34, 14:22–33
Mark 4:35–41
Luke 1:26–38, 12:22–32
Philippians 4:8–13
Romans 8:31–9

On Compassion

Luke 10:25–37, 15:11–24, 16:19–31
Luke 5:36–8, 23:33–43

A BRIEF DESCRIPTION OF INIGO OF LOYOLA

INIGO OF LOYOLA WAS a Basque nobleman, born in 1491 and brought up in the Spanish court from which he emerged in his early twenties, full of ambition and with a strong streak of Don Quixote in him. In his late twenties he was badly wounded in both knees while defending the city of Pamplona against very superior French troops. It was during his convalescence back home in Loyola that he experienced an inner conversion. He had a great gift for daydreaming and whiled away his time, at first, in dreams of the great deeds he would do when his wounds were healed and of the great lady whose love he would win. Then he grew bored and asked for novels. Novels were short in those days and Loyola had none: the only books they could find for him were *A Life of Christ* and *Lives of the Saints*. In his boredom he began reading these, then soon found himself on a new set of daydreams, imagining himself as St Inigo, outdoing all the saints, saying to himself, 'If Dominic can do it, so can I. If Francis can do it, so can I.'

For weeks he alternated between the two sets of daydreams – doing heroic deeds and winning the great lady, then outdoing the saints. Both sets of daydreams were pleasant at the time, but then he noticed something which was to change his life and is the reason why you are now reading this page: he noticed a qualitative difference in the after-effects of the daydreams. Dreams about his great deeds and winning the great lady left him bored, empty and sad: dreams about outdoing the saints left him hopeful, happy and strengthened. Later, he called this experience his first lesson in discernment. He decided he must become a saint, but was a little vague as to how to begin!

He decided that a pilgrimage to Jerusalem (he was still limping from his wounds), there to see the Holy Land and convert the Muslims, might be a modest beginning to his saintly career! In those days, long-distance pilgrims were advised to make a general confession before starting. Inigo stopped at the Benedictine monastery of Montserrat, found a patient Benedictine and, after three days' preparation, made his general confession. He then limped down to nearby Manresa where he spent nine months living in a cave and underwent a series of inner experiences of darkness and of light, out of which he eventually wrote his book *The Spiritual Exercises*, a series of Scripture-based, Christ-centred meditations and contemplations, designed to help us to get in touch with our inner self, the Christ-self. By praying these passages, then reflecting on our felt experience during the prayer and speaking of it to a retreat-giver, we can become more aware of the creative movements within us and of the destructive. By following the creative and avoiding the destructive, we discover God's will for us.

Inigo got to the Holy Land, made no conversions, as far as we know, and was sent back to Europe by the Franciscans who were in charge of the Christian sites. On his return, the Inquisition forbade him to give the Spiritual Exercises until he had some academic qualifications, so he learned Latin and studied in Salamanca, Alacala and eventually in Paris, where he met up with a group of companions who were later to form the nucleus of the Society of Jesus, which today numbers about 21,000.

THE TWO STANDARDS
MEDITATION

('THIS IS AN ABRIDGED version and free translation of the two standards meditation from Ignatius Loyola's *Spiritual Exercises*. The comments Ignatius offers in this and in his other meditations/contemplations are to help us discover for ourselves: they can help us to focus our attention if it strays from prayer, but there is no need to follow the text slavishly. For example, read his description of Lucifer and his smoky throne, but then try to find your own image. Similarly, read the address of Lucifer and of Christ as given in the text, but then hear their words in your own imagination.)

Preparatory Prayer: 'Lord, grant that my whole being may be directed purely to your service and praise.'

1 Consider how Christ calls and desires all human beings to be drawn to his standard, and how Lucifer, the enemy of our human nature, wants to drag all to his.
2 Put yourself in the scene, imagining a great plain near Jerusalem where Jesus gathers his followers; then see another plain near Babylon where Lucifer is enthroned.

3 Pray for what you desire. Beg Christ to show you his attractiveness and the wisdom of his teaching so that loving and being enlightened by him, you are able to detect the deceits of Lucifer, who does evil under the appearance of doing good.

Part 1: Lucifer's Standard

1 Imagine Lucifer in the great plain of Babylon, seated on a smoky throne, looking hideous and menacing.
2 See how he summons innumerable devils, dispersing them everywhere throughout the world, omitting no region, country, place, and no individual person.
3 Hear the instructions he gives the devils. They are to ensnare and bind all human beings by encouraging them first to crave for riches, then leading them on to long for honours, status, power over others, and finally to all-consuming pride in their own self-importance. In this way they can be enticed to all other vices.

Part 2: The Standard of Christ

1 See how Jesus takes his place in the great plain round Jerusalem, a place beautiful and attractive.
2 Watch how he chooses so many people, apostles, disciples, men and women, sending them throughout the world to bring his good news to people of all kinds and conditions.
3 Hear what he is saying to his servants and friends whom he is sending on this expedition. They are to work for the good of all those they encounter, first by attracting them to the most perfect spiritual poverty, which is to live with a total trust in God at work in all life's circumstances. They are also to attract people to a life of actual poverty, if that seems to be the best service this individual can give to God, and if they feel drawn to this way of life. Second they are to attract them to a desire for reproaches and contempt, because from these comes humility which is the root of all virtue.

A Conversation

1 During the prayer and at the end of it, I should talk with Our Lady, asking her to obtain from her Son the grace that may be received under his standard in total spiritual poverty, and even in actual poverty, if that is what God wants of me; second that I should bear reproaches and injuries, so that I may become more like her Son. Then say a Hail Mary.
2 Have the same conversation and make the same request of Christ, and pray the 'Anima Christi'.
3 Finally, make the same request of God the Father, and end with the 'Our Father'.

(Ignatius recommends the retreatant to repeat this same conversation in all the meditations/contemplations on Christ's public life, passion and death which follow. He also recommends that this meditation should be made once and then repeated three times by those who are making the full *Spiritual Exercises*.)

Some Scripture texts that can be helpful in praying this meditation:

Mark 4:1–20, 10:35–45
Luke 6:17–26, 18:18–30
Galatians 5:16–25
Ephesians 6:10–20
Philippians 2:1–18, 3:7–16
1 John 4:1–6
1 Peter 4:1–5:11